GED Prep **X**celerator Mathematics WORKBOOK

PAXEN

Chris Ramsey

PAXEN

Melbourne, Florida
www.paxen.com

Acknowledgements

For each of the selections and images listed below, grateful acknowledgement is made for permission to excerpt and/or reprint original or copyrighted material, as follows:

Images

(cover, astronomical clock) Fribus Ekaterina, Shutterstock Images. **(cover, architecture)** iStockphoto. **(cover, drawing compass)** Carlos Alvarez, iStockphoto. **(cover, circuit board)** iStockphoto. **v** iStockphoto. **vi** iStockphoto.

ISBN-13: 978-1-934350-29-4
ISBN-10: 1-934350-29-X

2 3 4 5 6 7 8 9 10 GEDXWB2 16 15 14 13 12 11 10

Printed in the U.S.A.

GED PREP X CELERATOR

Mathematics Workbook

Table of Contents

About the GED Tests

Simply by turning to this page, you've made a decision that will change your life for the better. Each year, thousands of people just like you decide to pursue the General Educational Development (GED) certificate. Like you, they left school for one reason or another. And now, just like them, you've decided to continue your education by studying for and taking the GED Tests.

However, the GED Tests are no easy task. The tests—five in all, spread across the subject areas of Language Arts/Reading, Language Arts/Writing, Mathematics, Science, and Social Studies—cover slightly more than seven hours. Preparation takes considerably longer. The payoff, however, is significant: more and better career options, higher earnings, and the sense of achievement that comes with a GED certificate. Employers and colleges and universities accept the GED certificate as they would a high school diploma. On average, GED recipients earn $4,000 more per year than do employees without a GED certificate.

The American Council on Education (ACE) has constructed the GED Tests to mirror a high school curriculum. Although you will not need to know all of the information typically taught in high school, you will need to answer a variety of questions in specific subject areas. In Language Arts/Writing, you will need to write an essay on a topic of general knowledge.

In all cases, you will need to effectively read and follow directions, correctly interpret questions, and critically examine answer options. The table below details the five subject areas, the number of questions within each of them, and the time that you will have to answer them. Since different states have different requirements for the number of tests you may take in a single day, you will need to check with your local adult education center for requirements in your state or territory.

The original GED Tests were released in 1942 and have since been revised a total of three times. In each case, revisions to the tests have occurred as a result of educational findings or workplace needs. All told, more than 17 million people have received a GED certificate since the tests' inception.

SUBJECT AREA TEST	CONTENT AREAS	ITEMS	TIME LIMIT
Language Arts/Reading	Literary texts—75% Nonfiction texts—25%	40 questions	65 minutes
Language Arts/Writing (Editing)	Organization—15% Sentence Structure—30% Usage—30% Mechanics—25%	50 questions	75 minutes
Language Arts/Writing (Essay)	Essay	Essay	45 minutes
Mathematics	Number Sense/Operations—20% to 30% Data Measurement/Analysis—20% to 30% Algebra—20% to 30% Geometry—20% to 30%	Part I: 25 questions (with calculator) Part II: 25 questions (without calculator)	90 minutes
Science	Life Science—45% Earth/Space Science—20% Physical Science—35%	50 questions	80 minutes
Social Studies	Geography—15% U.S. History—25% World History—15% U.S. Government/Civics—25% Economics—20%	50 questions	70 minutes

Three of the subject-area tests—Language Arts/Reading, Science, and Social Studies—will require you to answer questions by interpreting passages. The Science and Social Studies tests also require you to interpret tables, charts, graphs, diagrams, timelines, political cartoons, and other visuals. In Language Arts/Reading, you also will need to answer questions based on workplace and consumer texts. The Mathematics Test will require you to use basic computation, analysis, and reasoning skills to solve a variety of word problems, many of them involving graphics. On all of the tests, questions will be multiple-choice with five answer options. An example follows:

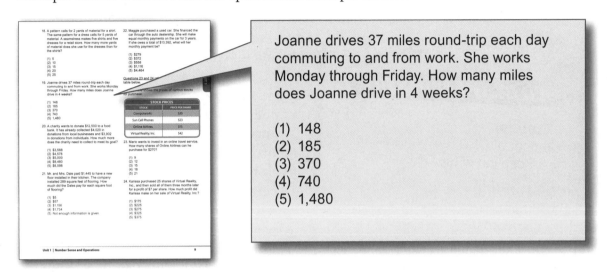

On the Mathematics Test, you will have additional ways in which to register your responses to multiple-choice questions. See p. ix for more information about the three ways of recording responses on the GED Mathematics Test.

As the table on p. iv indicates, the Language Arts/ Writing Test contains two parts, one for editing and the other for essay. In the editing portion of Language Arts/ Writing, you will be asked to identify and correct common errors in various passages and texts while also deciding on the most effective organization of a text. In the essay portion, you will write an essay that provides an explanation or an opinion on a single topic of general knowledge.

So now that you understand the task at hand—and the benefits of a GED certificate— you must prepare for the GED Tests. In the pages that follow, you will find a recipe of sorts that, if followed, will help guide you toward successful completion of your GED certificate. So turn the page. The next chapter of your life begins right now.

About *GED Prep Xcelerator*

Along with choosing to pursue your GED certificate, you've made another smart decision by selecting *GED Prep Xcelerator* as your main study and preparation tool. Simply by purchasing *GED Prep Xcelerator*, you've joined an elite club with thousands of members, all with a common goal—earning their GED certificates. In this case, membership most definitely has its privileges.

For more than 65 years, the GED Tests have offered a second chance to people who need it most. To date, 17 million Americans like you have studied for and earned GED certificates and, in so doing, jump-started their lives and careers. Benefits abound for GED holders: Recent studies have shown that people with GED certificates earn more money, enjoy better health, and exhibit greater interest in and understanding of the world around them than do those without.

In addition, more than 60 percent of GED recipients plan to further their educations, which will provide them with more and better options. As if to underscore the point, U.S. Department of Labor projections show that 90 percent of the fastest growing jobs through 2014 will require postsecondary education.

Your pathway to the future—a *brighter* future—begins now, on this page, with *GED Prep Xcelerator*, an intense, accelerated approach to GED preparation. Unlike other programs, which take months to teach the GED Tests through a content-based approach, *Xcelerator* gets to the heart of the GED Tests—and quickly—by emphasizing *concepts*. At their core, the majority of the GED Tests are reading-comprehension exams. Students must be able to read and interpret excerpts, passages, and various visuals—tables, charts, graphs, timelines, and so on—and then answer questions based upon them.

Xcelerator shows you the way. By emphasizing key reading and thinking concepts, *Xcelerator* equips learners like you with the skills and strategies you'll need to correctly interpret and answer questions on the GED Tests. Two-page micro-lessons in each student book provide focused and efficient instruction, while callout boxes, sample exercises, and test-taking and other thinking strategies aid in understanding complex concepts. For those who require additional support, we offer the *Xcelerator* workbooks, which provide *twice* the support and practice exercises as the student books.

Unlike other GED materials, which were designed *for* the classroom, *Xcelerator* materials were designed *from* the classroom, using proven educational theory and cutting-edge classroom philosophy. The result: More than 90 percent of people who study with *Xcelerator* earn their GED certificates. For learners who have long had the deck stacked against them, the odds are finally in their favor. And yours.

GED BY THE NUMBERS

17 million
Number of GED recipients since the inception of the GED Tests

1.23 million
Number of students who fail to graduate from high school each year

700,000
Number of GED test-takers each year

451,759
Total number of students who passed the GED Tests in 2007

$4,000
Additional earnings per year for GED recipients

About *GED Prep Xcelerator Mathematics*

For those who think the GED Mathematics Test is a breeze, think again. The GED Mathematics Test is a rigorous exam that will assess your ability to answer a range of mathematics questions about various topics, such as estimation, ratio, and proportion. About half of the GED Mathematics Test involves answering questions using tables, charts, graphs, diagrams, and drawings. Tables, for example, organize and group complex data using rows and columns. As you can see on the sample page below, rows are read from top to bottom, and columns from left to right. Tables often include headings that describe the data they contain.

All told, you will have a total of 90 minutes in which to answer 50 multiple-choice items organized across four main content areas, each of which makes up between 20% and 30% of all questions: Number Sense and Operations; Measurement/Data Analysis; Algebra, Patterns, and Functions; and Geometry. Material in *GED Prep Xcelerator Mathematics* has been organized with these percentages in mind.

GED Prep Xcelerator Mathematics helps learners like you build and develop core mathematics skills. A combination of targeted strategies, informational callouts and sample questions, assorted test-taking tips, and ample assessment help to clearly focus study efforts in needed areas, all with an eye toward success on the GED Tests.

You will use a site-issued calculator to answer questions in Part I of the GED Mathematics Test. In addition, a formulas page, such as that on p. viii in this book, will be supplied. It includes all of the formulas needed to succeed on the GED Mathematics Test.

The **Review the Skill** section reviews and provides additional information about the skill to be studied.

Callouts provide strategies and information that you may use to understand and interpret various passages or graphics.

Test-Taking Tips offer broad or specific support for answering multiple-choice questions.

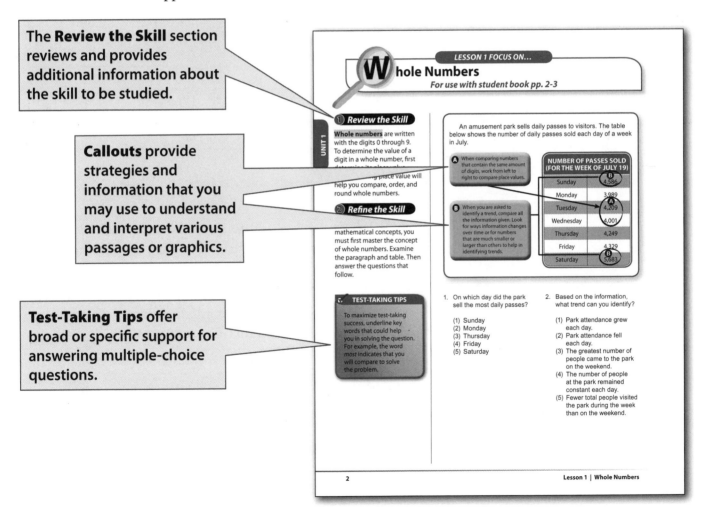

Formulas for GED Mathematics Test

Area of a...

Square:	Area = side^2
Rectangle:	Area = length × width
Parallelogram:	Area = base × height
Triangle:	Area = $\frac{1}{2}$ × base × height
Trapezoid:	Area = $\frac{1}{2}$ × (base$_1$ + base$_2$) × height
Circle:	Area = π × radius^2; π equals about 3.14

Perimeter of a...

Square:	Perimeter = 4 × side
Rectangle:	Perimeter = 2 × length + 2 × width
Triangle:	Perimeter = side$_1$ + side$_2$ + side$_3$

Circumference of a...

Circle:	Circumference = π × diameter

Volume of a...

Cube:	Volume = edge^3
Rectangular prism:	Volume = length × width × height
Square pyramid:	Volume = $\frac{1}{3}$ × (base edge)^2 × height
Cylinder:	Volume = π × radius^2 × height
Cone:	Volume = $\frac{1}{3}$ × π × radius^2 × height

Coordinate geometry

Distance between points = $\sqrt{(x_2 - x_1)^2 + (y_2 - y_1)^2}$

Slope of a line = $\dfrac{y_2 - y_1}{x_2 - x_1}$

Pythagorean relationship

$a^2 + b^2 = c^2$; a and b are legs, and c is the hypotenuse

Central measures

Mean = $\dfrac{x1 + x2 + ... + xn}{n}$;	where x's are the individual values, and n is the total number of values for x.
Median =	The middle value of an odd number of ordered scores, and halfway between the two middle values of an even number of ordered scores.
Mode =	The most common number in a set.

Simple interest

Interest =	Principal × rate × time

Distance

Distance =	Rate × time

Total cost

Total cost =	(Number of units) × (Price per unit)

Response Options for the GED Mathematics Test

Once you read each question, apply any formulas, and determine the correct answer, you then must mark the answer correctly on the GED answer sheet. On the GED Mathematics Test, you will have three options to use, all of which will be explained below and on the test itself. The Unit Reviews in *GED Prep Xcelerator Mathematics* have been organized to provide you with practice in using all three response styles.

The horizontal-response format requires you to fill in the numbered circle that corresponds to the answer you select for each question on the GED Mathematics Test. Mark your answer completely, making no stray or unnecessary marks. If you change an answer, erase your first mark completely. Mark only one answer space for each question; multiple answers will be scored as incorrect.

To record your answers in the alternate-response format, you must do the following:

- Begin in any column that will allow your answer to be entered;
- Write your answer in the boxes in the top row;
- In the column beneath a fraction bar or decimal point (if any) and each number in your answer, fill in the bubble representing that character;
- Leave blank any unused columns.

Points to consider when recording an answer on the coordinate grid:

- To record an answer, you must have an *x* and *y* value.
- No answer will have a value that is a fraction or a decimal.
- Mark only one circle that represents your answer.

Calculator Directions

The GED Mathematics Test has two sections, one of which allows for the use of a calculator. Therefore, calculators are permitted in certain lessons of this book. When you see a 🖩 symbol within a *GED Prep Xcelerator* student book or workbook lesson, this means that calculator use is allowed. When you do not see a 🖩 symbol, then calculators should not be used. The Unit Reviews contain a representative sampling of problems from all lessons in a unit. Therefore, each item in a Unit Review that permits the use of a calculator will show a 🖩 symbol.

The Casio FX-260 Solar is the featured calculator for the GED Mathematics Test. Your testing center will provide this calculator when you take the test. The calculator is shown below, along with callouts that indicate some of its most important keys.

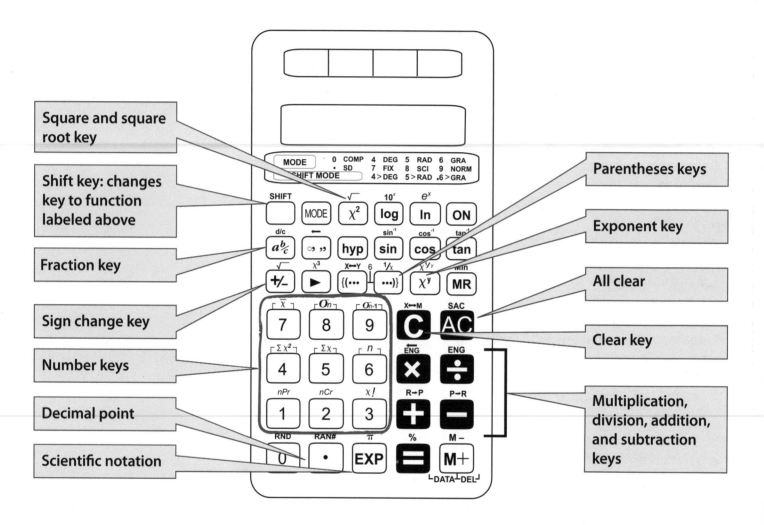

Square and square root key

Shift key: changes key to function labeled above

Fraction key

Sign change key

Number keys

Decimal point

Scientific notation

Parentheses keys

Exponent key

All clear

Clear key

Multiplication, division, addition, and subtraction keys

Getting Started

Press the **ON** key to turn on the calculator. Check the display screen for "DEG" in the upper center and 0 at the right. If you do not see "DEG," then press **MODE** 4.

- Use the **AC** key when you wish to clear all numbers and operations from the screen.
- Use the **C** key when you only wish to delete the last number or operation shown on the screen.

Order of Operations

Note that the calculator uses the order of operations to perform calculations. For example, if you wish to find the mean of 5, 9, 3, 4, and 2, you would need to make sure that you divide the *sum* by 5. If you entered 5 **+** 9 **+** 3 **+** 4 **+** 2 ÷ 5, the calculator would interpret this as $5 + 9 + 3 + 4 + \frac{2}{5}$.

Signed Numbers

Press the **+/−** key when you wish to change a positive number to a negative number, or vice versa. For example, to solve 4 − (−5), enter "4 **−** 5 **+/−** **=**." Note that although the minus symbol and negative sign may look similar on paper, there is a different calculator key for each symbol.

> Use your calculator to simplify −7 − (−9).
> The correct answer is 2.

Parentheses

Use the **((··)** and **(··))** keys to group numbers and symbols. For example, to solve $\frac{-4 + 9}{5 \times 2}$, enter "**((··)** 4 **+/−** **+** 9 **(··))** **÷** **((··)** 5 **×** 2 **(··))** **=**."

> Use your calculator to simplify $9 + \frac{4 - 20}{-3 + 5}$.
> The correct answer is 1.

Squares, Square Roots, and Exponents

Use the **x²** key to raise a number to the second power. For example, to solve $(-6)^2$, enter "6 **+/−** **x²**."

- To find the square root of a number, use the **SHIFT** and **x²** keys. For example, to find the square root of 200, enter "200 **SHIFT** **x²**." The **SHIFT** key changes the function from x^2 to $\sqrt{\ }$.
- To raise a number to a power, use the **xʸ** key. For example, to find 6^4, enter "6 **xʸ** 4."

Note that when squaring numbers or finding square roots, you do not need to press **=**.

> Use your calculator to simplify $3^4 - \sqrt{25} + (-3)^2$.
> The correct answer is 85.

Test-Taking Tips

The GED Tests include 240 questions across the five subject-area exams of Language Arts/Reading, Language Arts/Writing, Mathematics, Science, and Social Studies. In each of the GED Tests, you will need to apply some amount of subject-area knowledge. However, because all of the questions are multiple-choice items largely based on text or visuals (such as tables, charts, or graphs), the emphasis in *GED Prep Xcelerator* is on helping learners like you build and develop core reading and thinking skills. As part of the overall strategy, various test-taking tips are included below and throughout the book to help you improve your performance on the GED Tests. For example:

◆ *Always thoroughly read the directions so that you know exactly what to do.* In Mathematics, for example, one part of the test allows for the use of a calculator. The other part does not. If you are unsure of what to do, ask the test provider if the directions can be explained.

◆ *Read each question carefully so that you fully understand what it is asking.* Some questions, for example, may present more information than you need to correctly answer them. Other questions may note emphasis through capitalized and boldfaced words (Which of the following is **NOT** an example of photosynthesis?).

◆ *Manage your time with each question.* Because the GED Tests are timed exams, you'll want to spend enough time with each question, but not *too* much time. For example, on the GED Mathematics Test, you have 90 minutes in which to answer 50 multiple-choice questions. That works out to less than two minutes per item. You can save time by first reading each question and its answer options before reading the passage or examining the graphic. Once you understand what the question is asking, review the passage or visual for the appropriate information.

◆ *Note any unfamiliar words in questions.* First, attempt to reread the question by omitting the unfamiliar word(s). Next, try to substitute another word in its place.

◆ *Answer all questions, regardless of whether you know the answer or are guessing at it.* There is no benefit in leaving questions unanswered on the GED Tests. Keep in mind the time that you have for each test and manage it accordingly. For time purposes, you may decide to initially skip questions. However, note them with a light mark beside the question and try to return to them before the end of the test.

◆ *Narrow answer options by rereading each question and the text or graphic that goes with it.* Although all five answers are *possible*, keep in mind that only one of them is *correct*. You may be able to eliminate one or two answers immediately; others may take more time and involve the use of either logic or assumptions. In some cases, you may need to make your best guess between two options. If so, keep in mind that test makers often avoid answer patterns; that is, if you know the previous answer is (2) and are unsure of the answer to the next question but have narrowed it to options (2) and (4), you may want to choose (4).

◆ *Read all answer choices.* Even though the first or second answer choice may appear to be correct, be sure to thoroughly read all five answer choices. Then go with your instinct when answering questions. For example, if your first instinct is to mark (1) in response to a question, it's best to stick with that answer unless you later determine that answer to be incorrect. Usually, the first answer you choose is the correct one.

◆ *Correctly complete your answer sheet by marking one numbered space on the answer sheet beside the number that corresponds to it.* Mark only one answer for each item; multiple answers will be scored as incorrect. If time permits, double-check your answer sheet after completing the test to ensure that you have made as many marks—no more, no less—as there are questions.

You've already made two very smart decisions in trying to earn your GED certificate and in purchasing *GED Prep Xcelerator* to help you to do so. The following are additional strategies to help you optimize your success on the GED Tests.

3 weeks out ...

- Set a study schedule for the GED Tests. Choose times in which you are most alert, and places, such as a library, that provide the best study environment.

- Thoroughly review all material in *GED Prep Xcelerator,* using the *GED Prep Xcelerator Mathematics Workbook* to extend understanding of concepts in the *GED Prep Xcelerator Mathematics Student Book.*

- Make sure that you have the necessary tools for the job: sharpened pencils, pens, paper, and, for Mathematics, the Casio FX-260 Solar calculator.

- Keep notebooks for each of the subject areas that you are studying. Folders with pockets are useful for storing loose papers.

- When taking notes, restate thoughts or ideas in your own words rather than copying them directly from a book. You can phrase these notes as complete sentences, as questions (with answers), or as fragments, provided you understand them.

1 week out ...

- Take the pretests, noting any troublesome subject areas. Focus your remaining study around those subject areas.

- Prepare the items you will need for the GED Tests: admission ticket (if necessary), acceptable form of identification, some sharpened No. 2 pencils (with erasers), a watch, eyeglasses (if necessary), a sweater or jacket, and a high-protein snack to eat during breaks.

- Map out the course to the test center, and visit it a day or two before your scheduled exam. If you drive, find a place to park at the center.

- Get a good night's sleep the night before the GED Tests. Studies have shown that learners with sufficient rest perform better in testing situations.

The day of ...

- Eat a hearty breakfast high in protein. As with the rest of your body, your brain needs ample energy to perform well.

- Arrive 30 minutes early to the testing center. This will allow sufficient time in the event of a change to a different testing classroom.

- Pack a sizeable lunch, especially if you plan to be at the testing center most of the day.

- Focus and relax. You've come this far, spending weeks preparing and studying for the GED Tests. It's your time to shine.

Whole Numbers

For use with student book pp. 2-3

UNIT 1

① Review the Skill

Whole numbers are written with the digits 0 through 9. To determine the value of a digit in a whole number, first determine its place value. Understanding place value will help you compare, order, and round whole numbers.

② Refine the Skill

To understand more complex mathematical concepts, you must first master the concept of whole numbers. Examine the paragraph and table. Then answer the questions that follow.

☑ TEST-TAKING TIPS

To maximize test-taking success, underline key words that could help you in solving the question. For example, the word *most* indicates that you will compare to solve the problem.

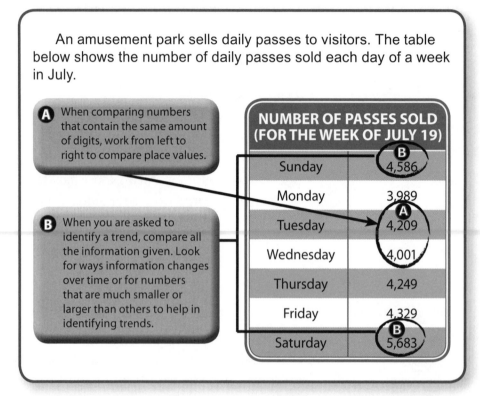

An amusement park sells daily passes to visitors. The table below shows the number of daily passes sold each day of a week in July.

A When comparing numbers that contain the same amount of digits, work from left to right to compare place values.

B When you are asked to identify a trend, compare all the information given. Look for ways information changes over time or for numbers that are much smaller or larger than others to help in identifying trends.

NUMBER OF PASSES SOLD (FOR THE WEEK OF JULY 19)	
Sunday	4,586
Monday	3,989
Tuesday	4,209
Wednesday	4,001
Thursday	4,249
Friday	4,329
Saturday	5,683

1. On which day did the park sell the most daily passes?

    (1) Sunday
    (2) Monday
    (3) Thursday
    (4) Friday
    (5) Saturday

2. Based on the information, what trend can you identify?

    (1) Park attendance grew each day.
    (2) Park attendance fell each day.
    (3) The greatest number of people came to the park on the weekend.
    (4) The number of people at the park remained constant each day.
    (5) Fewer total people visited the park during the week than on the weekend.

Directions: Choose the <u>one best answer</u> to each question.

<u>Questions 3 through 5</u> refer to the following information and table.

The seats in a large auditorium are identified by both numbers and letters. The range of numbers for each letter row is shown in the chart.

SEAT NUMBERS	
LETTER OF ROW	NUMBER RANGE
A	100–250
B	251–500
C	501–750
D	751–1000
E	1001–1250
F	1251–1500

3. In which row will you sit if your seat number is 1107?

    (1) Row A
    (2) Row B
    (3) Row C
    (4) Row E
    (5) Row F

4. Which row has the fewest number of seats?

    (1) Row A
    (2) Row B
    (3) Row C
    (4) Row E
    (5) Row F

5. How many rows have seat numbers in the thousands?

    (1) 1
    (2) 2
    (3) 3
    (4) 4
    (5) 5

<u>Questions 6 and 7</u> refer to the following information.

In a dictionary, the following letters can be found on the following pages:

    P—pages 968–1096

    Q—pages 1097–1105

    R—pages 1105–1178

    S—pages 1178–1360

    T—pages 1360–1447

6. With which letter does a word found on page 1100 begin?

    (1) P
    (2) Q
    (3) R
    (4) S
    (5) T

7. Words that begin with the letter S can be found on what pages?

    (1) 998–1045
    (2) 1046–1105
    (3) 1117–1165
    (4) 1234–1287
    (5) 1293–1376

8. Callie's job involves data entry. Which digits should she type in for the number twelve thousand, eight hundred two?

    (1) 1, 2, 8, 0, 2
    (2) 1, 2, 8, 2, 0
    (3) 1, 2, 8, 0, 0, 2
    (4) 1, 2, 0, 8, 0, 2
    (5) 1, 2, 0, 8, 2, 0

9. Romy's scores for her five social studies quizzes this semester are shown below.

98, 75, 84, 92, 95

What is the order of her social studies quiz scores from greatest to least?

(1) 75, 84, 92, 95, 98
(2) 75, 92, 95, 84, 98
(3) 95, 92, 98, 84, 75
(4) 98, 95, 84, 92, 75
(5) 98, 95, 92, 84, 75

10. Calvin is writing an essay. He wants to write the sentence "150,218 people lived in the city in 2005," but a good rule for writing is to avoid beginning a sentence with a numeral. What is a better way for Calvin to write his sentence?

(1) One hundred fifty thousand, two eighteen people lived in the city in 2005.
(2) One hundred fifty, two hundred eighteen people lived in the city in 2005.
(3) One thousand fifty, two hundred eighteen people lived in the city in 2005.
(4) One hundred fifty thousand, twenty-one eight people lived in the city in 2005.
(5) One hundred fifty thousand, two hundred eighteen people lived in the city in 2005.

11. A museum tracks its visitors each month. For its records, the museum rounds the number of monthly visitors to the nearest hundred. If 8,648 people visited the museum in July, what number will the museum record?

(1) 8,500
(2) 8,600
(3) 8,650
(4) 8,700
(5) 9,000

Questions 12 and 13 refer to the table below.

The table shows the number of people in different age groups who lived in San Francisco in 2000.

AGE GROUPS IN SAN FRANCISCO	
AGE GROUP	POPULATION
Under 5 years	31,633
5 to 9 years	31,564
10 to 14 years	30,813
15 to 19 years	33,334
20 to 24 years	56,054
25 to 34 years	180,418
35 to 44 years	133,804
45 to 54 years	107,718
55 to 59 years	35,026
60 to 64 years	30,258
65 to 74 years	53,955
75 to 84 years	37,929
85 years and over	14,227

12. Which age group had the fewest number of people?

(1) Under 5 years
(2) 10 to 14 years
(3) 15 to 19 years
(4) 60 to 64 years
(5) 85 years and over

13. Based on the table, the greatest number of people in San Francisco in 2000 were how old?

(1) 9 years or younger
(2) 10 to 24 years old
(3) 15 to 24 years old
(4) 25 to 54 years old
(5) 75 years or older

14. During jury selection, a clerk calls juror numbers. When a juror hears his or her number, he or she steps forward to speak with the judge. Bryan is juror number 807. When should he step forward to speak with the judge?

(1) when the clerk says "eighty-seven"
(2) when the clerk says "eight and seven"
(3) when the clerk says "eight hundred seven"
(4) when the clerk says "eight hundred seventy"
(5) when the clerk says "eighty hundred and seven"

Questions 15 and 16 refer to the information and table below.

Some people believe that, if you double the height of a child at age 2, the figure will equal the child's full height as an adult. The table below shows the heights of five children at age 2.

HEIGHT OF 2-YEAR-OLDS	
CHILD	HEIGHT (IN.)
Ellie	32
Jake	34
George	33
Charlie	35
Kiera	34
Melanie	31

15. According to the above belief, which child will be the tallest adult?

(1) Ellie
(2) Jake
(3) George
(4) Charlie
(5) Kiera

16. If the belief holds true, which child will be the same height as Kiera in adulthood?

(1) Ellie
(2) Jake
(3) George
(4) Charlie
(5) Melanie

17. A professional cyclist bicycled 22,755 miles in 2005, 20,564 miles in 2006, and 23,804 miles in 2007. What is the order of the miles bicycled each year from least to greatest?

(1) 20,564, 22,755, 23,804
(2) 20,564, 23,804, 22,755
(3) 22,755, 23,804, 20,564
(4) 23,804, 20,564, 22,755
(5) 23,804, 22,755, 20,564

Question 18 refers to the information and table below.

The table shows weekly sales of an automobile dealership over five weekends in the month of May.

WEEKLY SALES IN MAY	
WEEKEND	SALES
Weekend 1	$168,000
Weekend 2	$102,000
Weekend 3	$121,000
Weekend 4	$119,000
Weekend 5	$305,000

18. On which weekend did the automobile dealership most likely run a promotion to sell more cars?

(1) Weekend 1
(2) Weekend 2
(3) Weekend 3
(4) Weekend 4
(5) Weekend 5

Question 19 refers to the information and table below.

Tom's Toy Store released its quarterly sales figures for the recent year. Sales are shown below.

QUARTERLY SALES	
MONTHS	SALES
Quarter 1 (January through March)	$79,000
Quarter 2 (April through June)	$131,000
Quarter 3 (July through September)	$119,000
Quarter 4 (October through December)	$151,000

19. What is the store's order of quarterly toy sales from least to greatest?

(1) Quarter 1, Quarter 2, Quarter 3, Quarter 4
(2) Quarter 2, Quarter 3, Quarter 4, Quarter 1
(3) Quarter 1, Quarter 3, Quarter 2, Quarter 4
(4) Quarter 3, Quarter 2, Quarter 4, Quarter 1
(5) Quarter 4, Quarter 2, Quarter 3, Quarter 1

Operations

For use with student book pp. 4-5

1 Review the Skill

Select an operation(s) based on the information you need to find. Add to find a sum. Subtract to find a difference. Multiply to add the same number many times. Divide to separate a quantity into equal groups.

2 Refine the Skill

You will use one or more of the four basic operations to solve many problems on the GED Mathematics Test. You must understand what each operation does, and when to use each operation to solve problems effectively. Examine the information and table. Then answer the questions that follow.

The table shows the number of boxes of cereal that a company produced each day in one week.

COMPANY CEREAL PRODUCTION	
DAY OF WEEK	NUMBER OF BOXES
Monday	A 4,596
Tuesday	4,025
Wednesday	3,548
Thursday	4,250
Friday	B 3,115

A To add, align place values. Then add the numbers in each column to find the sum. If the sum of a column exceeds 9, you must regroup.

B Sometimes, words in the question provide clues about the needed operation. For example, question 2 states that production of cereal increased *3 times* from the previous week. The word *times* suggests that multiplication is the operation to use to solve the problem.

☑ TEST-TAKING TIPS

Addition and subtraction are opposites. Use addition to check your answer to a subtraction problem, and use subtraction to check your answer to an addition problem. Multiplication and division are related in the same way. Use multiplication to check division answers, and division to check multiplication answers.

1. What was the total number of boxes of cereal produced on Monday and Tuesday?

(1) 8,144
(2) 8,611
(3) 8,620
(4) 8,621
(5) 8,846

2. The following Friday, the factory increased production and produced 3 times as many boxes of cereal as the previous Friday. How many boxes of cereal were produced the following Friday?

(1) 6,230
(2) 7,730
(3) 9,345
(4) 9,430
(5) 12,460

Directions: Choose the <u>one best answer</u> to each question.

3. Alex saves $325 each month for college tuition. How much will he have saved after 6 months?

   (1) $331
   (2) $975
   (3) $1,300
   (4) $1,625
   (5) $1,950

4. Angelo has paid $1,560 toward his car loan. If his loan is $2,750, how much does he still owe?

   (1) $190
   (2) $990
   (3) $1,190
   (4) $1,290
   (5) Not enough information is given.

5. Tara pays the same amount for her electric bill each month. If she pays $72 per month, what is the total cost of her electricity for one year?

   (1) $84
   (2) $216
   (3) $720
   (4) $864
   (5) Not enough information is given.

6. Four roommates equally share their monthly rent. Their monthly rent is $1,080. How much does each roommate pay per month?

   (1) $270
   (2) $250
   (3) $240
   (4) $216
   (5) $207

7. A city budgets $567,800 for parks and recreation and $258,900 for facility maintenance. How much is spent on these two parts altogether?

   (1) $308,900
   (2) $358,900
   (3) $700,000
   (4) $801,900
   (5) $826,700

8. Mara gave 22 shirts, 14 pairs of pants, and 12 scarves to charity. How many clothing items did she give away altogether?

   (1) 26
   (2) 30
   (3) 32
   (4) 48
   (5) 54

9. Eli is writing a 1,500-word essay for English class. He has written 892 words so far. How many words must he still write?

   (1) 408
   (2) 508
   (3) 608
   (4) 708
   (5) 808

Question 10 refers to the table below.

The table shows the cost of attending a professional football game.

COST OF GAME	
PRODUCT/SERVICE	COST
Gasoline and parking	$50
Tickets	$335
Food	$80
Souvenirs	$75

10. If five friends decided to evenly share the costs, how much would each person expect to pay?

    (1) $106
    (2) $107
    (3) $108
    (4) $109
    (5) $110

Questions 11 through 13 refer to the following information and table.

The table shows part of Antonio's monthly budget.

MONTHLY BUDGET	
Rent	$825
Utilities	$220
Food	$285
Recreation	$100
Auto Loan	$179
Auto Insurance	$62

11. What is the total amount included in Antonio's budget for rent, utilities, and food?

    (1) $540
    (2) $605
    (3) $1,045
    (4) $1,110
    (5) $1,330

12. How much more money does Antonio allow in his budget for food than for his auto loan?

    (1) $41
    (2) $65
    (3) $106
    (4) $185
    (5) $464

13. How much does Antonio pay toward his auto loan each year?

    (1) $179
    (2) $372
    (3) $744
    (4) $1,074
    (5) $2,148

14. Annette works 5 days per week, 6 hours per day. She earns $13 per hour. How much does Annette earn in 4 weeks?

    (1) $1,560
    (2) $1,180
    (3) $390
    (4) $260
    (5) $120

15. Andrew worked 54 hours one week and 39 hours the next week. He earns $11 per hour. How much did he earn in the 2 weeks?

    (1) $429
    (2) $594
    (3) $945
    (4) $1,023
    (5) $2,106

16. In January, the Wilsons spent $458 on groceries. They spent $397 in February and $492 in March. What is the total amount the Wilsons spent on groceries for the three months?

    (1) $800
    (2) $855
    (3) $950
    (4) $1,250
    (5) $1,347

17. A sports store ran a promotion on a specific tent. During the promotion, the store had tent sales of $23,870. If each tent cost $385, how many tents did the store sell during the promotion?

    (1) 59
    (2) 60
    (3) 61
    (4) 62
    (5) 63

18. A pattern calls for 2 yards of material for a shirt. The same pattern for a dress calls for 5 yards of material. A seamstress makes five shirts and five dresses for a retail store. How many more yards of material does she use for the dresses than for the shirts?

(1) 5
(2) 10
(3) 15
(4) 20
(5) 25

19. Joanne drives 37 miles round-trip each day commuting to and from work. She works Monday through Friday. How many miles does Joanne drive in 4 weeks?

(1) 148
(2) 185
(3) 370
(4) 740
(5) 1,480

20. A charity wants to donate $12,500 to a food bank. It has already collected $4,020 in donations from local businesses and $3,902 in donations from individuals. How much more does the charity need to collect to meet its goal?

(1) $3,588
(2) $4,578
(3) $5,000
(4) $8,480
(5) $8,598

21. Mr. and Mrs. Dale paid $1,445 to have a new floor installed in their kitchen. The company installed 289 square feet of flooring. How much did the Dales pay for each square foot of flooring?

(1) $5
(2) $57
(3) $1,156
(4) $1,734
(5) Not enough information is given.

22. Maggie purchased a used car. She financed the car through the auto dealership. She will make equal monthly payments on the car for 3 years. If she owes a total of $13,392, what will her monthly payment be?

(1) $279
(2) $372
(3) $558
(4) $1,116
(5) $4,464

Questions 23 and 24 refer to the information and table below.

The table shows the prices of various stocks for purchase.

STOCK PRICES	
STOCK	PRICE PER SHARE
Computers4U	$30
Sun Cell Phones	$23
Online Airlines	$15
Virtual Reality, Inc.	$42

23. Mario wants to invest in an online travel service. How many shares of Online Airlines can he purchase for $270?

(1) 9
(2) 12
(3) 15
(4) 18
(5) 21

24. Karissa purchased 25 shares of Virtual Reality, Inc., and then sold all of them three months later for a profit of $7 per share. How much profit did Karissa make on her sale of Virtual Reality, Inc.?

(1) $175
(2) $225
(3) $275
(4) $325
(5) $375

ord Problems

For use with student book pp. 6-7

① Review the Skill

To solve a word problem, first read carefully to find out what you are being asked. Next, determine the information that you need to solve the problem. Then decide which operation or operations to use. Finally, solve the problem and check your answer.

② Refine the Skill

Remember to add when combining amounts. Subtract when finding the difference or finding "how many more." Multiply when adding the same number several times, and divide when a total is being split into groups. Examine the information and table. Then answer the questions that follow.

The Ryersons are going on vacation. The table shows the amount of money they have budgeted for their vacation.

MONEY BUDGETED FOR VACATION	
Airfare	$1,650
Food	$810
Lodging	$720
Entertainment	$375
Souvenirs	$250

Ⓐ

Ⓑ

Ⓐ The key to solving word problems is to first read and understand them before performing any calculations. Sometimes this will involve reading tables or graphs as well as text. Here, the Ryersons' vacation budget is divided into five categories, with costs listed for each.

Ⓑ Sometimes, word problems involve multiple operations in order to solve them. Here, you must add two areas and then subtract them from another to arrive at the correct answer.

☑ TEST-TAKING TIPS

Look for key words in word problems to help you determine what to do. The word *approximately* indicates that you need to find an estimate. The word *combined* indicates that one of your operations will be addition.

1. Approximately how much money have the Ryersons budgeted for food and lodging?

   (1) $1,400
   (2) $1,500
   (3) $1,600
   (4) $1,700
   (5) $1,800

2. How much more money do the Ryersons expect airfare to cost than food and lodging combined?

   (1) $120
   (2) $180
   (3) $840
   (4) $930
   (5) Not enough information is given.

UNIT 1

Directions: Choose the <u>one best answer</u> to each question.

3. José is training for a triathlon. He needs to eat 3,500 calories per day to maintain his level of fitness. He ate 1,250 calories at breakfast. He ate another 780 calories at lunch. How many calories must he still eat today to maintain his level of fitness?

   (1) 780
   (2) 1,250
   (3) 1,470
   (4) 2,250
   (5) 2,720

4. A large factory has 2,391 employees. Of these employees, 2,012 work on the production lines, 157 work in shipping, and the rest of the employees work in administration. How many employees work in administration?

   (1) 157
   (2) 222
   (3) 379
   (4) 2,548
   (5) 4,403

5. Stella pays $126 per month on her car loan. She pays $57 per month for auto insurance. What is the cost of her car loan per year?

   (1) $183
   (2) $684
   (3) $828
   (4) $1,512
   (5) $2,196

6. Five friends carpool to work together. Each week, the gas, parking, and tolls cost $95. If the friends split the cost equally, how much does each person pay toward the weekly carpool costs?

   (1) $17
   (2) $18
   (3) $19
   (4) $20
   (5) $21

Questions 7 and 8 refer to the table below.

The table shows Grace's weekly time sheet.

GRACE'S WEEKLY TIME SHEET					
	HOURS WORKED PER DAY				
Employee	Mon	Tues	Wed	Thu	Fri
Grace D.	6	5	7	8	8

7. If Grace makes $8 per hour, how much money did she earn for the week?

   (1) $48
   (2) $144
   (3) $240
   (4) $264
   (5) $272

8. The following week, Grace worked 6 more hours than the week before. She also received a raise to $9 per hour. How much did Grace earn the following week?

   (1) $272
   (2) $304
   (3) $320
   (4) $360
   (5) $369

9. Theo and two friends went out for lunch. The bill was $30. They also left a tip. If they split the cost evenly, how much did each of them pay?

   (1) $12
   (2) $14
   (3) $16
   (4) $18
   (5) Not enough information is given.

10. Naomi has $913 in her checking account. She deposits $130, writes two checks for $75 apiece, and withdraws $50 with her bank card. How much money is left in Naomi's account?

   (1) $843
   (2) $893
   (3) $923
   (4) $973
   (5) $1,043

11. The mileage on Marla's car was 41,868 when she last had her tires changed. She bought new tires that are advertised to last for 40,000 miles. Marla now has 97,634 miles on her car. How many miles over 40,000 has Marla driven on these tires?

(1) 15,766
(2) 15,776
(3) 15,867
(4) 16,766
(5) 16,776

12. Charlotte can drive 400 miles on one tank of gas. Her gas tank holds 16 gallons of gas. If gas is $3 per gallon, how much will it cost her to drive 800 miles?

(1) $48
(2) $96
(3) $133
(4) $144
(5) $1,200

13. Karen owns three apartments. She rents each apartment for $895 per month. If she raises the rent to $950 per month, how much rent will she collect each month?

(1) $165
(2) $2,520
(3) $2,550
(4) $2,685
(5) $2,850

14. Trisha and her three siblings inherited $4,598 from an uncle. The lawyer's fees to settle the estate were $1,354. The remainder was split equally. How much money did Trisha and each of her siblings inherit?

(1) $811
(2) $1,081
(3) $1,150
(4) $1,622
(5) $3,244

Question 15 and 16 refer to the table below.

The table shows how many skeins of each color yarn that a craft store has in stock.

SKEINS OF YARN	
YARN COLOR	NUMBER OF SKEINS
Blue	3,156
Red	2,634
Green	1,920
White	4,208
Off-white	983
Yellow	732
Orange	531
Brown	1,828
Purple	935

15. About how many more skeins of white yarn than off-white yarn does the store have in stock? Round to the nearest thousand.

(1) 1,000
(2) 2,000
(3) 3,000
(4) 4,000
(5) 5,000

16. The white, blue, and red skeins are the craft store's most popular colors of yarn. Added together, the number of white, blue, and red skeins exceeds the combined amount of the other six skeins. How many more white, blue, and red skeins are there than the other skeins combined? Round the difference to the nearest hundred.

(1) 2,500
(2) 3,100
(3) 3,600
(4) 3,800
(5) 4,500

17. A furniture store is offering a payment plan for a dining table and chairs. The cost of the set is $1,620. The payment plan is $150 per month for 12 months. How much more will you pay if you choose the payment plan instead of purchasing the set up front?

(1) $1,800
(2) $1,620
(3) $180
(4) $135
(5) $0

18. Cody works at an electronics store. On Sunday, he sold four televisions for $757 each and three speaker systems for $533 each. He earns $50 commission for each television and $30 commission for each speaker system that he sells. How much money in commissions did Cody make on Sunday?

(1) $560
(2) $290
(3) $270
(4) $80
(5) Not enough information is given.

19. Angela bought $250 worth of fencing supplies, $207 worth of paving blocks, and 18 bags of mulch. What was the total cost of the mulch and paving blocks?

(1) $43
(2) $268
(3) $457
(4) $475
(5) Not enough information is given.

20. Hernando plans to make 12 monthly payments on his computer. The total cost of the computer plus interest is $1,476. How much will he pay per month?

(1) $112
(2) $123
(3) $131
(4) $139
(5) $147

Questions 21 and 22 refer to the information and table below.

Gretchen ordered T-shirts for the participants in a triathlon. The table shows how many boxes of each size T-shirt that she ordered. There are 35 T-shirts in each box of women's T-shirts and 25 T-shirts in each box of men's T-shirts.

BOXES OF T-SHIRTS ORDERED	
SIZE	NUMBER OF BOXES
Women's Small	5
Women's Medium	6
Women's Large	5
Men's Medium	3
Men's Large	8
Men's Extra Large	14

21. How many more men's T-shirts than women's T-shirts did Gretchen order?

(1) 9
(2) 10
(3) 65
(4) 475
(5) 1,185

22. How many shirts would Gretchen order if she only ordered medium and large sizes?

(1) 550
(2) 600
(3) 625
(4) 660
(5) 910

23. The Millersville Youth Athletic Center has children's sports leagues. Last fall, 460 children (242 boys, 218 girls) signed up to play basketball. In the spring, 540 children (295 boys, 245 girls) signed up to play soccer. How many more girls signed up to play soccer than signed up to play basketball?

(1) 17
(2) 27
(3) 37
(4) 47
(5) 57

F ractions

For use with student book pp. 8-9

① **Review the Skill**

A **fraction** shows part of a whole or part of a group. An **improper fraction** has a numerator that is greater than the denominator. It shows an amount greater than one whole. A **mixed number** has a whole number part and a fraction part. To compare and order fractions, first find a common denominator.

② **Refine the Skill**

Before you can perform operations with fractions, you must first understand how to compare, order, and rename fractions. You will use these skills to help you solve problems successfully on the GED Mathematics Test. Examine the table. Then answer the questions that follow.

The table below shows the fraction of employees who work the night shift at each of five auto plants.

A To answer certain questions, you may need to find equivalent fractions. Scan the answer options and determine whether, by simply reducing the fraction, you can successfully answer the question.

B Some problems will ask you to compare fractions with different denominators. These fractions are called unlike fractions. To solve problems with unlike fractions, rename the fractions using one common denominator. Then subtract the numerators to find the difference.

AUTO PLANTS AND THEIR NIGHT-SHIFT EMPLOYEES

AUTO PLANT	FRACTION OF EMPLOYEES WHO WORK THE NIGHT SHIFT
Plant A	$\frac{1}{3}$
Plant B	$\frac{1}{6}$
Plant C	**B** $\frac{3}{4}$
Plant D	$\frac{2}{3}$
Plant E	$\frac{1}{4}$

✓ **TEST-TAKING TIPS**

When the numerator and the denominator of a fraction are close in value, the value of the fraction is close to 1. For example, $\frac{3}{4}$ has a value close to 1, whereas $\frac{1}{6}$ does not.

A 1. At which auto plant do $\frac{2}{6}$ of the employees work the night shift?

(1) Auto Plant A
(2) Auto Plant B
(3) Auto Plant C
(4) Auto Plant D
(5) Auto Plant E

B 2. Which auto plant has the greatest fraction of nightly workers?

(1) Auto Plant A
(2) Auto Plant B
(3) Auto Plant C
(4) Auto Plant D
(5) Auto Plant E

③ Master the Skill

Directions: Choose the <u>one best answer</u> to each question.

3. Two out of every five students in a high school are male. What fraction of the high school students are male?

(1) $\frac{1}{6}$

(2) $\frac{1}{5}$

(3) $\frac{2}{5}$

(4) $\frac{4}{5}$

(5) $\frac{5}{2}$

4. There are 64 students in the school band. There are 16 trumpet players. What fraction of the band are trumpet players?

(1) $\frac{1}{4}$

(2) $\frac{3}{8}$

(3) $\frac{5}{8}$

(4) $\frac{3}{4}$

(5) $\frac{7}{8}$

5. Anna withdrew $50 from her checking account. She spent $28 on a pair of shoes. What fraction of her money does Anna have left?

(1) $\frac{28}{50}$

(2) $\frac{14}{25}$

(3) $\frac{26}{50}$

(4) $\frac{23}{50}$

(5) $\frac{11}{25}$

6. A restaurant served 72 customers for breakfast. Of those, 18 had omelets. What fraction of the customers had omelets?

(1) $\frac{1}{54}$

(2) $\frac{1}{18}$

(3) $\frac{1}{4}$

(4) $\frac{2}{3}$

(5) $\frac{6}{7}$

7. There were 3,000 fans at a football game. Of those, 2,000 were fans of the Hawks. What fraction of the fans rooted for the Hawks?

(1) $\frac{1}{4}$

(2) $\frac{1}{3}$

(3) $\frac{1}{2}$

(4) $\frac{2}{3}$

(5) $\frac{3}{4}$

8. The school chess club celebrated its recent championship. The 15-member team went out for dessert. Five members ordered pie, 4 ordered ice cream, 3 ordered cake, and 3 ordered milkshakes. What fraction of the chess club members ordered ice cream?

(1) $\frac{1}{5}$

(2) $\frac{1}{4}$

(3) $\frac{4}{15}$

(4) $\frac{1}{3}$

(5) $\frac{11}{15}$

9. Janine's answers to a math quiz are shown below.

$$1. \frac{12}{17} \quad 2. \frac{7}{8} \quad 3. \frac{4}{7} \quad 4. \frac{8}{18} \quad 5. \frac{3}{5}$$

Janine's teacher marked one of her answers as incorrect because she did not write the fraction in lowest terms. Which question did her teacher mark as incorrect?

(1) Question 1
(2) Question 2
(3) Question 3
(4) Question 4
(5) Question 5

10. There are 248 students in a school. The student population includes 172 females. What fraction of the students are male?

(1) $\frac{19}{248}$

(2) $\frac{43}{248}$

(3) $\frac{19}{62}$

(4) $\frac{43}{62}$

(5) $\frac{172}{184}$

11. To show their school spirit, students were to wear red, white, or blue colors to the Patriots' next game. Of the 2,500 students in attendance, 750 wore red, 850 wore white, and the rest wore blue. What fraction of students wore blue to the game?

(1) $\frac{3}{10}$

(2) $\frac{17}{50}$

(3) $\frac{9}{25}$

(4) $\frac{2}{5}$

(5) $\frac{1}{2}$

Questions 12 and 13 refer to the table below.

The table lists five students and the fraction of homework that each student completed.

VARIOUS STUDENTS' HOMEWORK COMPLETION	
STUDENT	FRACTION OF HOMEWORK COMPLETED
Dara	$\frac{2}{5}$
Natalia	$\frac{7}{10}$
Miguel	$\frac{1}{2}$
Ethan	$\frac{9}{10}$
Walt	$\frac{4}{5}$

12. Which student completed the most amount of homework?

(1) Dara
(2) Natalia
(3) Miguel
(4) Ethan
(5) Walt

13. The fraction of homework completed by which two students in the table equals the fraction of homework completed by Ethan?

(1) Dara and Natalia
(2) Miguel and Walt
(3) Dara and Miguel
(4) Natalia and Walt
(5) Natalia and Miguel

14. The GED Mathematics pretest features 25 questions. Erik answered $\frac{1}{5}$ of the questions incorrectly. How many questions did Erik correctly answer?

(1) 17
(2) 18
(3) 19
(4) 20
(5) 21

Lesson 4 | Fractions

15. Rachel needs $7\frac{1}{2}$ cups of flour to make pizzas. How many $\frac{1}{2}$ cups of flour are in $7\frac{1}{2}$ cups?

   (1) 5
   (2) 7
   (3) 8
   (4) 14
   (5) 15

16. On a quiz, Alexandra answered eight questions correctly and two questions incorrectly. What fraction of the questions did she answer correctly?

   (1) $\frac{1}{8}$

   (2) $\frac{2}{8}$

   (3) $\frac{2}{5}$

   (4) $\frac{4}{5}$

   (5) $\frac{5}{8}$

17. Quentin is filling a glass that holds $1\frac{3}{4}$ cups of water. He is using a $\frac{1}{4}$-cup measuring cup. How many times will he have to fill the smaller measuring cup to equal $1\frac{3}{4}$ cups?

   (1) 5
   (2) 6
   (3) 7
   (4) 8
   (5) 9

18. Marta is tripling a recipe. The recipe calls for $2\frac{3}{8}$ cups of flour. Before she multiplies by three, she writes the mixed number as an improper fraction. What is $2\frac{3}{8}$ written as an improper fraction?

   (1) $\frac{5}{8}$

   (2) $\frac{13}{8}$

   (3) $\frac{19}{8}$

   (4) $\frac{23}{8}$

   (5) $\frac{30}{8}$

19. An employee is packing shirts into boxes for shipping. On his inventory sheet, he marks that he is shipping $\frac{23}{4}$ boxes of shirts. What is $\frac{23}{4}$ written as a mixed number?

   (1) $4\frac{3}{4}$

   (2) $5\frac{1}{23}$

   (3) $5\frac{1}{4}$

   (4) $5\frac{1}{2}$

   (5) $5\frac{3}{4}$

20. Downtown Hardware advertised a weekend sale in the newspaper. On Saturday, 85 people visited the store. Of those, 34 had viewed the store's sale advertisement. What fraction of shoppers saw the store's advertisement?

   (1) $\frac{1}{2}$

   (2) $\frac{4}{9}$

   (3) $\frac{3}{7}$

   (4) $\frac{2}{5}$

   (5) $\frac{1}{3}$

21. Matt earns $2,750 per month in take-home pay. He spends $825 per month on rent. What fraction of his take-home earnings does Matt spend on rent?

   (1) $\frac{1}{10}$

   (2) $\frac{1}{5}$

   (3) $\frac{1}{4}$

   (4) $\frac{3}{10}$

   (5) $\frac{1}{3}$

UNIT 1

① Review the Skill

To add or subtract fractions, the fractions first must have common denominators. Then add or subtract the numerators. To multiply fractions, multiply the numerators and multiply the denominators. To divide fractions, multiply the dividend by the reciprocal of the divisor. To find the reciprocal, switch the numerator and the denominator.

② Refine the Skill

Problems relating to fractions often appear on the GED Mathematics Test. To successfully solve these problems, you must understand how to choose and perform the correct operation. Answers must be in simplified form. Examine the table. Then answer the questions that follow.

The following chart shows the yards of fabric needed for each size of a dress pattern.

YARDS OF FABRIC NEEDED FOR DRESS PATTERNS		
SIZE	45-INCH FABRIC (YD)	60-INCH FABRIC (YD)
XS	$3\frac{1}{4}$	$2\frac{3}{4}$
S	$3\frac{1}{2}$	$3\frac{1}{4}$
M	$3\frac{5}{8}$	$3\frac{3}{4}$
L	$3\frac{7}{8}$	$4\frac{1}{8}$
XL	$4\frac{1}{8}$	$4\frac{3}{8}$

Ⓐ When finding "how much more," subtract the amounts. In question 1, it may be helpful to write the mixed numbers as improper fractions, since $\frac{1}{8} < \frac{1}{4}$.

Ⓑ When you see a fraction followed by the word *of*, multiply. For example, to find $\frac{1}{5}$ of $\frac{3}{4}$, multiply $\frac{1}{5} \times \frac{3}{4}$.

☑ TEST-TAKING TIPS

You can reduce some fractions before you multiply or divide to make your calculations simpler. To simplify, divide the numerator and denominator by the same number.

$$\frac{1}{2} \times \frac{4}{5} = \frac{1 \times \overset{2}{\cancel{4}}}{\underset{1}{\cancel{2}} \times 5} = \frac{2}{5}$$

1. Sharon is sewing an extra-small dress for her daughter and an extra-large dress for herself using 45-inch fabric. **Ⓐ** <u>How much more fabric</u> will she need for the extra-large dress than for the extra-small dress?

(1) $\frac{1}{8}$ yd

(2) $\frac{1}{4}$ yd

(3) $\frac{1}{2}$ yd

(4) $\frac{3}{4}$ yd

(5) $\frac{7}{8}$ yd

2. **Ⓑ** Sharon has $\frac{1}{2}$ of the 60-inch fabric she needs to make an extra-small dress. How much 60-inch fabric does she have?

(1) $1\frac{1}{8}$ yd

(2) $1\frac{1}{4}$ yd

(3) $1\frac{3}{8}$ yd

(4) $2\frac{1}{8}$ yd

(5) $2\frac{3}{4}$ yd

③ Master the Skill

<u>Directions</u>: Choose the <u>one best answer</u> to each question.

3. Chandra has 8 sick days per year. If she has already used $3\frac{1}{2}$ sick days, how many sick days does she have left?

   (1) $3\frac{1}{2}$

   (2) 4

   (3) $4\frac{1}{2}$

   (4) 5

   (5) $5\frac{1}{2}$

4. Todd keeps track of the water he uses in his garden every week. One week he used $3\frac{3}{4}$ gallons, $5\frac{1}{2}$ gallons, and $4\frac{1}{4}$ gallons. How many gallons of water did he use in his garden that week?

   (1) $4\frac{1}{2}$

   (2) $8\frac{1}{4}$

   (3) $9\frac{1}{2}$

   (4) $12\frac{1}{2}$

   (5) $13\frac{1}{2}$

5. Last year, a farmer used 6 gallons of pesticide on his vegetable gardens. This year, he only used $1\frac{1}{3}$ gallons. How much more pesticide did he use last year than this year?

   (1) $4\frac{1}{8}$

   (2) $4\frac{1}{3}$

   (3) $4\frac{1}{2}$

   (4) $4\frac{2}{3}$

   (5) Not enough information is given.

6. In one year, Elias earns \$29,400. His semi-monthly paycheck is $\frac{1}{24}$ of this amount. What is the amount of his semi-monthly paycheck?

   (1) \$12.25
   (2) \$122.50
   (3) \$1,225.00
   (4) \$12,250.00
   (5) Not enough information is given.

7. A chef uses $\frac{1}{4}$ pound of ground beef to make each dinner special. How many specials can the chef prepare from 24 pounds of ground beef?

   (1) 48
   (2) 64
   (3) 80
   (4) 96
   (5) 112

8. Mike owns a lawnmowing business. He can mow one lawn in about 15 minutes. If Mike works 30 hours per week, how many lawns can he mow?

   (1) 30
   (2) 60
   (3) 90
   (4) 120
   (5) 150

9. Amy works as an editor at a publishing house. It takes her 35 minutes to edit one textbook page. How many hours would it take Amy to edit a 300-page book?

   (1) 150
   (2) 175
   (3) 200
   (4) 225
   (5) 250

10. Forty people are part of a tour group in London. One day, $\frac{1}{2}$ of the group opted to go for a cruise on the River Thames. Of the $\frac{1}{2}$ that did not go on the cruise, $\frac{2}{3}$ visited the Tower of London. What fraction of the group chose to visit the Tower of London that day?

(1) $\frac{1}{6}$

(2) $\frac{1}{3}$

(3) $\frac{4}{6}$

(4) $\frac{2}{3}$

(5) $\frac{3}{4}$

11. Ed purchased $25\frac{7}{8}$ yd of fencing for his yard. He only used $17\frac{5}{6}$ yd. How many yards of fencing does he have left?

(1) $8\frac{1}{48}$

(2) $8\frac{1}{24}$

(3) $9\frac{1}{8}$

(4) $9\frac{1}{12}$

(5) $9\frac{1}{2}$

12. A group of 30 people attended a baseball game. Of those, $\frac{1}{5}$ sat in blue seats, $\frac{1}{2}$ sat in yellow seats, and the rest sat in red seats. What fraction of the people sat in red seats?

(1) $\frac{1}{3}$

(2) $\frac{3}{10}$

(3) $\frac{1}{4}$

(4) $\frac{1}{5}$

(5) $\frac{1}{10}$

Questions 13 and 14 refer to the table below.

The table below shows the number of miles that Luke rode his bicycle over the course of one week.

LUKE'S WEEKLY BICYCLING MILEAGE	
DAY	NUMBER OF MILES
Sunday	$18\frac{2}{3}$
Monday	$25\frac{9}{10}$
Tuesday	$15\frac{1}{2}$
Wednesday	$12\frac{7}{8}$
Thursday	$32\frac{5}{6}$
Friday	$19\frac{7}{8}$
Saturday	$24\frac{5}{6}$

13. How many miles did Luke ride on the weekend?

(1) 42

(2) $42\frac{1}{2}$

(3) $43\frac{1}{2}$

(4) $44\frac{1}{2}$

(5) $44\frac{17}{24}$

14. How many fewer miles did Luke ride on Wednesday than he rode on Monday?

(1) $12\frac{1}{40}$

(2) $12\frac{1}{20}$

(3) $13\frac{1}{40}$

(4) $13\frac{1}{10}$

(5) $14\frac{1}{20}$

UNIT 1

15. Ginny has 26 tests to correct. It takes her $\frac{1}{9}$ of an hour to correct each test. How many hours will it take Ginny to correct all of the tests?

(1) $2\frac{1}{4}$

(2) $2\frac{1}{3}$

(3) $2\frac{1}{2}$

(4) $2\frac{2}{3}$

(5) $2\frac{8}{9}$

16. Scott cut a board for a cabinet. The original board was $3\frac{7}{8}$ feet long. The board is now $3\frac{1}{4}$ feet long. If he cut the board $\frac{3}{8}$ of an inch too short, how many feet long is the board supposed to be?

(1) $2\frac{5}{8}$

(2) $3\frac{1}{4}$

(3) $3\frac{5}{8}$

(4) $7\frac{1}{8}$

(5) Not enough information is given.

17. Caroline has $50\frac{1}{2}$ feet of rope. She wants to divide it into 2 equal sections. Before she divides, she writes $50\frac{1}{2}$ as an improper fraction. Which shows the correct improper fraction form for $50\frac{1}{2}$?

(1) $\frac{51}{2}$

(2) $\frac{53}{2}$

(3) $\frac{100}{2}$

(4) $\frac{101}{2}$

(5) $\frac{501}{2}$

18. Riley and Maggie hiked a trail that is $4\frac{3}{4}$ miles long. If they hiked $2\frac{1}{4}$ miles each hour, how many hours did it take them to hike the trail?

(1) $2\frac{1}{9}$

(2) $2\frac{1}{8}$

(3) $2\frac{1}{4}$

(4) $2\frac{1}{3}$

(5) $2\frac{1}{2}$

19. Scott writes a 200-word blog in $\frac{3}{4}$ of an hour. How many hours would it take Scott to write a 500-word blog?

(1) $1\frac{3}{8}$

(2) $1\frac{5}{8}$

(3) $1\frac{7}{8}$

(4) $2\frac{1}{8}$

(5) $2\frac{3}{8}$

20. Mario needs to work $32\frac{5}{6}$ hours this week. He has worked $19\frac{7}{8}$ hours so far. How many more hours must Mario work this week?

(1) $13\frac{23}{24}$

(2) $13\frac{3}{4}$

(3) $12\frac{23}{24}$

(4) $12\frac{7}{8}$

(5) $11\frac{7}{8}$

21. It takes the drive-through staff $\frac{2}{3}$ of a minute to process a fast-food order. How many orders can they process in 18 minutes?

(1) 6
(2) 12
(3) 18
(4) 27
(5) 36

Ratios and Proportions

For use with student book pp. 12-13

UNIT 1

① Review the Skill

A **ratio** compares two numbers. The second or bottom number of a ratio does not necessarily represent the whole. A ratio with a denominator of 1 is known as a **unit rate**. When two ratios are written as equal, the equation is a **proportion**.

② Refine the Skill

You may write a ratio as a fraction, using the word *to* or with a colon (:). In all cases remember to reduce a ratio to its simplest terms. Understanding how to write ratios and how to write and solve proportions will help you to efficiently and accurately solve problems on the GED Mathematics Test. Examine the table. Then answer the questions that follow.

The number of students who play a given instrument in the school band is shown below.

BAND MEMBERS AND THEIR INSTRUMENTS

INSTRUMENT	NUMBER OF STUDENTS
Flute	Ⓐ 8
Percussion	5
Saxophone	4
Clarinet	Ⓑ 12
Trumpet	5
Trombone	4
Tuba	2

Ⓐ Write the proportion $\frac{3}{4} = \frac{x}{8}$ and then solve for x to solve the problem.

Ⓑ This is a multi-step problem. Before you can write a ratio, you first need to find the number of girls who play clarinet. Next, subtract the number of boys from the total number of clarinet players.

✓ TEST-TAKING TIPS

Include labels in your ratio to make sure you are writing the numbers in the correct order. After you have written your ratio, read it in words. Check to make sure that it matches the problem.

1. The ratio of girls to total number of students in the band is 3 to 4. At that ratio, how many girls would you expect to play flute?

   (1) 5
   (2) 6
   (3) 7
   (4) 8
   (5) 9

2. There are four male clarinet players. What is the ratio of male clarinet players to female clarinet players?

   (1) $\frac{1}{1}$

   (2) $\frac{8}{4}$

   (3) $\frac{8}{12}$

   (4) $\frac{4}{12}$

   (5) $\frac{1}{2}$

Directions: Choose the <u>one best answer</u> to each question.

3. On a swimming skills test, Olive performed 12 skills correctly. She performed 4 skills incorrectly. What is the ratio of incorrect skills to total skills?

   (1) $\frac{1}{4}$

   (2) $\frac{1}{2}$

   (3) $\frac{2}{1}$

   (4) $\frac{4}{1}$

   (5) Not enough information is given.

4. Joe's baseball team won 38 games and lost 4 games this season. What is the ratio of games lost to games won?

   (1) 1:8
   (2) 38:4
   (3) 4:38
   (4) 19:2
   (5) 2:19

5. A box of soup contains 8 cans. If the box costs $16, what is the unit rate?

   (1) $0.50 per can
   (2) $1 per can
   (3) $2 per can
   (4) $3 per can
   (5) $4 per can

6. A scale drawing of a living room has a scale of 1 inch : 3 feet. If one wall is 4 inches long on the drawing, how long is the actual wall?

   (1) 4 inches
   (2) 4 feet
   (3) 7 feet
   (4) 12 inches
   (5) 12 feet

7. Annie drove 96 miles on Monday and 60 miles on Tuesday. What is the ratio of miles she drove on Monday to miles she drove on Tuesday?

   (1) $\frac{1}{2}$

   (2) $\frac{2}{1}$

   (3) $\frac{5}{8}$

   (4) $\frac{8}{5}$

   (5) $1\frac{3}{5}$

8. A pancake recipe that serves 30 people calls for 12 eggs. Marti wants to make enough to serve only 10 people. What is ratio of eggs to servings for the reduced recipe?

   (1) 2 to 5
   (2) 3 to 5
   (3) 2 to 3
   (4) 3 to 4
   (5) 4 to 5

9. The ratio of wins to losses for the Wildcats rugby team was 8:3. If the team won 24 games, how many did they lose?

   (1) 7
   (2) 8
   (3) 9
   (4) 10
   (5) 12

10. There are 30 full-time and 12 part-time employees at the tire plant. What is ratio of full-time to part-time workers?

   (1) 2:1
   (2) 5:2
   (3) 3:1
   (4) 7:2
   (5) 4:1

11. A map scale states that 2 inches equal 150 miles. If two cities are 6 inches apart on a map, how many miles separate them?

   (1) 154
   (2) 300
   (3) 450
   (4) 600
   (5) 900

12. For each $5 given to a charity by an individual, the Bay Company will give $15 to that same charity. If individual contributions total $275, how many dollars will the Bay Company contribute?

   (1) $75
   (2) $825
   (3) $1,375
   (4) $4,125
   (5) Not enough information is given.

13. One out of every five dogs that is brought to an animal shelter is adopted within one week. If 35 dogs arrive one week, how many dogs would you expect to be adopted within that week?

   (1) 175
   (2) 40
   (3) 35
   (4) 7
   (5) 5

14. Stuck in traffic, Trevor drove 48 miles in 3 hours. What was the unit rate of his speed?

   (1) 16 miles per hour
   (2) 24 miles per hour
   (3) 45 miles per hour
   (4) 48 miles per hour
   (5) 144 miles per hour

15. A recipe for a dessert sauce calls for 2 teaspoons of chocolate sauce and 3 teaspoons of caramel sauce. If Mary made 20 total teaspoons of dessert sauce, how many teaspoons of caramel did she use?

   (1) 10
   (2) 11
   (3) 12
   (4) 13
   (5) 14

16. There are 460 students in an elementary school. Of the students, $\frac{4}{5}$ ride the bus to school. How many students use a different method of transportation?

   (1) 8
   (2) 9
   (3) 92
   (4) 368
   (5) 575

17. Thirty people were surveyed about their type of work. Two of every five people work in a field related to education. How many of the people surveyed work in education?

   (1) 5
   (2) 8
   (3) 12
   (4) 15
   (5) 30

18. In a school, the ratio of students to teachers is 14 to 1. If there are 406 students, how many teachers work at the school?

   (1) 14
   (2) 29
   (3) 406
   (4) 570
   (5) 5,684

19. A person can burn about 110 calories by walking one mile. How many calories will a person burn by walking $4\frac{1}{2}$ miles?

   (1) 415
   (2) 435
   (3) 455
   (4) 475
   (5) 495

20. In a 30-person office, 16 people drive to work and the rest walk or ride their bicycles. What is ratio of people who drive to people who do not drive?

   (1) 8:7
   (2) 7:6
   (3) 6:5
   (4) 4:3
   (5) 3:2

21. The ratio of cars to parking spots at a local business is 2:3. If there are 26 cars, how many parking spots are there?

(1) 33
(2) 36
(3) 39
(4) 42
(5) 45

Questions 22 and 23 refer to the information and table below.

The table shows the number of miles Leila drove each week on a full tank of gas.

LEILA'S WEEKLY MILEAGE	
Week 1	420 miles
Week 2	414 miles
Week 3	389 miles
Week 4	421 miles
Week 5	396 miles

22. If Leila's gas tank holds 18 gallons of gasoline, how many miles per gallon did her car get during Week 2?

(1) 21
(2) 22
(3) 23
(4) 24
(5) 25

23. What is the ratio of the number of miles Leila drove during Week 1 to the total number of miles she drove over the 5 weeks?

(1) 2:9
(2) 1:4
(3) 8:29
(4) 16:57
(5) 7:34

24. The ratio of lifeguards to swimmers at a pool is 1:22. If there are 176 swimmers in the pool, how many lifeguards are there?

(1) 38
(2) 30
(3) 22
(4) 8
(5) 2

25. The ratio of cats to people in a town is 3 to 8. How many people live in the town if there are 387 registered cats?

(1) 1,032
(2) 1,161
(3) 1,935
(4) 3,096
(5) 4,257

26. Ayla bought an 8-pound turkey for $24. How much would he spend for a 12-pound turkey?

(1) $4
(2) $6
(3) $12
(4) $18
(5) $36

Questions 27 and 28 refer to the table below.

The table shows job openings and the number of applicants at Booksmart Publishing.

BOOKSMART PUBLISHING		
POSITION	OPENINGS	APPLICANTS
Graphic designer	5	25
Project manager	2	15
Art researcher	3	27
Staff writer	4	48
Editor	2	12

27. Which position shows a ratio of 12 applicants to 1 opening?

(1) Graphic designer
(2) Project manager
(3) Art researcher
(4) Staff writer
(5) Editor

28. Due to an increase in workload, Booksmart recently announced plans to hire a total of five, rather than three, art researchers. How many additional applicants can it expect to receive?

(1) 9
(2) 12
(3) 18
(4) 21
(5) 24

Decimals

For use with student book pp. 14-15

① **Review the Skill**

A **decimal** shows a fraction of a number using the place value system. Decimal places to the right have less value than do decimal places to the left. When you are solving problems involving money, you must know how to round decimals. Unless you are told otherwise, round answers involving money to the nearest penny, or hundredth.

② **Refine the Skill**

Comparing, ordering, and rounding decimals are important skills for solving decimal problems. Examine the table. Then answer the questions that follow.

☑ **TEST-TAKING TIPS**

When working with decimals, use estimation to check your answers. Round numbers to the nearest whole.

The Peterman family bowls once a week. Each member of the family has his or her own bowling ball. The mass of each bowling ball is shown in the table below.

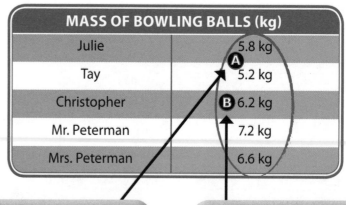

MASS OF BOWLING BALLS (kg)	
Julie	5.8 kg
Tay	5.2 kg
Christopher	6.2 kg
Mr. Peterman	7.2 kg
Mrs. Peterman	6.6 kg

A To answer question 1, first compare the whole numbers. Notice that Julie and Tay both have bowling balls weighing less than 6 kg. Compare 5.8 and 5.2 to find the lightest bowling ball.

B To compare a decimal to the tenths place with a decimal to the hundredths place, write a zero to fill the hundredths place. For example, 6.2 equals 6.20. You can now compare the hundredths digits.

1. Whose bowling ball is lightest?

   (1) Julie
   (2) Tay
   (3) Christopher
   (4) Mr. Peterman
   (5) Mrs. Peterman

2. How many of the Petermans' bowling balls have a mass greater than 6.25 kg?

   (1) 5
   (2) 4
   (3) 3
   (4) 2
   (5) 1

3. How many kilograms do the Petermans' bowling balls weigh altogether?

   (1) 21
   (2) 24.3
   (3) 25
   (4) 28.9
   (5) 31

4. How much more does Mr. Peterman's ball weigh than Tay's ball?

   (1) 1 kg
   (2) 1.5 kg
   (3) 2 kg
   (4) 2.5 kg
   (5) 3 kg

Directions: Choose the <u>one best answer</u> to each question.

<u>Questions 5 and 6</u> refer to the information below.

Kate recorded the miles she drove each day on her commute to and from work.

KATE'S DRIVING LOG	
DAY	**MILEAGE**
Monday	37.5 miles
Tuesday	38.1 miles
Wednesday	37.8 miles
Thursday	37.7 miles
Friday	38.3 miles

5. On which day did Kate drive the least number of miles?

(1) Monday
(2) Tuesday
(3) Wednesday
(4) Thursday
(5) Friday

6. Kate listed the number of miles she commuted each day in order from least to greatest. Which shows her list?

(1) 38.3, 38.1, 37.8, 37.7, 37.5
(2) 37.5, 37.7, 37.8, 38.1, 38.3
(3) 37.5, 37.7, 38.1, 37.8, 38.3
(4) 38.3, 38.1, 37.8, 37.5, 37.7
(5) 37.7, 37.8, 38.1, 38.3, 37.5

7. In a dive meet, Morgan finished in second place. The first-place diver scored 218.65 points. The third-place diver scored 218.15 points. Which of the following could be Morgan's score?

(1) 218.00 points
(2) 218.05 points
(3) 218.45 points
(4) 218.75 points
(5) 218.85 points

8. Natalia completed her balance beam routine in a gymnastics meet with a score of 15.975. The table shows the scores of four of Natalia's competitors. In what place did Natalia finish the competition?

BALANCE BEAM SCORES	
GYMNAST	**SCORE**
Johnson	15.995
Hen	15.98
Kalesh	15.97
Ryder	15.965

(1) first
(2) second
(3) third
(4) fourth
(5) fifth

9. A gallon of milk costs $3.89. About how many gallons of milk could Anne buy with $12?

(1) 1
(2) 2
(3) 3
(4) 4
(5) 5

10. Strawberries at a farmer's market are $2.99 per pound. About how much would 5.17 pounds of strawberries cost?

(1) $8
(2) $10
(3) $12
(4) $13
(5) $15

11. A soft drink at an amusement park costs $1.79. Dylan has $8. About how many soft drinks could Dylan buy at the amusement park?

(1) 1
(2) 2
(3) 3
(4) 4
(5) 5

UNIT 1

Questions 12 and 13 refer to the information and table below.

A library shelves its books by using decimal numbers. The table below shows the locations of the books in the library.

BOOK NUMBER LOCATIONS	
FLOOR AND SECTION	BOOK NUMBER RANGE
Floor 1, Section A	14.598–17.654
Floor 1, Section B	17.655–21.584
Floor 2, Section A	22.500–28.645
Floor 3, Section B	31.858–35.784
Floor 3, Section C	35.785–42.955

12. Where would you find a book labeled with the number 35.783?

(1) Floor 1, Section A
(2) Floor 1, Section B
(3) Floor 2, Section A
(4) Floor 3, Section B
(5) Floor 3, Section C

13. Mrs. Cafferty needs to shelve a book with the number 17.778. Where will she find the shelf for this book?

(1) Floor 1, Section A
(2) Floor 1, Section B
(3) Floor 2, Section A
(4) Floor 3, Section B
(5) Floor 3, Section C

14. The scale at a doctor's office shows a person's weight to the thousandth of a pound. On a patient's chart, the nurse writes the weight to the nearest tenth. If a child weighs 42.468 pounds on the scale, what will the nurse record on the chart?

(1) 42.35
(2) 42.4
(3) 42.47
(4) 42.5
(5) 43.0

15. Isaiah works in quality-control at an ice cream factory. Each half-gallon container of ice cream must weigh more than 1.097 kg and less than 1.103 kg. Which of the following containers of ice cream would Isaiah reject?

(1) Sample A—1.099 kg
(2) Sample B—1.101 kg
(3) Sample C—1.121 kg
(4) Sample D—1.098 kg
(5) Sample E—1.102 kg

Questions 16 and 17 refer to the table below.

The batting averages of five baseball players are shown in the table.

BATTING AVERAGES	
PLAYER	BATTING AVERAGE
A	0.279
B	0.350
C	0.305
D	0.298
E	0.289

16. Which player has the highest batting average?

(1) Player A
(2) Player B
(3) Player C
(4) Player D
(5) Player E

17. The players with the top three batting averages are first in the batting lineup. They will bat in order from the lowest batting average to the highest batting average. Which lists the correct batting order?

(1) Player D, Player B, Player C
(2) Player B, Player D, Player C
(3) Player C, Player B, Player D
(4) Player B, Player C, Player D
(5) Player D, Player C, Player B

Questions 18 and 19 refer to the information below.

Dierdre compared the price per gallon of gasoline at 5 different gas stations. She organized her information in the table below.

GAS STATION PRICES	
GAS STATION	**PRICE PER GALLON**
Lindy's Quick Stop	$2.45
Super Gasoline	$2.52
Triple Bay Gas	$2.49
Rudy's Petro	$2.59
Stop and Gas	$2.29

18. To which gas station should Dierdre go if she wants to pay the lowest price for gas?

    (1) Lindy's Quick Stop
    (2) Super Gasoline
    (3) Triple Bay Gas
    (4) Rudy's Petro
    (5) Stop and Gas

19. What is the cost of a gallon of gas, to the nearest ten cents, at Lindy's Quick Stop?

    (1) $2.00
    (2) $2.40
    (3) $2.45
    (4) $2.50
    (5) $2.60

20. Shauna scored 9.25, 8.75, and 9.5 on three math quizzes. Which shows her scores listed in order from lowest to highest?

    (1) 9.5, 8.75, 9.25
    (2) 8.75, 9.25, 9.5
    (3) 8.75, 9.5, 9.25
    (4) 9.5, 9.25, 8.75
    (5) 9.25, 8.75, 9.5

Questions 21 and 22 refer to the table below.

The table shows the shipping costs for packages of various weights.

SHIPPING COSTS	
PACKAGE WEIGHT RANGE (POUNDS)	**SHIPPING COST**
0–4.65	$3.95
4.66–7.85	$5.55
7.86–10.95	$8.99
10.96–15.40	$12.30
15.41–25.00	$15.75

21. Gary is shipping a package that weighs 8.37 pounds. How much will it cost?

    (1) $3.95
    (2) $5.55
    (3) $8.99
    (4) $12.30
    (5) $15.75

22. Stan needs to ship a package that weighs 16.54 pounds. About how much money will Stan need?

    (1) $4
    (2) $5
    (3) $9
    (4) $15
    (5) $16

23. Rachel pays $49.88 per month for auto insurance. About how much does she pay per year for auto insurance?

    (1) $1,000
    (2) $900
    (3) $800
    (4) $700
    (5) $600

Operations with Decimals

For use with student book pp. 16-17

① Review the Skill

To add or subtract decimals, align the decimal points and perform the operation. To multiply decimals, multiply as you would whole numbers. Then count the decimal places in the factors to determine the number of decimal places in the product. To divide decimals, set the problem up like you do with whole numbers. Adjust the problem so that there are no decimal places in the divisor. Then divide. Place the decimal in the quotient exactly above where it is in the dividend.

② Refine the Skill

When performing operations with decimals, you must know where to place the decimal point in the answer. Examine the menu. Then answer the questions that follow.

☑ TEST-TAKING TIPS

Use estimation to help you determine the placement of the decimal point in a solution. Round each number to the nearest whole.

Below is a list of lunch items from the menu at Ellie's Deli.

LUNCH MENU AT ELLIE'S DELI	
FOOD	**PRICE**
Reuben Sandwich	$5.49
Pastrami Sandwich	$4.99
Pasta Salad	$3.49
Potato Salad	$3.19
Soda	$1.29
Iced Tea	Ⓐ $1.59
Dessert of the Day	$2.89

Ⓐ Remember, to multiply by a power of 10, count the number of zeros and move the decimal point that amount of places to the right.

Ⓑ A whole number is understood to have a decimal point after the ones place. Write $10 as $10.00 to subtract.

1. The Kazmarek family purchased 10 iced teas. How much did they spend?

   (1) $17.49
   (2) $15.90
   (3) $14.31
   (4) $12.90
   (5) $12.72

2. Lydia purchases a pastrami sandwich and a soda. She pays with a $10 bill. How much change should she receive?

   (1) $8.71
   (2) $6.28
   (3) $5.01
   (4) $4.82
   (5) $3.72

UNIT 1

Directions: Choose the <u>one best answer</u> to each question.

3. Tara is paid twice per month. From each paycheck, $112.43 is deducted for income tax. How much income tax is deducted from Tara's earnings each month?

    (1) $2,698.32
    (2) $1,349.16
    (3) $674.58
    (4) $448.92
    (5) $224.86

4. A box of eight cans of baked beans sells for $5.89 at a discount warehouse. What is the price per can, rounded to the nearest penny?

    (1) $0.73
    (2) $0.74
    (3) $0.75
    (4) $0.76
    (5) $0.77

5. Evan purchased a computer for $589.45, a keyboard for $82.32, and a mouse for $14.99. How much did he spend in all?

    (1) $604.44
    (2) $671.66
    (3) $671.77
    (4) $686.76
    (5) $696.86

6. Alvarez Outdoor Furniture is selling Adirondack chairs for $89.79 each. In the Woods is selling the same chairs for $75.45 each. William buys 4 chairs at In the Woods. How much money did William save on 4 chairs by buying them at In the Woods instead of Alvarez Outdoor Furniture?

    (1) $75.45
    (2) $57.36
    (3) $48.78
    (4) $43.02
    (5) $14.34

7. Six packages of buns at a bakery cost $7.62. What is the cost of a single package of buns?

    (1) $1.09
    (2) $1.27
    (3) $1.52
    (4) $1.91
    (5) $2.54

8. Ariana has $37 in cash. She buys a book for $17.95 and a cup of coffee for $3.27. How much money does Ariana have left after her purchases?

    (1) $33.73
    (2) $21.22
    (3) $19.05
    (4) $15.78
    (5) $14.68

9. Carmen has $163.60 deducted from her paycheck and placed into a retirement account over an 8-week period. How much money is deducted from her paycheck each week?

    (1) $16.36
    (2) $18.18
    (3) $20.45
    (4) $23.37
    (5) $27.27

10. For lunch, Russell ordered a sandwich for $5.69, a salad for $3.98, and a drink for $1.99. How much did he spend on lunch?

    (1) $11.66
    (2) $10.46
    (3) $9.86
    (4) $9.67
    (5) $7.68

11. Timothy pays $143 per year to subscribe to his local newspaper. What is the cost per week of his subscription?

    (1) $2.75
    (2) $2.80
    (3) $2.86
    (4) $2.92
    (5) $2.98

12. Cedric has $597.16 in his checking account. He deposits a check for $217.98. He takes out $45 in cash at the same time. What is his new balance?

(1) $334.02
(2) $424.18
(3) $670.24
(4) $770.14
(5) $860.14

13. Salami at a deli costs $3.95 per pound. What is the cost, without sales tax, of 2.3 pounds of salami?

(1) $9.09
(2) $9.10
(3) $9.85
(4) $9.90
(5) $10.08

14. Sylvia bought a computer on a finance plan. She will make 12 equal payments altogether to pay for the computer. If the cost of the computer was $675.00, what is the amount of each month's payment?

(1) $56.25
(2) $57.30
(3) $58.00
(4) $58.25
(5) $58.30

15. At a home improvement store, Terese bought a new lamp for $14.89, a pack of light bulbs for $2.38, and a new light switch for $0.79. She paid with a $20 bill. How much change should be returned to her?

(1) $1.94
(2) $2.73
(3) $4.32
(4) $17.27
(5) $18.06

Questions 16 and 17 refer to the table below.

The table shows the costs of various services at a hair salon.

HAIR SALON SERVICES	
SERVICE	COST
Haircut	$22.95
Shampoo and Style	$14.85
Permanent Wave	$56.99
Color	$66.25

16. Lisa got a haircut and color at the hair salon. What was her total cost?

(1) $43.30
(2) $79.94
(3) $81.10
(4) $89.20
(5) $123.24

17. Mark is going to the hair salon before his wedding. He is trying to decide if he should get a haircut or just have his hair shampooed and styled. How much money would he save by only having his hair shampooed and styled?

(1) $2.10
(2) $6.85
(3) $8.10
(4) $9.20
(5) $37.80

18. Tim scored 95.75 on his first mathematics exam, 92.5 on his second exam, and 98.25 on his third exam. What is the combined total of his scores on the three exams?

(1) 285.95
(2) 286.05
(3) 286.5
(4) 286.75
(5) 287.5

Questions 19 and 20 refer to the table below.

The table shows the amount of Jonah's electric bill from July through December.

MONTHLY ELECTRIC BILL COSTS	
MONTH	**AMOUNT OF BILL**
July	$124.53
August	$118.92
September	$95.41
October	$88.73
November	$85.04
December	$86.29

19. What is the difference between Jonah's highest and lowest electric bills during these 6 months?

(1) $61.57
(2) $39.49
(3) $38.24
(4) $33.88
(5) $5.61

20. How much did Jonah pay for electricity from July through December?

(1) $386.84
(2) $474.39
(3) $510.24
(4) $512.63
(5) $598.92

21. Angel hair pasta at Hometown Foods normally costs $2.29. This week, it is on sale for $2.05. Lorenzo bought 5 boxes on sale. How much money did he save?

(1) $1.20
(2) $1.25
(3) $1.50
(4) $10.25
(5) $11.45

22. A diver's score is calculated by adding the scores of three judges and then multiplying this sum by the degree of difficulty of the dive. Craig performed a dive with a degree of difficulty of 3.2. He received scores of 8, 8.5, and 7.5. What was his total score for the dive?

(1) 67.8
(2) 68.7
(3) 76.8
(4) 78.6
(5) 86.7

23. A cyclist rode 115.02 miles in 5.4 hours. If he rode at a constant speed, how many miles per hour did he ride?

(1) 21.0
(2) 21.3
(3) 21.4
(4) 21.5
(5) 22.1

24. Alexis bought 6 fruit smoothies for $2.65 each. She paid with a $20.00 bill. How much change should be returned to her?

(1) $10.35
(2) $18.60
(3) $7.35
(4) $4.10
(5) $2.35

25. Walt took out a loan to buy his new car. He makes equal monthly payments. In a year, he pays $1,556.28. How much does he pay per month on his car loan?

(1) $128.29
(2) $129.69
(3) $130.99
(4) $131.09
(5) $132.89

26. A car traveled at a speed of 60.2 miles per hour for 3.5 hours. How many miles did the car travel?

(1) 18.5
(2) 21.7
(3) 180.5
(4) 200.7
(5) 210.7

Fractions, Decimals, and Percent
For use with student book pp. 18-19

UNIT 1

① Review the Skill

You can write fractions and decimals as percents. **Percents** are ratios that use the number 100 as the denominator. For example, 11 out of 100 is written as $\frac{11}{100}$. A percent is written with a percent sign, so $\frac{11}{100}$ is 11%.

② Refine the Skill

You can convert between fractions, decimals, and percents. This skill will enable you to efficiently solve problems involving fractions, decimals, and percents on the GED Mathematics Test. Examine the table. Then answer the questions that follow.

☑ TEST-TAKING TIPS

There were 50 people surveyed in all. When writing fractions, use 50 as the denominator. If necessary, double the denominator to arrive at the 100 percent figure.

Jeremy surveyed 50 people about their voting intentions in the upcoming state senate election. The results are shown in the table.

VOTER POLL	
SENATE CANDIDATE	**NUMBER OF VOTES**
Smith	6
Carlotti	Ⓐ 8
Jamieson	10
Hamilton	12
Sanchez	Ⓑ 14

Ⓐ To answer questions that involve percent, first write a fraction. In the case of question 1, a total of 50 people were surveyed. This is the denominator. Then convert the fraction to a percent.

Ⓑ To write a fraction as a decimal, divide the numerator by the denominator.

1. What percent of respondents plan to vote for Carlotti?

   (1) 8%
   (2) 16%
   (3) 20%
   (4) 22%
   (5) 37%

2. Jeremy wrote the fraction of votes each candidate is expected to receive as a decimal. What decimal did he write for Sanchez?

   (1) 0.06
   (2) 0.12
   (3) 0.16
   (4) 0.26
   (5) 0.28

3. What percent of the vote can Hamilton and Carlotti expect to receive together?

   (1) 40%
   (2) 36%
   (3) 32%
   (4) 24%
   (5) 12%

4. Which two candidates in combination would receive a majority of votes cast?

   (1) Hamilton and Smith
   (2) Sanchez and Hamilton
   (3) Smith and Sanchez
   (4) Carlotti and Hamilton
   (5) Sanchez and Carlotti

Directions: Choose the <u>one best answer</u> to each question.

5. One-eighth of the children in first grade are dropped off at school by their parents. What percentage of first-graders are dropped off at school?

   (1) 0.8%
   (2) 8.5%
   (3) 12%
   (4) 12.5%
   (5) 13%

6. At the local college, $\frac{2}{50}$ of all students have a full-time job while attending college. What percentage of students attend college and work full-time?

   (1) 0.4%
   (2) 2%
   (3) 4%
   (4) 8%
   (5) 40%

7. Of 140 sixteen-year-olds, 85% have taken driver's education and earned their driver's licenses. What fraction of the students received their licenses?

   (1) $\frac{15}{100}$

   (2) $\frac{3}{20}$

   (3) $\frac{17}{100}$

   (4) $\frac{17}{27}$

   (5) $\frac{17}{20}$

8. Each semester, about $\frac{3}{25}$ of students at a college study abroad. What percentage of students study abroad?

   (1) 3%
   (2) 9%
   (3) 12%
   (4) 21%
   (5) 25%

Questions 9 and 10 refer to the information below.

> # Refrigerator SALE
>
> # 10% OFF
>
> This promo is good while supplies last.

9. What fraction of the original price will customers pay for the refrigerator if they buy it during the store's sale?

   (1) $\frac{1}{10}$

   (2) $\frac{3}{5}$

   (3) $\frac{3}{4}$

   (4) $\frac{4}{5}$

   (5) $\frac{9}{10}$

10. Employees at the store receive a 30% discount on the original price. If the refrigerator ordinarily is priced at $580, how much will Sam, the store's manager, pay for it during the sale?

    (1) $348
    (2) $406
    (3) $435
    (4) $464
    (5) $522

11. Marie needs 500 fliers to be printed at a cost of $2 per flier. Because of the size of the order, the print shop is asking Marie to pay 30% up front. How much of a down payment must Marie make on the fliers?

    (1) $300
    (2) $320
    (3) $330
    (4) $360
    (5) $400

UNIT 1

12. On a test, 45% of the questions are related to science. What fraction of the questions on the test are science-related?

(1) $\frac{1}{45}$

(2) $\frac{9}{20}$

(3) $\frac{55}{100}$

(4) $\frac{45}{55}$

(5) $\frac{55}{45}$

13. The unit price of a can of soda is $22\frac{1}{2}$ cents. Aidan renames the mixed number as a decimal. What is the unit price in dollars when written as a decimal?

(1) $0.215
(2) $0.22
(3) $0.225
(4) $0.44
(5) $0.445

14. Nina biked $54\frac{1}{2}$ miles in two days. If she biked 22.8 miles the first day, how many miles did she bike the second day?

(1) 32.2
(2) 31.7
(3) 31.6
(4) 28.2
(5) 25.3

15. On Kennedy's income taxes, 5.5% of her income goes to pay her self-employment taxes. What fraction of her income is this?

(1) $\frac{1}{20}$

(2) $\frac{11}{200}$

(3) $\frac{1}{2}$

(4) $\frac{11}{20}$

(5) Not enough information is given.

16. Eighty-two percent of the employees at a food processing plant belong to an employee's union. How is this percent expressed as a decimal?

(1) 0.82%
(2) 0.82
(3) 8.2
(4) 82.0%
(5) 82.0

17. The Panthers won 22 of their 34 games. What percentage of the time did the Panthers win?

(1) 67.6%
(2) 64.7%
(3) 61.7%
(4) 58.8%
(5) 55.8%

18. On the GED Mathematics Test, Ted correctly answered 41 of 50 questions. What percentage of questions did Ted answer correctly?

(1) 80%
(2) 81%
(3) 82%
(4) 83%
(5) 84%

19. Bryon recently purchased a new laptop computer. He put 20 percent down on the purchase. If the computer cost $1,230, how much does Bryon owe after the down payment?

(1) $246
(2) $492
(3) $615
(4) $984
(5) $1,107

20. Jim makes and sells denim knapsacks for $10.50 apiece. The knapsacks cost $7 apiece to produce. What is the percentage of profit that Jim makes on each knapsack?

(1) 50%
(2) 75%
(3) 100%
(4) 125%
(5) 150%

The Clothing Depot is having a two-day sale on its most popular items. The table shows the discount on each type of clothing in the sale.

CLOTHING DISCOUNTS	
ITEM	**DISCOUNT**
Shirts	30% off
Shorts	25% off
Socks	10% off
Jackets	40% off
Vests	25% off

21. Maya buys a shirt. What fraction of the original price does she pay for the shirt?

(1) $\frac{3}{10}$

(2) $\frac{2}{3}$

(3) $\frac{14}{21}$

(4) $\frac{7}{10}$

(5) $\frac{5}{6}$

22. Carlos buys a jacket. What fraction of the original price will he save?

(1) $\frac{1}{5}$

(2) $\frac{1}{4}$

(3) $\frac{1}{3}$

(4) $\frac{2}{5}$

(5) $\frac{2}{3}$

23. Delia earns $28,500 per year. She budgets $\frac{1}{6}$ of this for food and 0.35 of this for housing expenses. What fraction of her earnings is left to budget for other items?

(1) $\frac{6}{35}$

(2) $\frac{8}{26}$

(3) $\frac{29}{60}$

(4) $\frac{31}{60}$

(5) Not enough information is given.

24. Elliott sells 8x10 color photographs for $12 apiece. His friends receive a 10% discount. What fraction of the original price do Elliott's friends pay?

(1) $\frac{1}{10}$

(2) $\frac{1}{9}$

(3) $\frac{9}{10}$

(4) $\frac{9}{1}$

(5) $\frac{10}{1}$

25. The Kickers soccer team played 24 matches and won 75 percent of them. How many matches did the Kickers win?

(1) 15
(2) 16
(3) 17
(4) 18
(5) 19

26. Jason paid $5\frac{1}{2}$% interest on his computer loan. What is this interest rate expressed as a decimal?

(1) 0.055
(2) 0.512
(3) 0.55
(4) 5.12
(5) 5.5

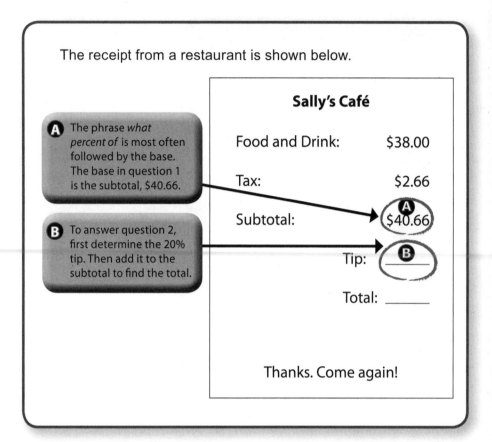

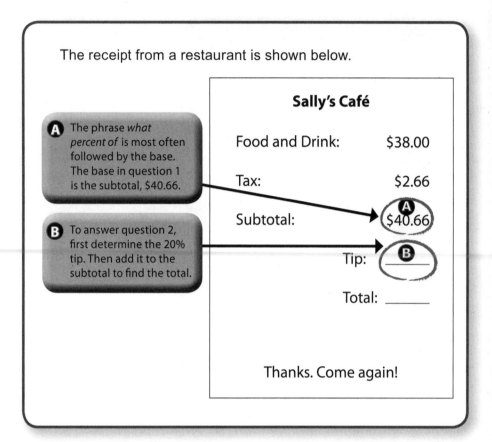

Percent Problems

For use with student book pp. 20-21

UNIT 1

① Review the Skill

The main pieces of a percent problem are the base, the rate, and the part. The **base** is the whole amount. The **rate** is the percent, and the **part** is a piece of the base.

② Refine the Skill

On the GED Mathematics Test, you will be asked to solve percent problems, including those involving simple interest. Read percent problems carefully to make sure you understand what the numbers in the problem correspond to—the base, the rate, or the part. Examine the receipt. Then answer the questions that follow.

☑ TEST-TAKING TIPS

A proportion can be used to solve percent-of-change problems. Write the amount of change over the original amount. Set this ratio equal to the rate over 100.

The receipt from a restaurant is shown below.

A The phrase *what percent of* is most often followed by the base. The base in question 1 is the subtotal, $40.66.

B To answer question 2, first determine the 20% tip. Then add it to the subtotal to find the total.

Sally's Café

Food and Drink: $38.00

Tax: $2.66

Subtotal: Ⓐ $40.66

Tip: Ⓑ _____

Total: _____

Thanks. Come again!

1. Ethan works as a waiter at Sally's. He received a $6.10 tip based on the subtotal of the check shown. About Ⓐ <u>what percent of</u> the subtotal was his tip?

   (1) 10%
   (2) 15%
   (3) 17%
   (4) 18%
   (5) 20%

2. A customer left a 20% tip Ⓑ on the check shown. What is the total?

   (1) $8.13
   (2) $32.53
   (3) $40.86
   (4) $45.60
   (5) $48.79

③ Master the Skill

Directions: Choose the <u>one best answer</u> to each question.

3. As of January 1, Theo's monthly rent increased from $585 to $615. What was the approximate percent increase of Theo's rent?

   (1) 4%
   (2) 5%
   (3) 6%
   (4) 7%
   (5) 8%

4. Pete paid $2.86 in sales tax on a purchase. If he paid 8% sales tax, what was the cost of the item?

   (1) $12.50
   (2) $15.36
   (3) $22.88
   (4) $28.60
   (5) $35.75

5. Ezra invested $3,000 for 18 months at 3% interest. How much interest will he earn on his investment?

   (1) $90.00
   (2) $135.00
   (3) $180.00
   (4) $900.00
   (5) $1,350.00

6. Dan paid 20% down on a new car that cost $16,584.00. He will pay the balance in 24 equal monthly installments. How much will he pay each month?

   (1) $135.00
   (2) $138.20
   (3) $552.80
   (4) $677.18
   (5) $691.00

7. Noelle bought a new jacket. The original price was $152.60. If the jacket was on sale for 40% off, how much did Noelle pay for the jacket?

   (1) $146.50
   (2) $122.08
   (3) $112.60
   (4) $91.56
   (5) $61.04

8. Last year, Cullen contributed $4\frac{1}{2}$% of his salary to charity. If he contributed $2,025.00 to charity, what was Cullen's salary?

   (1) $4,500
   (2) $9,125
   (3) $45,000
   (4) $91,125
   (5) $450,000

9. Remy took out a home-improvement loan to pay for new kitchen cabinets. The loan was for $10,000 at an annual interest rate of 5.6%. If Remy paid off the loan in 36 months, how much did she pay in all?

   (1) $10,680
   (2) $11,160
   (3) $11,680
   (4) $12,200
   (5) $12,760

10. Jae just bought her first car for $22,000. She put 20% down and financed the rest of the purchase over three years at 0% percent interest. What is the amount of Jae's monthly car payment?

    (1) $427.77
    (2) $488.89
    (3) $586.66
    (4) $611.11
    (5) $651.30

11. Jessica purchased a kayak in Florida, where the state sales tax is 6%. She paid $72 in sales tax. What was the retail price of the kayak?

    (1) $1,050
    (2) $1,100
    (3) $1,150
    (4) $1,200
    (5) $1,250

UNIT 1

Questions 12 and 13 refer to the following information and table.

A parts factory records the total number of each part sold in a monthly report. The report for May is shown below.

PARTS SOLD IN MAY	
PART NUMBER	AMOUNT SOLD
A056284	120,750
B057305	254,860
P183456	184,340
F284203	290,520
Q754362	308,205

12. What percent of the parts sold were part number Q754362? Round to the nearest whole percent.

(1) 23%
(2) 24%
(3) 25%
(4) 26%
(5) 27%

13. If combined, the sales of part numbers B057305 and F284203 equal what percentage of parts sold in May?

(1) 37%
(2) 39%
(3) 43%
(4) 47%
(5) 51%

14. Jay took out a small-business loan for $210,000. If the terms of the loan are 5% annual interest for four years, how much money will Jay pay back by the end of the four years?

(1) $420,000
(2) $252,000
(3) $210,000
(4) $168,000
(5) $42,000

15. Grace used to earn $11.00 per hour at her job. She recently received a 4% raise. What is Grace's new hourly wage?

(1) $0.44
(2) $10.56
(3) $11.04
(4) $11.44
(5) $11.88

16. In March, the average number of passengers on a commuter train line was 5,478 per day. In April, this number dropped to 4,380 due to construction on the train line. What is the approximate percent decrease in ridership from March to April?

(1) 15%
(2) 18%
(3) 20%
(4) 22%
(5) 25%

17. Michelle changed jobs this summer. Her new yearly salary is 15% more than her previous salary. If her new salary is $86,250.00, what was her previous salary?

(1) $97,500.00
(2) $75,000.00
(3) $73,312.50
(4) $63,750.00
(5) $11,250.00

18. There were 35 students signed up for an aerobics class. Then the class size increased by 20%. How many students are now in the class?

(1) 38
(2) 40
(3) 42
(4) 45
(5) 48

19. Quinn borrows $10,500 for 3 years to pay college tuition. If she pays $787.50 in interest on the loan, what is the interest rate of the loan?

(1) 1.5%
(2) 2%
(3) 2.5%
(4) 3%
(5) 3.5%

20. Seventy-two percent of the members of a teacher's union voted to accept the terms of a new contract. If 324 teachers voted in favor of the new contract, how many voted against it?

(1) 126
(2) 198
(3) 233
(4) 252
(5) 278

Question 21 refers to the advertisement below.

A clothing store has the following sign posted in the window:

SALE

5% off first item

15% off second item

25% off third item

21. Adam buys 3 shirts. If each shirt has an original price of $12, what is the total that he pays for the three shirts on sale?

(1) $9.00
(2) $25.20
(3) $27.00
(4) $29.40
(5) $30.60

22. A cheese factory had 850 employees at the beginning of the first quarter. By the beginning of the second quarter, they had hired 8% more employees. How many new employees did the cheese factory hire by the beginning of the second quarter?

(1) 67
(2) 68
(3) 69
(4) 70
(5) 71

23. The number of students at a school changed from 756 last year to 711 to this year. What is the approximate percent of change in the student population?

(1) increase of 6%
(2) decrease of 6%
(3) increase of 5%
(4) decrease of 5%
(5) increase of 4%

24. Judith took out a loan for $4,300 over 6 months. What is the total amount she will owe in 6 months?

(1) $4,300
(2) $4,450
(3) $4,600
(4) $4,900
(5) Not enough information is given.

Question 25 refers to the table below.

Dan is determining whether to do his holiday shopping in Maryland, where there is a 6% sales tax, or in Delaware, where there is no sales tax.

PRICES OF GIFT ITEMS		
GIFT ITEM	DELAWARE PRICE	MARYLAND PRICE
Women's jacket	$45	$43
Computer game	$32	$30
Hardcover book	$20.50	$19.50
Children's music CD	$10	$9.50

25. For which item would Dan pay less if he purchased it in Maryland?

(1) women's jacket
(2) computer game
(3) hardcover book
(4) children's music CD
(5) team sports jersey

LESSON 1 FOCUS ON...

Measurement Systems and Units of Measure
For use with student book pp. 30-31

① Review the Skill

The most commonly used **measurement systems** are the U.S. customary system and the metric system. You probably use the U.S. system in your daily life to measure lengths and to cook. Basic **units of measure** in the U.S. system include the foot, pound, and gallon. Basic units in the metric system include the meter, gram, and liter.

② Refine the Skill

When converting metric units, you multiply or divide by powers of 10—most often 10, 100, or 1,000. Examine the table and the conversion chart. Then answer the questions that follow.

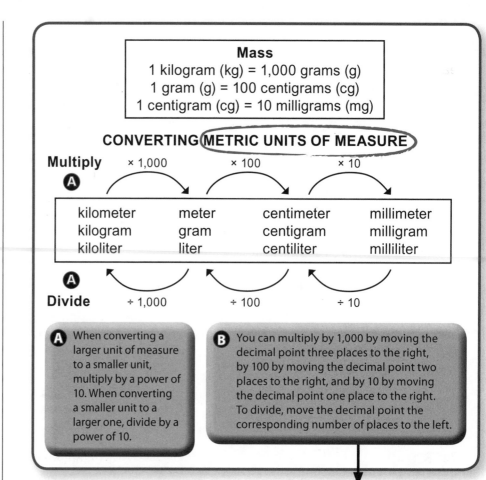

Mass
1 kilogram (kg) = 1,000 grams (g)
1 gram (g) = 100 centigrams (cg)
1 centigram (cg) = 10 milligrams (mg)

CONVERTING METRIC UNITS OF MEASURE

Multiply   × 1,000   × 100   × 10

Ⓐ

kilometer	meter	centimeter	millimeter
kilogram	gram	centigram	milligram
kiloliter	liter	centiliter	milliliter

Ⓐ

Divide   ÷ 1,000   ÷ 100   ÷ 10

Ⓐ When converting a larger unit of measure to a smaller unit, multiply by a power of 10. When converting a smaller unit to a larger one, divide by a power of 10.

Ⓑ You can multiply by 1,000 by moving the decimal point three places to the right, by 100 by moving the decimal point two places to the right, and by 10 by moving the decimal point one place to the right. To divide, move the decimal point the corresponding number of places to the left.

First, identify the unit of measure being called for in the answer. Then convert each unit as needed before performing any other calculations, such as addition or subtraction. In the first problem, the unit asked for is *centigrams*. Note that information such as units of measure sometimes may be housed in tables. For more information about tables, see p. vii and pp. 66–69.

1. A printmaker produces her own ink by mixing powdered pigments with water and alcohol. In the morning, she mixed 45 milligrams of red pigment. At noon, she mixed 2 grams of the same red pigment. Later in the afternoon, she mixed an additional 85 centigrams. How many centigrams of red powdered pigment did the printmaker use?

   (1) 33
   (2) 109.5
   (3) 289.5
   (4) 320
   (5) 735

2. For one print, an artist uses 50 milligrams of blue pigment, 55 centigrams of green pigment, and 3 grams of red pigment. How much greater is the mass of red pigment than the combined mass of the blue and green pigments?

   (1) 2.05 g
   (2) 2.4 g
   (3) 3.05 g
   (4) 12.5 g
   (5) 107 g

42   Lesson 1 | Measurement Systems and Units of Measure

Directions: Choose the <u>one best answer</u> to each question.

<u>Questions 3 through 5</u> refer to the following table and recipe.

Cedric is making punch to take to a family reunion. He wants to triple the following recipe for Pineapple Punch.

Pineapple Punch
2 cups tea
$\frac{1}{2}$ cup lemon juice
2 cups orange juice
1 cup sugar
5 pints ginger ale
4 pints carbonated water
8 slices canned pineapple

Liquid Capacity
1 cup (c) = 8 fluid ounces (fl oz)
1 pint (pt) = 2 cups
1 quart (qt) = 2 pints
1 gallon (gal) = 4 quarts

3. How many pints of orange juice will Cedric need?

   (1) 1 pt
   (2) 2 pt
   (3) 3 pt
   (4) 4 pt
   (5) 6 pt

4. How many quarts of carbonated water will Cedric need?

   (1) 2 qt
   (2) 3 qt
   (3) 4 qt
   (4) 6 qt
   (5) 12 qt

5. How many cups of ginger ale will Cedric need?

   (1) 7.5 c
   (2) 10 c
   (3) 13 c
   (4) 15 c
   (5) 30 c

<u>Questions 6 through 8</u> refer to the tables below.

Sabrina is marking the route for an upcoming cross-country foot race. She keeps a record of the number of meters she marks each day.

METERS MARKED FOR A CROSS-COUNTRY RACE				
DAY	1	2	3	4
METERS MARKED	700 m	600 m	800 m	1,000 m

Metric Units of Length
1 kilometer (km) = 1,000 meters (m)
1 meter (m) = 100 centimeters (cm)
1 centimeter (cm) = 10 millimeters (mm)

6. How many kilometers of the cross-country route did Sabrina mark on Day 1?

   (1) 0.0007 km
   (2) 0.007 km
   (3) 0.07 km
   (4) 0.7 km
   (5) 7.0 km

7. How many kilometers of the route had Sabrina marked by Day 4?

   (1) 0.31 km
   (2) 3.1 km
   (3) 31 km
   (4) 310 km
   (5) 3,100 km

8. On Day 5, Sabrina marked another 900 meters. How many kilometers must the runners race?

   (1) .04 km
   (2) .4 km
   (3) 4 km
   (4) 40 km
   (5) 400 km

Standard Measures of Length
1 foot (ft) = 12 inches (in.)
1 yard (yd) = 3 feet
1 mile (m) = 5,280 feet
1 mile = 1,760 yards

9. During a school track meet, Jason threw the javelin 63 feet. Hector threw the javelin 54 feet. What is the difference between the two throws?

(1) 3 yd
(2) 9 yd
(3) 21 yd
(4) 33 yd
(5) 39 yd

10. Hannah walks 875 yards on Monday, on Wednesday, and on Friday. She walks 2,625 yards on Tuesday and again on Thursday. How many miles has she walked by the end of the day Friday?

(1) 1.5
(2) 4
(3) 4.5
(4) 7.875
(5) 78.75

11. Each place setting requires 18 inches of ribbon. If Mara makes 24 place settings, how many feet of ribbon will she need?

(1) 12 ft
(2) 36 ft
(3) 144 ft
(4) 432 ft
(5) 5,184 ft

12. George ran for a school-record of 2,640 yards. About how many miles did George run during the football season?

(1) .5
(2) 1.5
(3) 3
(4) 5
(5) 26.4

Metric Measures of Capacity
1 kiloliter (kL) = 1,000 liters (L)
1 liter (L) = 100 centiliters (cL)
1 centiliter (cL) = 10 milliliters (mL)

13. Kyle is decorating his restaurant with tropical fish tanks. Three of the tanks each have a capacity of 448 L of water. Two of the tanks each have a capacity of 236 L of water. How many kiloliters of water will Kyle need to fill all of the tanks?

(1) 0.0186 kL
(2) 0.186 kL
(3) 1.816 kL
(4) 18.16 kL
(5) 1,816 kL

14. Microbiologists gathered 15 vials of pond water. They filled 5 vials with 10 milliliters of pond water each, 5 vials with 1 milliliter of pond water each, and 5 vials with 0.1 milliliters of pond water each. How many centiliters of pond water did they gather in all?

(1) 0.6 cL
(2) 1.11 cL
(3) 11.1 cL
(4) 5.55 cL
(5) 55.5 cL

15. The soccer team drank a combined 17 liters of water during the game. How many kiloliters did the team consume?

(1) .017 kL
(2) .17 kL
(3) 1.7 kL
(4) 170 kL
(5) 1,700 kL

UNIT 2

Questions 16 through 18 refer to the tables below.

Students in an ecology class are tracking the growth of saplings over the summer.

SAPLINGS' GROWTH OVER 4 MONTHS	MAY	JUNE	JULY	AUGUST
MAPLE	55 cm	62 cm	83 cm	101 cm
CHERRY	15 cm	18 cm	21 cm	23 cm
OAK	91 cm	98 cm	105 cm	121 cm
ASH	33 cm	38 cm	45 cm	57 cm

Metric Measures of Length
1 kilometer (km) = 1,000 meters (m)
1 meter (m) = 100 centimeters (cm)
1 centimeter (cm) = 10 millimeters (mm)

16. What was the height, in meters, of the tallest sapling in August?

    (1) 1.01 m
    (2) 1.21 m
    (3) 2.3 m
    (4) 5.7 m
    (5) 12.1 m

17. What is the difference between the ash's height in May and its height in August?

    (1) 0.24 m
    (2) 2.4 m
    (3) 24 m
    (4) 240 m
    (5) 2,400 m

18. The students measured the saplings' heights the following summer. How many more meters had the maple sapling grown than the cherry sapling?

    (1) 0.38 m
    (2) 0.46 m
    (3) 3.8 m
    (4) 4.6 m
    (5) Not enough information is given.

Questions 19 through 20 refer to the following table.

Metric Measures of Mass
1 kilogram (kg) = 1,000 grams (g)
1 gram (g) = 100 centigrams (cg)
1 centigrams (cg) = 10 milligrams (mg)

19. One serving of breakfast cereal contains 45 grams of carbohydrates. If there are 8 servings per box of cereal, how many kilograms of carbohydrates does one box contain?

    (1) 0.036 kg
    (2) 0.36 kg
    (3) 3.6 kg
    (4) 36 kg
    (5) 360 kg

20. A can of tuna contains 250 mg of sodium. If Jim eats half a can, how many centigrams sodium will he consume?

    (1) 12.5 cg
    (2) 25 cg
    (3) 100 cg
    (4) 125 cg
    (5) 1,250 cg

Question 21 refers to the following table.

Metric Units of Length
1 kilometer (km) = 1,000 meters (m)
1 meter (m) = 100 centimeters (cm)
1 centimeter (cm) = 10 millimeters (mm)

21. A building shown in a magazine is 50 millimeters tall. Darlene is making a scale drawing of the building. She wants her drawing to be four times the size shown in the magazine. How tall will her drawing of the building be?

    (1) 1 m
    (2) 2 m
    (3) 20 cm
    (4) 150 cm
    (5) Not enough information is given.

UNIT 2

Length, Perimeter, and Circumference

For use with student book pp. 32-33

UNIT 2

① Review the Skill

For questions that ask for a **perimeter** (distance around a polygon) or **circumference** (distance around a circle), you can use formulas that make solving a problem easier and quicker. Before you start the test, review the formulas in the test booklet.

② Refine the Skill

Questions about perimeter and circumference often include brief text followed by a figure or diagram. Use the data in the text and the figure to solve the problem. Then use the appropriate formula to answer each question.

✓ TEST-TAKING TIPS

The text and figure in a test item may provide data about two or more figures. However, the question may only ask about one of the figures. Read the question carefully to know exactly what you are being asked.

A farmer buys a plot of land. On a small part of the plot, he wants to build a house and fence off the yard. The following is a diagram of the farmer's plan.

VIEW OF FARMER'S LAND

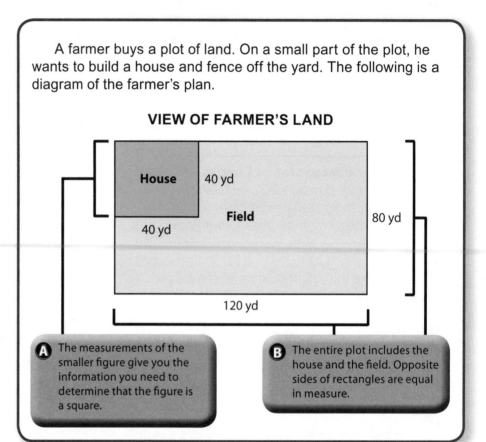

A The measurements of the smaller figure give you the information you need to determine that the figure is a square.

B The entire plot includes the house and the field. Opposite sides of rectangles are equal in measure.

1. What is the perimeter of the area that the farmer wants to use to build a house?

   (1) 40 yd
   (2) 80 yd
   (3) 120 yd
   (4) 160 yd
   (5) 2,000 yd

2. What is the perimeter of the entire plot of land?

   (1) 160 yd
   (2) 200 yd
   (3) 240 yd
   (4) 320 yd
   (5) 400 yd

Directions: Choose the <u>one best answer</u> to each question.

<u>Questions 3 through 5</u> refer to the following diagram.

The diagram shows Erica's rectangular yard and square garden.

ERICA'S YARD

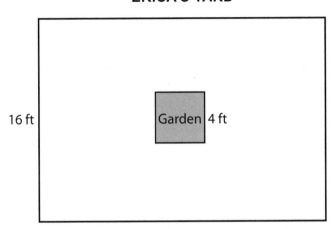

3. The perimeter of Erica's yard is 72 feet. The width is 16 feet. What is the length of each side of her yard?

   (1) 20 ft
   (2) 32 ft
   (3) 40 ft
   (4) 52 ft
   (5) 56 ft

4. What is the perimeter of the garden?

   (1) 8 ft
   (2) 12 ft
   (3) 16 ft
   (4) 20 ft
   (5) 32 ft

5. Erica wants to build a fence around her garden, and another fence around her entire yard. How much fencing will she need?

   (1) 16 ft
   (2) 20 ft
   (3) 64 ft
   (4) 72 ft
   (5) 88 ft

<u>Questions 6 through 8</u> refer to the following text and diagram.

Kevin mounted a circular mirror onto a square piece of wood, as shown in the diagram below. The diameter of the circular mirror is equal in length to the side of the square piece of wood.

KEVIN'S MIRROR

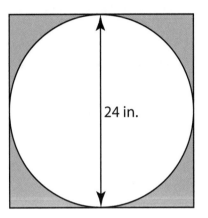

6. What is the circumference of the circular mirror?

   (1) 37.68 in.
   (2) 48 in.
   (3) 75.36 in.
   (4) 150.72 in.
   (5) 576 in.

7. What is the perimeter of the square piece of wood?

   (1) 24 in.
   (2) 48 in.
   (3) 72 in.
   (4) 96 in.
   (5) 576 in.

8. What is the difference between the perimeter of the square and circumference of the circle?

   (1) 15.72 in.
   (2) 20.64 in.
   (3) 27.36 in.
   (4) 48 in.
   (5) 171.36 in.

Questions 9 and 10 refer to the following diagram.

VIEW OF JULIO'S YARD WITH DIAGONAL FENCE

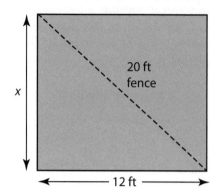

The width of the rectangle is 12 feet. The diagonal of the rectangle is 20 feet. The perimeter of the rectangle is 56 feet.

9. What is the value of x?

(1) 12 ft
(2) 16 ft
(3) 20 ft
(4) 32 ft
(5) 44 ft

10. What is the perimeter of one of the triangles?

(1) 32 ft
(2) 44 ft
(3) 48 ft
(4) 68 ft
(5) 96 ft

11. A rectangle has a perimeter of 54 cm. The length is 16 cm. What is the width of the rectangle?

(1) 11 cm
(2) 19 cm
(3) 38 cm
(4) 140 cm
(5) 864 cm

Questions 12 through 15 refer to the following diagram.

KAYLA'S FABRIC PATTERN

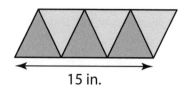

The triangles in the pattern are all the same size. Together, the triangles form a parallelogram with a length of 15 inches.

12. What is the length of one side of one of the equilateral triangles?

(1) 2 in.
(2) 3 in.
(3) 5 in.
(4) 10 in.
(5) 15 in.

13. What is the perimeter of one of the triangles?

(1) 5 in.
(2) 10 in.
(3) 15 in.
(4) 20 in.
(5) 30 in.

14. What is the perimeter of the parallelogram formed by the triangles?

(1) 20 in.
(2) 30 in.
(3) 35 in.
(4) 40 in.
(5) 45 in.

15. Kayla decided to add two more triangles to the pattern. What is the new perimeter of the parallelogram formed by the triangles?

(1) 40 in.
(2) 44 in.
(3) 50 in.
(4) 54 in.
(5) 60 in.

Lesson 2 | Length, Perimeter, and Circumference

UNIT 2

Question 16 through 18 refer to the following diagram and information.

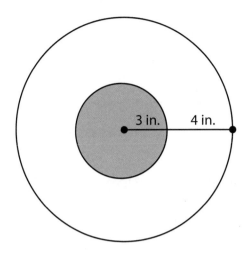

The circles have the same center. The radius of the smaller circle is 3 inches. The radius of the larger circle is 7 inches.

16. What is the circumference of the smaller circle?

(1) 9.42 in.
(2) 18.84 in.
(3) 21.98 in.
(4) 25.12 in.
(5) 43.96 in.

17. What is the diameter of the larger circle?

(1) 6 in.
(2) 7 in.
(3) 14 in.
(4) 21 in.
(5) 21.98 in.

18. What is the circumference of the larger circle?

(1) 9.42 in.
(2) 18.84 in.
(3) 21.98 in.
(4) 25.12 in.
(5) 43.96 in.

Questions 19 through 21 refer to the following diagram and information.

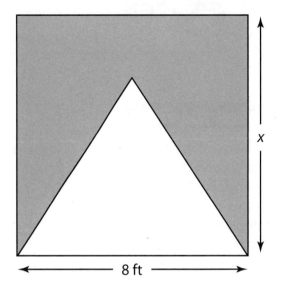

The triangle inside the rectangle is equilateral. The length of one side of the triangle is 8 feet. The perimeter of the rectangle is 36 feet.

19. What is the perimeter of the triangle?

(1) 18 ft
(2) 24 ft
(3) 28 ft
(4) 32 ft
(5) 36 ft

20. What is the length of x?

(1) 8 ft
(2) 10 ft
(3) 16 ft
(4) 20 ft
(5) 28 ft

21. What is the perimeter of the shaded area?

(1) 12 ft
(2) 24 ft
(3) 36 ft
(4) 44 ft
(5) Not enough information is given.

Area

For use with student book pp. 34-35

① Review the Skill

Area is the number of square units that cover a closed two-dimensional figure. Such figures include squares, rectangles, parallelograms, triangles, trapezoids, and circles. A square is a special kind of rectangle. Squares and rectangles are special forms of parallelograms.

② Refine the Skill

The units used to express area are based on units of length. For example, if the sides of a rectangle are measured in meters, the area will be expressed in square meters, or m^2. Read the text and examine the figure. Then answer the questions that follow.

✓ TEST-TAKING TIPS

You need information from both the text and the drawing to answer these questions. The text tells you that you need to find the area of either the rectangular or the whole figure. The drawing enables you to identify the kind of figure.

A park employee needs to spread grass seed over a new section of the park.

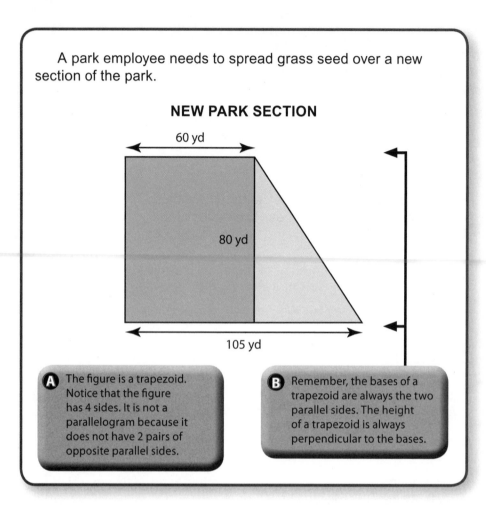

NEW PARK SECTION

A The figure is a trapezoid. Notice that the figure has 4 sides. It is not a parallelogram because it does not have 2 pairs of opposite parallel sides.

B Remember, the bases of a trapezoid are always the two parallel sides. The height of a trapezoid is always perpendicular to the bases.

1. How many square yards of grass seed will be needed to cover the rectangular area?

   (1) 4,200 yd²
   (2) 4,800 yd²
   (3) 5,600 yd²
   (4) 6,300 yd²
   (5) 8,400 yd²

2. How many square yards of grass seed will be needed to cover the entire area of land?

   (1) 4,200 yd²
   (2) 6,600 yd²
   (3) 8,400 yd²
   (4) 10,800 yd²
   (5) 13,200 yd²

Directions: Choose the one best answer to each question.

Questions 3 and 4 refer to the paragraph and diagram below.

Ian is planning to carpet his square living room floor. The floor has two air vents that will not be covered with carpeting. Each rectangular vent is 1 foot long.

IAN'S LIVING ROOM

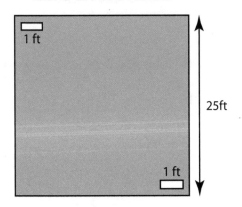

3. What is the area of Ian's living room floor, including the two vents?

   (1) 25 ft²
   (2) 50 ft²
   (3) 100 ft²
   (4) 625 ft²
   (5) 15,625 ft²

4. What is the area of the room that Ian will need to carpet?

   (1) 23 ft²
   (2) 48 ft²
   (3) 623 ft²
   (4) 15,623 ft²
   (5) Not enough information is given.

Questions 5 through 7 refer to the following text and diagram.

Cheryl is planning to paint a wall in her bedroom and needs to know how much paint to buy. Her wall has two square windows that will not need to be painted. A diagram of the wall is shown below.

WALL OF CHERYL'S ROOM

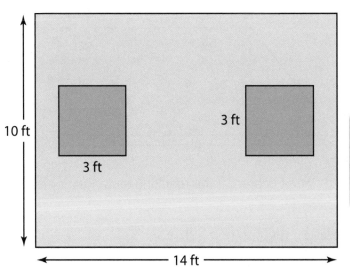

5. What is the area of the wall, including the two windows?

   (1) 24 ft²
   (2) 28 ft²
   (3) 48 ft²
   (4) 140 ft²
   (5) 196 ft²

6. What is the combined area of the two square windows?

   (1) 6 ft²
   (2) 9 ft²
   (3) 12 ft²
   (4) 18 ft²
   (5) 24 ft²

7. What is the area of the wall that Cheryl will need to paint?

   (1) 118 ft²
   (2) 122 ft²
   (3) 128 ft²
   (4) 131 ft²
   (5) 140 ft²

Questions 8 through 10 refer to the following diagram and text.

Leon has a piece of wood in the shape of a parallelogram. He wants to cut two triangular pieces off each end so that he ends up with three pieces of wood, one rectangular and two triangular.

LEON'S PLAN FOR CUTTING

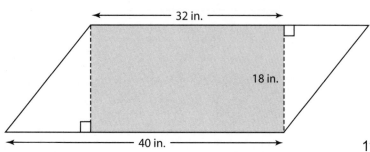

8. What is area of the resulting rectangular piece of wood?

    (1) 100 in.²
    (2) 324 in.²
    (3) 432 in.²
    (4) 576 in.²
    (5) 756 in.²

9. What is the combined area of the resulting two triangular pieces of wood?

    (1) 36 in.²
    (2) 72 in.²
    (3) 108 in.²
    (4) 144 in.²
    (5) 288 in.²

10. What is the area of the original parallelogram?

    (1) 116 in.²
    (2) 576 in.²
    (3) 720 in.²
    (4) 864 in.²
    (5) 1,280 in.²

Questions 11 through 14 refer to the following diagram and information.

The Miller family wants to pave a section of their backyard. The portion to be paved is shaded.

THE MILLER FAMILY'S BACKYARD

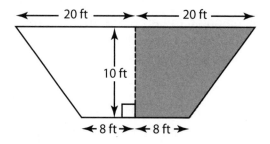

11. What is the total area of the Millers' backyard?

    (1) 140 ft²
    (2) 180 ft²
    (3) 240 ft²
    (4) 280 ft²
    (5) 560 ft²

12. What is the area of the lot that the Millers want to pave?

    (1) 140 ft²
    (2) 180 ft²
    (3) 240 ft²
    (4) 280 ft²
    (5) 560 ft²

13. The cost for pavers is $3 per square foot. How much will the Miller family spend to pave the shaded area of their backyard?

    (1) $400
    (2) $420
    (3) $600
    (4) $800
    (5) $840

14. The cost for pavers is $3 per square foot. How much would the Miller family spend to pave their entire backyard?

    (1) $400
    (2) $420
    (3) $600
    (4) $800
    (5) $840

Lesson 3 | Area

Questions 15 through 18 refer to the following information and diagram.

Jaime is creating a parallelogram-shaped flag for the local marching band. Below is a diagram of the flag. The triangles each have a base of 3 ft and a height of 4 ft.

JAIME'S FLAG DESIGN

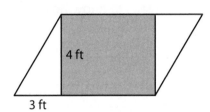

15. The area of the flag is 48 square feet. What is the base of the parallelogram?

    (1) 11 ft
    (2) 12 ft
    (3) 14 ft
    (4) 16 ft
    (5) 20 ft

16. What is the area of one of the triangles?

    (1) 6 ft²
    (2) 7 ft²
    (3) 12 ft²
    (4) 14 ft²
    (5) 24 ft²

17. What is the total area of the triangles?

    (1) 6 ft²
    (2) 7 ft²
    (3) 12 ft²
    (4) 14 ft²
    (5) 16 ft²

18. What is the area of the shaded region?

    (1) 42 ft²
    (2) 36 ft²
    (3) 16 ft²
    (4) 12 ft²
    (5) Not enough information is given.

Questions 19 through 21 refer to the diagram below.

HIGHWAY BILLBOARD

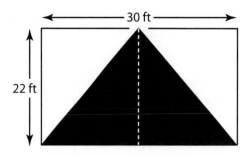

The billboard is 30 feet wide and 22 feet high. A dashed line divides the billboard in half.

19. What is the area of the shaded section?

    (1) 82.5 ft²
    (2) 104 ft²
    (3) 165 ft²
    (4) 330 ft²
    (5) 660 ft²

20. What is the area of the unshaded section?

    (1) 82.5 ft²
    (2) 104 ft²
    (3) 165 ft²
    (4) 330 ft²
    (5) 660 ft²

21. What is the area of the entire billboard?

    (1) 82.5 ft²
    (2) 104 ft²
    (3) 165 ft²
    (4) 330 ft²
    (5) 660 ft²

22. A triangle has an area of 33.84 cm². The base of the triangle is 14.1 cm. What is the height of the triangle?

    (1) 2.4 cm
    (2) 4.8 cm
    (3) 238.6 cm
    (4) 477.1 cm
    (5) Not enough information is given.

LESSON 4 FOCUS ON...

Volume

For use with student book pp. 36-37

① Review the Skill

Volume is the amount of space within a three-dimensional figure. The volume, which is measured in cubic units, tells how many cubes of a given size would be needed to fill the figure.

The GED Mathematics Test provides formulas for finding the volume of various three-dimensional figures, including rectangular prisms and cubes.

② Refine the Skill

People find the volume of various items such as storage crates and boxes used for mailing. Read the text and examine the figure. Then answer the questions that follow.

☑ TEST-TAKING TIPS

To find the volume is to find the number of cubic units it would take to fill a container. Imagine stacking cubic feet inside the bin. The bottom layer would consist of 6 by 8 cubes. It would take twelve and a half layers to fill the container.

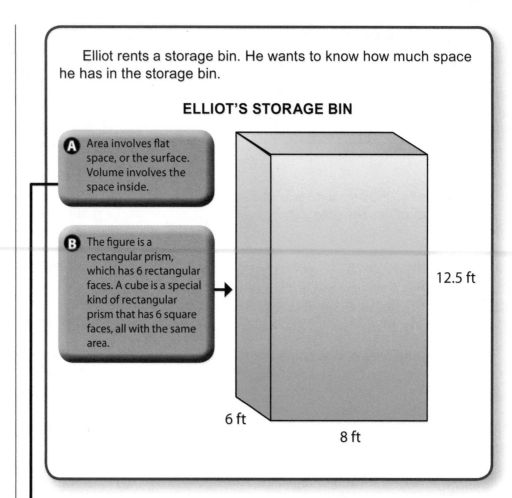

Elliot rents a storage bin. He wants to know how much space he has in the storage bin.

ELLIOT'S STORAGE BIN

A Area involves flat space, or the surface. Volume involves the space inside.

B The figure is a rectangular prism, which has 6 rectangular faces. A cube is a special kind of rectangular prism that has 6 square faces, all with the same area.

12.5 ft

6 ft

8 ft

1. To find the amount of space, Elliot needs to calculate which measurement?

   (1) area
   (2) volume
   (3) perimeter
   (4) circumference
   (5) diameter

2. What is the volume of the storage bin that Elliot rented?

   (1) 100 ft³
   (2) 260 ft³
   (3) 600 ft³
   (4) 6,000 ft³
   (5) Not enough information is given.

Directions: Choose the <u>one best answer</u> to each question.

Questions 3 through 5 refer to the paragraph and figures below.

Carmen wants to buy an above-ground swimming pool. She is trying to decide between two models. A diagram of the models is shown below.

TWO SWIMMING POOLS

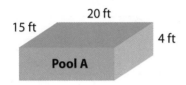

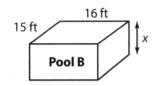

Each model holds the same amount of water. The height of pool B is represented by *x*.

3. What is the volume of swimming pool A?

(1) 80 ft³
(2) 300 ft³
(3) 1,000 ft³
(4) 1,200 ft³
(5) 1,527 ft³

4. What is the value of *x*?

(1) 4 ft
(2) 5 ft
(3) 6 ft
(4) 8 ft
(5) Not enough information is given.

5. Carmen only wanted to fill her pool halfway. What is the volume of the pool?

(1) 400 ft³
(2) 600 ft³
(3) 800 ft³
(4) 1,000 ft³
(5) 1,200 ft³

Questions 6 and 7 refer to the following text and figures.

A company is shipping goods by air to Europe. The airline has provided three different container sizes.

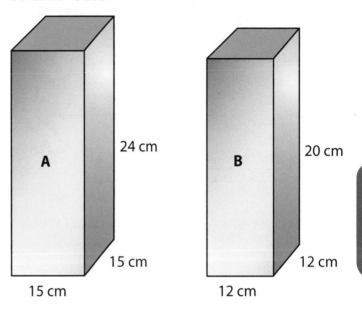

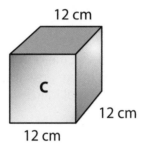

6. What is the volume of the smallest container?

(1) 36 cm³
(2) 156 cm³
(3) 1,560 cm³
(4) 1,728 cm³
(5) 2,880 cm³

7. What is difference in volume between the medium container and the large container?

(1) 576 cm³
(2) 1,440 cm³
(3) 2,520 cm³
(4) 3,672 cm³
(5) 5,400 cm³

Questions 8 and 9 refer to the following text and diagram.

Angela measured the dimensions of her living room. The dimensions are labeled below.

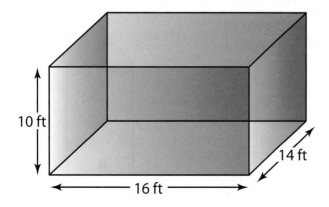

8. What is the size of Angela's living room in cubic feet?

   (1) 40
   (2) 160
   (3) 1,420
   (4) 2,240
   (5) 22,400

9. What would be the volume of Angela's living room if she sealed off an area that is 4 feet wide, 10 feet high, and 14 feet long?

   (1) 560 ft³
   (2) 1,400 ft³
   (3) 1,680 ft³
   (4) 2,240 ft³
   (5) 2,800 ft³

10. What is the volume of a box that is 3 feet wide, 5 feet long, and 10 feet high?

   (1) 30 ft³
   (2) 45 ft³
   (3) 80 ft³
   (4) 150 ft³
   (5) 300 ft³

Questions 11 through 13 refer to the following figures.

Each box shown below is a cube. One side of the larger box is twice the length of the side of the smaller one.

TWO PACKING BOXES

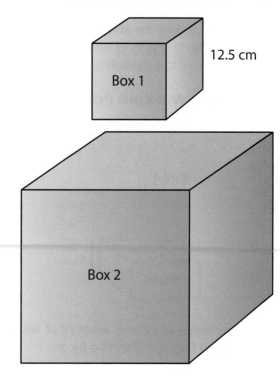

11. What is the volume of Box 1?

   (1) 37.5 cm³
   (2) 156.3 cm³
   (3) 1,875.0 cm³
   (4) 1,953.13 cm³
   (5) Not enough information is given.

12. What is the volume of Box 2?

   (1) 15,625.0 cm³
   (2) 7,812.5 cm³
   (3) 3,906.3 cm³
   (4) 1,953.2 cm³
   (5) 650.0 cm³

13. What is the difference in volume between Box 1 and Box 2?

   (1) 1,953.13 cm³
   (2) 3,906.3 cm³
   (3) 7,812.5 cm³
   (4) 13,671.87 cm³
   (5) 15,625 cm³

Questions 14 through 16 refer to the following information and figures.

Terry wants to replace his old toolbox with a newer model. The old toolbox is 16 inches deep. The new model is 12 inches deep.

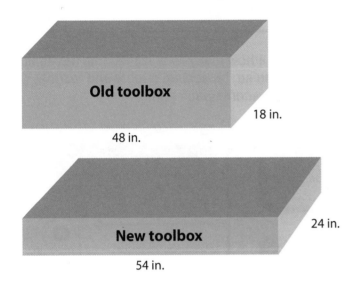

14. What is the volume of the old toolbox?

   (1) 768 in.³
   (2) 840 in.³
   (3) 6,724 in.³
   (4) 10,368 in.³
   (5) 13,824 in.³

15. What is the volume of the new toolbox?

   (1) 648 in.³
   (2) 1,296 in.³
   (3) 13,824 in.³
   (4) 15,552 in.³
   (5) 20,736 in.³

16. What is the difference in volume between the old and new toolboxes?

   (1) 432 in.³
   (2) 1,728 in.³
   (3) 13,824 in.³
   (4) 15,552 in.³
   (5) Not enough information is given.

Questions 17 through 19 refer to the following paragraph and diagram.

Owen has a garage shaped like a rectangular prism. He built an addition in the shape of a cube.

OWEN'S GARAGE AND NEW ADDITION

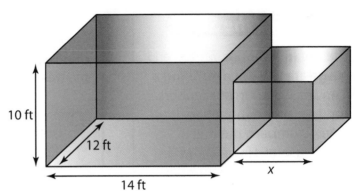

17. What is the volume of Owen's garage without the addition?

   (1) 120 ft³
   (2) 140 ft³
   (3) 168 ft³
   (4) 1,680 ft³
   (5) 2,800 ft³

18. The volume of the addition is 512 ft³. What is the value of x?

   (1) 6 ft
   (2) 8 ft
   (3) 11 ft
   (4) 23 ft
   (5) Not enough information is given.

19. Owen wanted to add a drop ceiling to the garage that would reduce the ceiling height by 2 feet. What is the volume of the garage with the drop ceiling but without the addition?

   (1) 1,344 ft³
   (2) 1,400 ft³
   (3) 1,440 ft³
   (4) 1,536 ft³
   (5) 1,680 ft³

ean, Median, and Mode

For use with student book pp. 38-39

① Review the Skill

The **mean**, **median**, **mode**, and **range** are ways of describing a data set, or group of numbers. For data sets without very high or low numbers, the mean can be useful. However, when a data set contains a number much greater or much less than the others, the median can give a more accurate average.

② Refine the Skill

The median is the number that falls in the middle of a data set. When a data set consists of an even number of data values, there are two middle numbers. To find the median, add the two middle numbers and divide the sum by 2. Read the text and the table. Then answer the questions that follow.

Kyle wants to know about how many runs his favorite baseball team scores per game. To do so, he sets up a table and records the number of runs the team scores each game.

A To find the range, identify the greatest number and the least number. Then subtract the least from the greatest.

B To determine the mean, add all the data and then divide by the amount of numbers in the data set. When a data set consists of an even number of data values, there are two middle numbers. In that case, the median is the number that falls in the middle of a data set.

RUNS SCORED BY THE PATRIOTS	
GAME	RUNS SCORED
1	3
2	9 **A**
3	3
4	4
5	7
6	5
7	6
8	3
9	1 **A**
10	5

B

☑ TEST-TAKING TIPS

Questions on the GED Mathematics Test may ask you to determine the more accurate average of a data set. This requires you to think about the mean, median, and mode.

1. What is the range of the data set that Kyle collected?

   (1) 1
   (2) 3
   (3) 5
   (4) 7
   (5) 8

2. Kyle wants to determine the average number of runs scored by the Patriots. What is the mean of Kyle's data?

   (1) 3
   (2) 4.5
   (3) 4.6
   (4) 5.5
   (5) 9

③ Master the Skill

Directions: Choose the one best answer to each question.

Questions 3 through 5 refer to the table below.

FINAL EXAM SCORES	
STUDENT	GRADES
David	87
Marla	72
Elena	75
Jeff	85
Tyrell	89
Jasmine	93
Kim	68
Chris	97
Jessica	85
Mel	70
Jean	91

3. What is the range of grades for the exam?

   (1) 29
   (2) 68
   (3) 72
   (4) 85
   (5) 97

4. What is the mode for the set of exam grades?

   (1) 29.0
   (2) 82.9
   (3) 85.0
   (4) 93.0
   (5) 97.0

5. What is the difference between Elena's grade and the median grade on the exam?

   (1) 7
   (2) 8
   (3) 10
   (4) 22
   (5) 24

Questions 6 through 8 refer to the following table.

Fred's Bike Shop kept track of its sales for one year. Its monthly sales (rounded to the nearest ten dollars) are shown in the table below.

BICYCLE SALES	
MONTH	SALES
Jan.	$8,320
Feb.	$7,200
March	$11,820
April	$18,560
May	$23,630
June	$26,890
July	$24,450
Aug.	$22,110
Sept.	$23,450
Oct.	$19,300
Nov.	$15,340
Dec.	$16,980

6. What is the median for January through June?

   (1) $15,190
   (2) $16,070
   (3) $18,560
   (4) $18,930
   (5) $19,690

7. What is the mean sale for July through December? Round to the nearest dollar.

   (1) $9,110
   (2) $18,171
   (3) $20,272
   (4) $20,705
   (5) $22,110

8. What is the range of sales throughout the year?

   (1) $15,310
   (2) $17,250
   (3) $18,570
   (4) $19,690
   (5) $26,890

Questions 9 through 14 refer to the following information and table.

Jessica is conducting a random survey to find out how much time people spend on the Internet. The following table shows the results in hours per day.

HOURS PER DAY SPENT ON INTERNET							
	MON	TUES	WED	THURS	FRI	SAT	SUN
Jen	3	4.25	5	1	1.5	5.5	6
Mila	4	3.5	5.5	2.5	4	6	5.5
Trang	2	1.5	0.5	0.25	0.75	3	3
Ron	3.5	4.25	5	5.5	2.25	6.25	7
Yusef	2.5	1	1	1.5	0.5	5.25	7.5

9. What is the range for the data set showing the number of hours spent per day on the Internet?

(1) 0.0
(2) 3.4
(3) 5.5
(4) 7.0
(5) 7.25

10. What is the mode of the data set?

(1) 1.0
(2) 1.5
(3) 3.5
(4) 5.5
(5) 7.5

11. What is the median number of hours spent on the Internet over a weekend (Sat. and Sun.)?

(1) 4.50
(2) 5.50
(3) 5.75
(4) 6.00
(5) 6.25

12. What is the range for the number of hours per day that Ron spends on the Internet?

(1) 7
(2) 5
(3) 4.75
(4) 3.5
(5) 2.25

13. What is the median number of hours Trang spends on the Internet in a day?

(1) 1.1
(2) 1.5
(3) 1.6
(4) 3.0
(5) 2.8

14. What is the difference between the mean of Wednesday's data and the mean of Sunday's data?

(1) 1.25
(2) 1.5
(3) 2.0
(4) 2.4
(5) 2.5

Questions 15 and 16 refer to the following information.

The table shows the number of points scored by the Pirates football team for the first six games of the season.

FOOTBALL SCORES		
GAME	POINTS SCORED BY THE PIRATES	POINTS SCORED BY OPPONENTS
1	24	0
2	7	14
3	13	21
4	12	6
5	0	12
6	36	30

15. What is the average number of points scored by the Pirates?

(1) 12.50
(2) 13.83
(3) 15.33
(4) 17.67
(5) 18.40

16. What is the median number of points scored by the Pirates' opponents?

(1) 12.5
(2) 13
(3) 13.8
(4) 14
(5) 16.5

Lesson 5 | Mean, Median, and Mode

Questions 17 and 18 refer to the following information and table.

The table shows the results of a cross-country team's times in a recent 3-mile race.

CROSS-COUNTRY RUNNING TIMES	
NAME	TIMES (MINUTES:SECONDS)
Holly	25:21
Karen	21:07
Ana	20:58
Jessie	26:10
Sonya	23:27

17. Which teammate ran the fastest?

(1) Holly
(2) Karen
(3) Ana
(4) Jessie
(5) Sonya

18. What is the median time of the team's results?

(1) 4:37
(2) 20:58
(3) 23:27
(4) 23:41
(5) Not enough information is given.

19. Which data set has a range of $6\frac{1}{2}$?

(1) $3, 0, 6\frac{1}{2}, 4\frac{1}{2}$

(2) $6, \frac{1}{2}, 3, 4\frac{1}{2}$

(3) $4, 6\frac{1}{2}, 3, \frac{1}{2}$

(4) $3\frac{1}{2}, 6\frac{1}{2}, 6, \frac{1}{2}$

(5) Not enough information is given.

Questions 20 through 23 refer to the paragraph and table below.

A survey was taken of the students in Mr. Macon's class to determine the number of pets owned by each student over his or her lifetime.

PET OWNERSHIP	
NUMBER OF PETS	NUMBER OF STUDENTS
1	II
2	ЖТ
3	ЖТ II
4	II
5	I

20. What is the mode for the data set?

(1) 1
(2) 2
(3) 3
(4) 4
(5) 5

21. What is the median for the data set?

(1) 1
(2) 2
(3) 3
(4) 5
(5) Not enough information given

22. What is the mean for the data set?

(1) 2.7
(2) 3.0
(3) 3.4
(4) 4.0
(5) 9.2

23. If one more student in the class had 5 pets, what would be the mean?

(1) 2.7
(2) 2.83
(3) 3.0
(4) 4.0
(5) 5.0

Probability

For use with student book pp. 40-41

① Review the Skill

Probability is a way to describe the chance that some event may occur. Probability compares the number of favorable outcomes to the number of total outcomes. Probability can be written as a ratio, fraction, or percent.

② Refine the Skill

If an event has a probability of 0%, it is said to be *impossible*. If the probability is less than 50%, the event is *unlikely*. If the chances are greater than 50%, it is *likely*. If the probability of an event is 100%, it is *certain*. Read the text and examine the spinner. Then answer the questions that follow.

The spinner shown below has five equal sections.

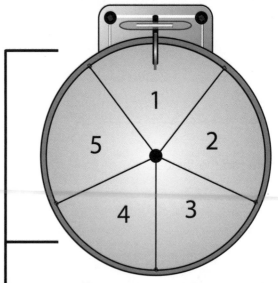

A Question 1 means that spinning 1, 4, and 5 are all favorable outcomes. Increasing the number of favorable outcomes generally increases the overall probability.

B Choice 3 is incorrect because it implies that there are four possible outcomes, when there are actually five possible outcomes.

TEST-TAKING TIPS

Compute and express the probability of an event in the way that is easiest for you. You may find it easiest to determine probability as a fraction. You always can convert your answer to a ratio, percent, or decimal as needed.

1. Which word best describes the chances of spinning a 1, 4, or 5?

   (1) impossible
   (2) unlikely
   (3) likely
   (4) certain
   (5) Not enough information is given.

2. What is the probability of spinning a 3?

   (1) 1:1
   (2) 1:2
   (3) 1:4 **B**
   (4) 1:5
   (5) 4:5

Directions: Choose the one best answer to each question.

Questions 3 and 4 refer to the following information and drawing.

Jay uses this spinner to conduct probability experiments.

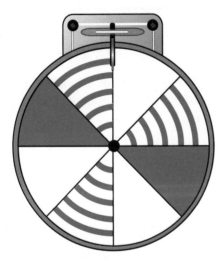

3. What is the probability that the spinner will land on a striped or white wedge?

   (1) 2:8
   (2) 3:8
   (3) 3:4
   (4) 6:6
   (5) Not enough information is given.

4. What is the probability that the spinner will land on a red or striped wedge?

   (1) $\frac{1}{4}$

   (2) $\frac{3}{8}$

   (3) $\frac{1}{2}$

   (4) $\frac{5}{8}$

   (5) $\frac{1}{1}$

Questions 5 through 7 refer to the following drawing.

Jenna has a bag of marbles that contains 7 striped marbles and 5 black marbles.

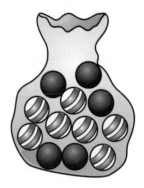

5. What is the probability that Jenna will pick a black marble?

   (1) 1:6
   (2) 5:12
   (3) 1:2
   (4) 7:12
   (5) 1:1

6. Jenna picks a striped marble and does not replace it. Then Jenna picks a black marble and does not replace it. What is the probability that she will pick a striped marble in the third event?

   (1) 41%
   (2) 50%
   (3) 60%
   (4) 100%
   (5) Not enough information is given.

7. In another experiment, Jenna wants to find the probability of picking a striped marble. In the first event, she picks a black marble and places it back in the bag. In the second and third events, she picks a striped marble, replacing the marble after each pick. What is the experimental probability at this point of picking a striped marble?

   (1) $\frac{1}{3}$

   (2) $\frac{2}{3}$

   (3) $\frac{1}{2}$

   (4) $\frac{3}{4}$

   (5) $\frac{1}{1}$

Questions 8 through 10 refer to the following information and drawing.

Marta uses this spinner to conduct probability experiments.

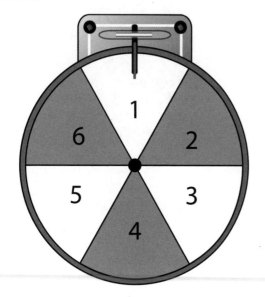

Questions 11 through 13 refer to the following information and figure.

Chuck is conducting probability experiments using a single die.

11. Chuck rolls the die once, and it lands on 2. What is the probability that Chuck will roll a 2 on his second turn?

    (1) 1:6
    (2) 1:3
    (3) 1:2
    (4) 2:3
    (5) Not enough information is given.

8. What is the probability that Marta will land on either a red wedge or an odd number?

    (1) 20%
    (2) 40%
    (3) 50%
    (4) 100%
    (5) Not enough information is given.

12. Chuck rolls the die once, and it lands on 3. He rolls it again, and it lands on a 5. What is the experimental probability so far for landing on an odd number?

    (1) 0:2
    (2) 1:6
    (3) 1:3
    (4) 2:3
    (5) 1:1

9. Marta spins and lands on 4. What is the probability that on her second spin, she will land on 4?

    (1) 1:2
    (2) 1:4
    (3) 1:6
    (4) 2:5
    (5) 2:6

13. What is the probability that Chuck will roll an even number?

    (1) 16.7%
    (2) 33.3%
    (3) 50.0%
    (4) 66.7%
    (5) 83.3%

10. What is the probability that Marta will land on 6, 2, or one of the white wedges?

    (1) 1:6
    (2) 1:2
    (3) 2:3
    (4) 5:6
    (5) 6:6

Ryan took a random survey of 100 cars. The following table displays the results.

SURVEY OF CARS	
COLOR OF CAR	AMOUNT
Black	32
Blue	15
Red	25
White	18
Other	10

14. Based on Ryan's survey, what is the probability that the next car he spots will be blue or red?

    (1) 0.15
    (2) 0.40
    (3) 0.60
    (4) 0.75
    (5) 0.85

15. What is the probability that the next car Ryan sees will be a color other than black, blue, red, or white?

    (1) 0%
    (2) 10%
    (3) 30%
    (4) 50%
    (5) 100%

16. The probability is greatest for seeing which color of car next?

    (1) blue
    (2) red
    (3) black
    (4) white
    (5) other

Julian has a bag of marbles. He knows that the bag contains 10 marbles, some black and some red. He conducts experiments to predict how many of each color marble is in the bag.

17. In the first event, Julian picks a black marble. He replaces the marble. In the second and third events, he picks a red marble. He replaces the marble after each event. What is the experimental probability that he will pick a red marble next?

    (1) $\frac{1}{5}$

    (2) $\frac{3}{10}$

    (3) $\frac{1}{3}$

    (4) $\frac{2}{3}$

    (5) $\frac{3}{4}$

18. In the first event, Julian picks a black marble out of the bag. He does not replace it. In the second event, he picks another black marble out of the bag and does not replace it. What is the probability that the next marble he picks out of the bag will be black?

    (1) $\frac{1}{10}$

    (2) $\frac{1}{5}$

    (3) $\frac{4}{5}$

    (4) $\frac{1}{1}$

    (5) Not enough information is given.

UNIT 2

Tables

For use with student book pp. 42-43

UNIT 2

① Review the Skill

Data organized and presented in a **table** are usually easier to interpret than if the same data were presented in a paragraph. Before using a table, be sure to understand its purpose and how the data are organized. Reading the title, column and row headings, and any labels can provide information and insight as to a table's purpose.

② Refine the Skill

Apart from their presence on the GED Mathematics Test, tables also frequently appear on maps, in nonfiction books, and in magazine articles. The business and sports sections of newspapers usually contain several tables. Read the text and examine the table. Then answer the questions that follow.

Tara regularly eats Good Morning cereal for breakfast. She is interested in comparing it with other recommended cereals.

HEALTHY CEREALS FOR A HEALTHY LIFE

Ⓐ CEREAL	AMOUNT PER 1 CUP SERVING			Ⓑ
	CALORIES	TOTAL FAT	TOTAL CARBOHYDRATE	DIETARY FIBER
Good Morning	110	3 g	22 g	3 g
Valley Oats	150	2.5 g	27 g	4 g
Puffs	105	4 g	20 g	6 g
Healthy Wheat	165	3 g	22 g	4.5 g
Rise 'n' Shine	120	3.5 g	24 g	5 g

Ⓐ The category of the column on the far left is "Cereal." The names of five cereals appear below this label. All the values that appear in the other columns relate to the category that appears at the top of each column.

Ⓑ Tables usually contain more information than you need to answer a question. You only need to look at the fiber column for question 2.

✔ **TEST-TAKING TIPS**

Certain words help you determine what a question is asking. In question 1, the words *two, fewest,* and *calories* help you understand what to look for in the table.

1. Which two cereals contain the fewest number of calories per serving?

   (1) Good Morning and Valley Oats
   (2) Puffs and Rise 'n' Shine
   (3) Good Morning and Healthy Wheat
   (4) Valley Oats and Healthy Wheat
   (5) Good Morning and Puffs

2. If Tara wants the most dietary fiber, which cereal should she eat for breakfast?

   (1) Good Morning
   (2) Rise 'n' Shine
   (3) Puffs
   (4) Healthy Wheat
   (5) Valley Oats

③ Master the Skill

Directions: Choose the one best answer to each question.

Questions 3 and 4 refer to the information and table below.

Ernesto works for a moving company based in Portland. He uses the following mileage chart to determine the amount of gasoline for each trip.

MILEAGE CHART					
CITY	EUREKA	REDDING	SACRA.	SAN FRAN.	PORTLAND
Portland	414	422	581	636	—
Eureka	—	154	281	296	414
Redding	154	—	165	217	422
Sacramento	296	165	—	91	581
San Fran.	281	217	91	—	636

3. Ernesto drives from Portland to San Francisco, where he spends the night. The following day, he drives to Sacramento. How many miles has he driven altogether?

   (1) 91
   (2) 545
   (3) 636
   (4) 727
   (5) 818

4. Ernesto plans to move a business from Redding to Eureka. It will take two trips to complete the move. He first will have to drive from Sacramento to Redding and from Redding to Eureka and back, and then make a final trip to Eureka. How many miles will he have to drive in all?

   (1) 165
   (2) 317
   (3) 473
   (4) 627
   (5) 781

Questions 5 through 7 refer to the following text and table.

The following table shows the results of a commuting survey. The survey asked 200 commuters to keep track of the average amount of time they spend commuting each day.

TIME SPENT COMMUTING					
HOURS PER DAY	1995	1997	1999	2001	2003
1 or less	65	62	58	45	19
1 to 2	53	55	53	49	60
2 to 3	61	62	64	77	77
3 to 4	21	21	22	24	29
4 or more	0	0	3	5	15

5. Between which two years did the category "2 to 3" hours increase the most?

   (1) between 1995 and 1997
   (2) between 1997 and 1999
   (3) between 1999 and 2001
   (4) between 2001 and 2003
   (5) Not enough information is given.

6. In which year did more than 60% of the commuters spend 2 or more hours commuting?

   (1) 1995
   (2) 1997
   (3) 1999
   (4) 2001
   (5) 2003

7. Which category showed the greatest decrease in the number of drivers over the 8-year period?

   (1) 1 or less
   (2) 1 to 2
   (3) 2 to 3
   (4) 3 to 4
   (5) 4 or more

UNIT 2

Inez kept track of the type and amount of traffic on her street for 5 days.

A WEEK OF TRAFFIC ON ELM STREET						
	DAY 1	DAY 2	DAY 3	DAY 4	DAY 5	TOTAL
BICYCLES	11	20	8	3	0	**42**
MOTORCYCLES	18	25	28	16	5	**92**
CARS	81	90	101	75	35	**382**
TRUCKS	65	73	84	58	21	**301**
TOTAL	**175**	**207**	**221**	**152**	**61**	**817**

8. On which day were there exactly twice as many cars as motorcycles and bicycles combined?

   (1) Day 1
   (2) Day 2
   (3) Day 3
   (4) Day 4
   (5) Day 5

9. Which sentence best describes the total amount of traffic for the 5 days?

   (1) The amount stayed the same.
   (2) The amount increased.
   (3) The amount decreased.
   (4) The amount increased, then decreased.
   (5) The amount decreased, then increased.

10. The total for Day 1 is approximately three times the total for which day?

    (1) Day 2
    (2) Day 3
    (3) Day 4
    (4) Day 5
    (5) Not enough information is given.

Questions 11 through 14 refer to the following paragraph and table.

A shopping mall took a poll of 100 employees to find out whether the mall should extend its hours. The results of the poll are shown in the table below.

SHOPPING MALL EMPLOYEE POLL		
	FAVOR EXTENDED HOURS	OPPOSE EXTENDED HOURS
WOMEN	15	30
MEN	25	30

11. What percent of the employees polled were male?

    (1) 15%
    (2) 25%
    (3) 30%
    (4) 55%
    (5) 60%

12. What percentage of employees favored extending the hours?

    (1) 15%
    (2) 25%
    (3) 30%
    (4) 35%
    (5) 40%

13. What percentage of women opposed extended hours?

    (1) 15%
    (2) 33%
    (3) 40%
    (4) 45%
    (5) 67%

14. The decision about whether to extend hours is based on a simple majority of the employees polled. How many opposed employees would need to change their votes for the mall to extend its hours?

    (1) 10
    (2) 11
    (3) 12
    (4) 15
    (5) 18

UNIT 2

Questions 15 through 18 refer to the following paragraph and table.

The Northside Bowling Club recorded its nightly scores in the frequency table below.

BOWLING SCORES	
SCORE	FREQUENCY
100–119	3
120–139	5
140–159	8
160–179	9
180–199	5

15. How many bowlers scored between 100 and 139?

(1) 3
(2) 5
(3) 8
(4) 13
(5) Not enough information is given.

16. What score range had the highest frequency?

(1) 100–119
(2) 120–139
(3) 140–159
(4) 160–179
(5) 180–199

17. How many bowlers scored between 157 and 189?

(1) 1
(2) 3
(3) 8
(4) 9
(5) Not enough information is given.

18. What percentage of bowlers scored between 160 and 179?

(1) 10%
(2) 20%
(3) 30%
(4) 33%
(5) 40%

Questions 19 through 21 refer to the following paragraph and table.

Kendra runs a small online bookstore. Her sales for the year are shown in the table below.

SALES FOR 2008	
MONTHS	SALES
Jan–Feb	$483.70
Mar–Apr	$586.81
May–June	$523.25
July–Aug	$459.09
Sept–Oct	$910.45
Nov–Dec	$1,141.85

19. During which months did Kendra roughly double her sales of the previous months?

(1) Jan–Feb
(2) Mar–Apr
(3) May–June
(4) July–Aug
(5) Sept–Oct

20. How much more did Kendra sell in November and December than she did between January and April?

(1) $71.34
(2) $103.11
(3) $555.04
(4) $658.25
(5) $1,070.51

21. What trend can you infer from the table?

(1) Sales increased throughout the year.
(2) Sales decreased throughout the year.
(3) Sales remained the same throughout the year.
(4) Sales were highest toward the end of the year.
(5) Sales were highest in summer months, but dipped in the fall and winter.

Bar and Line Graphs

For use with student book pp. 44-45

UNIT 2

1 Review the Skill

In **single-bar graphs** and **double-bar graphs**, the bars show how pieces of data compare to one another. A **line graph**, which can contain one or more lines, helps you see how data increase or decrease over time. A **scatter plot** is a type of line graph that shows how one data set can affect another. This relationship may be positive or negative, or it may not exist at all.

2 Refine the Skill

Bar graphs and line graphs can show how different data sets compare. Read the paragraph and examine the double-bar graph. Then answer the questions that follow.

✓ TEST-TAKING TIPS

Double-check your answer to ensure that you used and correctly interpreted the proper bar on the double-bar graph.

The manager of the concession stands at a minor-league baseball stadium wants to know how sales of items compare. He also wants to see how the sales of individual items from the first to fifth innings of the game compare to sales from the sixth to ninth innings.

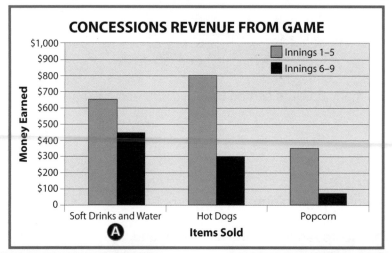

CONCESSIONS REVENUE FROM GAME

A Question 1 tells you the category to focus on for the answer. It also tells you what you are looking for: the amount of change and the nature of the change.

B Carefully examine all the elements of the double-bar graph. The categories on the horizontal axis, the scale on the vertical axis, and the key give essential information.

1. What was the change in sales for soft drinks and water from the first part of the game to the latter part of the game?

   (1) an increase of $100
   (2) a decrease of $200
   (3) an increase of $250
   (4) a decrease of $300
   (5) a decrease of $500

2. Which statement about the double-bar graph is true?

   (1) Soft drinks and water sold better in the latter part of the game.
   (2) Hot dogs sold better throughout the game than soft drinks and water.
   (3) Hot dogs show the greatest decrease in sales from the first part of the game to the latter part of the game.
   (4) The sales of all products increased in the latter part of the game.
   (5) Soft drinks and water are the most popular products.

Directions: Choose the <u>one best answer</u> to each question.

Questions 3 through 5 refer to the following information and graph.

The bar graph shows the population of a city over a 50-year period.

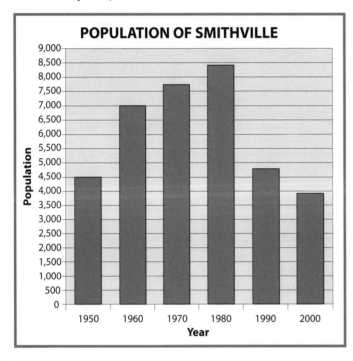

3. The sharpest decrease in Smithville's population occurred between which years?

   (1) 1950 to 1960
   (2) 1960 to 1970
   (3) 1970 to 1980
   (4) 1980 to 1990
   (5) 1990 to 2000

4. In which two years was the population roughly the same?

   (1) 1950, 1960
   (2) 1950, 1990
   (3) 1970, 2000
   (4) 1980, 1990
   (5) 1980, 2000

5. Which sentence best describes the population trend between 1950 and 2000?

   (1) The population increased.
   (2) The population decreased.
   (3) The population increased, then decreased.
   (4) The population decreased, then increased.
   (5) The population remained the same.

Questions 6 and 7 refer to the scatter plot.

A local marketing company conducted a study that compared annual earnings of workers with their ages. Their findings are shown on the scatter plot below.

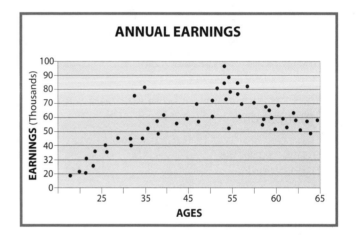

6. According to the study, at what age do workers earn the highest annual salaries?

   (1) 25
   (2) 35
   (3) 45
   (4) 55
   (5) 65

7. What correlation can you draw from the information on the scatter plot?

   (1) Employees with less experience tend to earn the highest salaries.
   (2) Higher levels of experience result in greater levels of pay, up to a certain point.
   (3) Experience plays no role in workers' salaries.
   (4) Employees with 10 years of experience earn more than employees with 20 years of experience.
   (5) Workers earn their highest salaries immediately before retirement.

Questions 8 through 10 refer to the following information and bar graph.

Every five years, ecologists record the type and number of mammals living in Pond Park. The bar graph below shows their counts for 1995 and 2000.

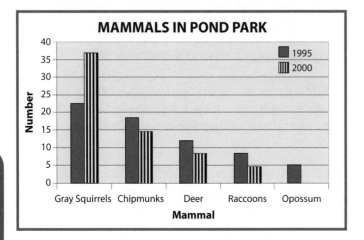

8. Which mammal increased in numbers over the 5-year period?

(1) gray squirrels
(2) chipmunks
(3) deer
(4) raccoons
(5) opossum

9. Which mammal was not seen at Pond Park in 2000?

(1) gray squirrels
(2) chipmunks
(3) deer
(4) raccoons
(5) opossum

10. The number of deer in 2000 is equal to the number of which animal in 1995?

(1) gray squirrels
(2) chipmunks
(3) deer
(4) raccoons
(5) opossum

Questions 11 through 13 refer to the following paragraph and graph.

The line graph compares the average yearly rainfall for Anchorage, Alaska, to the average yearly rainfall in the United States.

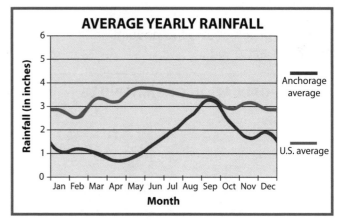

11. In which month is the average rainfall for Anchorage and the United States about the same?

(1) January
(2) March
(3) June
(4) September
(5) December

12. During which month is the difference between the two average rainfall amounts the greatest?

(1) January
(2) February
(3) May
(4) September
(5) November

13. What trend can you determine from the graph?

(1) Average rainfall amounts are about the same in Anchorage as in the rest of the United States.
(2) Average rainfall in Anchorage is consistently less than rainfall in the United States.
(3) Average rainfall in Anchorage is consistently greater than rainfall in the United States.
(4) Average rainfall in Anchorage and the United States is about the same in the winter, but quite different in the summer.
(5) Both Anchorage and the United States have average rainfalls of less than 3 inches.

Questions 14 through 16 refer to the following information and bar graph.

The following bar graph shows the occupations of women in Centre City.

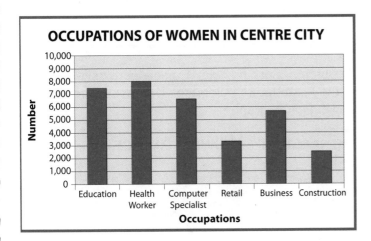

14. About how many more women work in education than in construction?

    (1) 3,000
    (2) 5,000
    (3) 7,000
    (4) 10,000
    (5) 11,000

15. What occupation is held by about twice the number of women who hold occupations in retail?

    (1) business
    (2) education
    (3) health worker
    (4) computer specialist
    (5) construction

16. Based on the bar graph, which occupation is likely to show an increase in numbers over the next ten years?

    (1) education
    (2) health worker
    (3) computer specialist
    (4) retail
    (5) Not enough information is given.

Questions 17 through 19 refer to the information and graph below.

The line graph shows the average amount of daylight throughout the year in Pine Town.

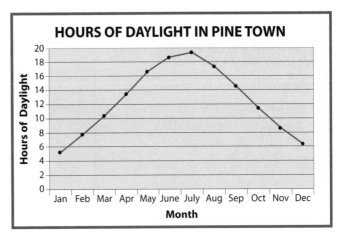

17. During which months are there more than 17 hours of sunlight?

    (1) January, February, March
    (2) March, April, May
    (3) June, July, August
    (4) September, October
    (5) November, December

18. Rounded to the nearest hour, what is the approximate difference between the number of daylight hours in August and the number of daylight hours in December?

    (1) 8
    (2) 9
    (3) 10
    (4) 11
    (5) 12

19. Which month has about double the hours of daylight as the month of January?

    (1) February
    (2) March
    (3) April
    (4) November
    (5) December

Circle Graphs

For use with student book pp. 46-47

1 Review the Skill

A **circle graph** shows how different parts of a whole compare both to one another and to the whole. The circle represents one whole, or 100%. If a section is half of the whole, it represents 50%, 0.50, or $\frac{1}{2}$. If a section is a quarter of the circle, it represents 25%, 0.25, or $\frac{1}{4}$. The values of each section, or category, in a circle graph also may be written as whole numbers.

2 Refine the Skill

Sometimes, exact values are given for the categories in a circle graph. When they are not provided, estimate the value. Read the text and examine the circle graph. Then answer the questions that follow.

The first 100 customers at Sandwich Palace were asked which menu item they planned to purchase. The results are shown in the following circle graph.

PURCHASES AT SANDWICH PALACE

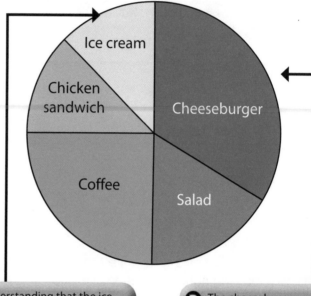

A Understanding that the ice cream and chicken sandwich categories combine to make up a quarter of the circle can help you determine the answer to question 1.

B The cheeseburger section of the graph covers more than 25%, or $\frac{1}{4}$. As a result, answer choices 1, 2, and 3 are not reasonable.

☑ TEST-TAKING TIPS

When answering questions about circle graphs, estimate the value of a category in the way that is easiest for you. For example, you could estimate the value of the coffee category as $\frac{1}{4}$, 25%, 0.25, or 25. You then can convert as necessary.

1. Based on the graph, about what percentage of people wanted to buy ice cream?

(1) 1%
(2) 5%
(3) 12%
(4) 25%
(5) 30%

2. Which fraction shows the people who wanted cheeseburgers?

(1) $\frac{1}{10}$

(2) $\frac{1}{5}$

(3) $\frac{1}{4}$

(4) $\frac{1}{3}$

(5) $\frac{2}{3}$

③ Master the Skill

Directions: Choose the <u>one best answer</u> to each question.

<u>Questions 3 through 5</u> refer to the following information and circle graph.

As part of a civics project, Randall created a circle graph showing the most commonly used heating fuels in Smallsburg.

SOURCES OF HEATING FUEL IN SMALLSBURG

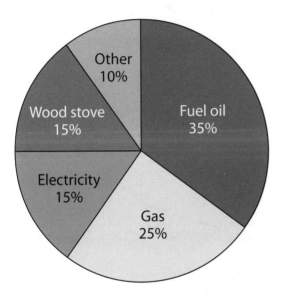

3. Which two sources of fuel together represent more than 50% of the total commonly used heating fuels?

    (1) gas and wood stove
    (2) fuel oil and electricity
    (3) wood stove and fuel oil
    (4) fuel oil and gas
    (5) gas and electricity

4. Which two sources of fuel are used by the same percentage of the population?

    (1) wood stove and gas
    (2) electricity and other
    (3) fuel oil and gas
    (4) gas and electricity
    (5) electricity and wood stove

5. What percentage of the population uses a source other than gas?

    (1) 25%
    (2) 35%
    (3) 50%
    (4) 75%
    (5) Not enough information is given.

<u>Questions 6 and 7</u> refer to the information and circle graph below.

The following circle graph shows the voting habits of the residents of Middlesburg.

HOW MIDDLESBURG VOTES

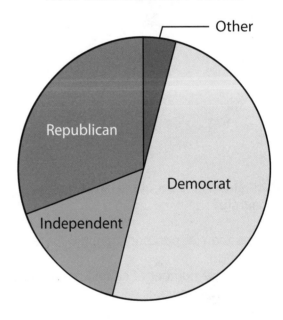

6. For which party did half of the population vote?

    (1) Republican
    (2) Independent
    (3) Democrat
    (4) Other
    (5) Not enough information is given.

7. About what percentage of the population voted for either Independent or Republican candidates?

    (1) 15%
    (2) 30%
    (3) 35%
    (4) 45%
    (5) 50%

Questions 8 through 10 refer to the following paragraph and circle graph.

Tom asked 100 of his friends and family members to name their favorite form of exercise. The circle graph below displays his findings.

FAVORITE WAY TO EXERCISE

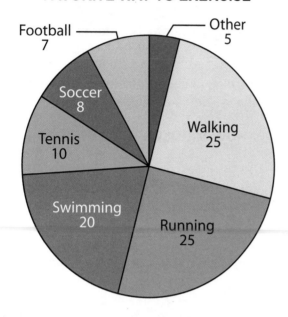

8. Which statement about the circle graph is accurate?

   (1) Less than 20 percent of people prefer walking.
   (2) The same number of people prefer soccer as prefer swimming.
   (3) About half of the people prefer either running or walking.
   (4) Fewer than 10 people fall into the category "swimming."
   (5) About 70 people prefer an exercise other than swimming.

9. About what fraction of people prefer an exercise other than running?

   (1) $\frac{1}{4}$

   (2) $\frac{1}{2}$

   (3) $\frac{3}{4}$

   (4) $\frac{4}{5}$

   (5) $\frac{9}{10}$

10. About what percentage of the people prefer skiing?

    (1) more than 4%
    (2) more than 10%
    (3) more than 25%
    (4) more than 50%
    (5) Not enough information is given.

Questions 11 and 12 refer to the information and graph below.

The circle graph shows the percentages of tree species in a state park.

TREE SPECIES

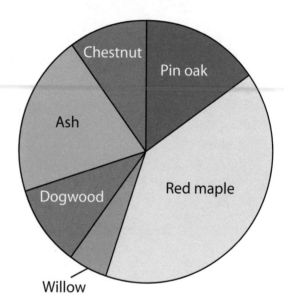

11. What percentage of trees are red maples?

    (1) 5%
    (2) 10%
    (3) 20%
    (4) 30%
    (5) 40%

12. If there were 300 trees in the park, how many red maple trees would you expect there to be?

    (1) 40
    (2) 80
    (3) 120
    (4) 160
    (5) 200

Questions 13 through 15 refer to the following paragraph and circle graph.

The circle graph shows the languages spoken by students at the Marbletown International High School.

LANGUAGES SPOKEN BY STUDENTS

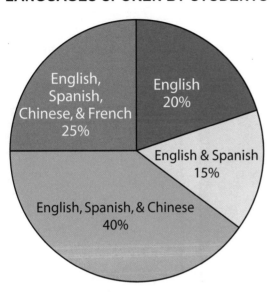

Questions 16 through 18 refer to the circle graph below.

DIEGO'S MONTHLY BUDGET

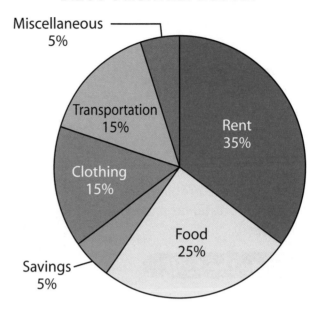

13. What percentage of students speak more than two languages?

   (1) 15%
   (2) 20%
   (3) 25%
   (4) 40%
   (5) 65%

14. What percentage of students do not speak Chinese?

   (1) 15%
   (2) 20%
   (3) 30%
   (4) 35%
   (5) 65%

15. Based on the circle graph, which of the following statements is accurate?

   (1) Half of the students speak French.
   (2) One-fourth of the students speak Spanish.
   (3) All students speak English.
   (4) Less than half of the students speak two or more languages.
   (5) More than half of the students speak exactly two languages.

16. For every $100, about how much should Diego spend on food?

   (1) $5
   (2) $15
   (3) $25
   (4) $35
   (5) Not enough information is given.

17. If Diego earns $2,200 this month, how much should he put into savings?

   (1) $5
   (2) $50
   (3) $100
   (4) $110
   (5) $1,100

18. Based on the graph, which of the following statements is accurate?

   (1) Diego spends most of his monthly budget on food.
   (2) Diego spends more on transportation and miscellaneous expenses than on food.
   (3) Diego spends more on transportation than on clothing costs.
   (4) Diego saves more than 10% of his monthly income.
   (5) Food and rent make up the largest percentage of Diego's monthly expenses.

UNIT 2

Time

For use with student book pp. 48-49

① Review the Skill

On the GED Mathematics Test, you will solve problems that involve time, including those that involve elapsed time. You also may solve problems involving time, distance, and rate (or speed).

② Refine the Skill

Solving problems involving time may require that you convert minutes to a fraction or a decimal, or vice versa. When converting a decimal or fraction of an hour to minutes, remember that an hour is 60 minutes.

$$15 \text{ min} = \frac{15}{60} \text{ hr} = 0.25 \text{ hr}$$

$$30 \text{ min} = \frac{30}{60} \text{ hr} = 0.5 \text{ hr}$$

$$45 \text{ min} = \frac{45}{60} \text{ hr} = 0.75 \text{ hr}$$

Read the paragraph and examine the clocks. Then answer the questions that follow.

☑ TEST-TAKING TIPS

After you use the distance formula, check your answer by multiplying the time by the rate. The product should be the distance. If it is not, go back and check your work.

A plane flies from Buffalo, New York, to Miami, Florida. The flight leaves at 10:28 A.M. and arrives in Miami at 1:40 P.M. The distance covered by the plane is approximately 1,190 miles.

Departure Time

Arrival Time

A To solve question 1, think:
10:28–10:30 is 2 mins
10:30–11:00 is 30 mins
11:00–1:00 is 2 hours
1:00–1:40 is 40 mins

B If you are using the distance formula to find miles per hour, you must substitute the number of hours for time, not minutes.

A

1. How long was the flight?

   (1) 2.28 hr
   (2) 2.4 hr
   (3) 3.12 hr
   (4) 3.2 hr
   (5) 4.1 hr

2. What was the average speed of the plane?

   (1) 372 mph
   (2) 382 mph
   (3) 452 mph
   (4) 500 mph
   (5) Not enough information is given.

Directions: Choose the <u>one best answer</u> to each question.

<u>Questions 3 through 5</u> refer to the paragraph and map below.

Ron, Cheryl, and Max are all attending a picnic at Bob's house. The picnic starts at 3:30 P.M. Ron lives 10 miles away from Bob's house and plans to ride his bicycle to the party. Cheryl lives 60 miles away. Max lives 20 miles away.

MAP TO THE PICNIC

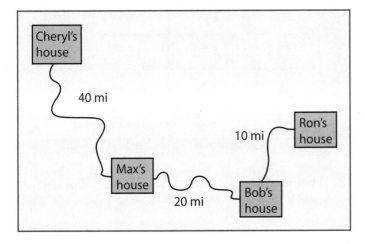

3. If Ron averages 7 miles per hour on his bike, what time should he leave his home in order to arrive at 3:30 P.M.?

   (1) 12:24 P.M.
   (2) 1:48 P.M.
   (3) 2:04 P.M.
   (4) 2:18 P.M.
   (5) 2:48 P.M.

4. If Cheryl leaves at 2:30 P.M. and travels at an average speed of 45 miles per hour, what time will she arrive at the picnic?

   (1) 3:15 P.M.
   (2) 3:30 P.M.
   (3) 3:50 P.M.
   (4) 4:15 P.M.
   (5) 4:45 P.M.

5. Cheryl offers to take Max to the picnic. She drives 40 miles to Max's house at an average speed of 50 miles per hour. She and Max spend 30 minutes at his house preparing a dish. Then they drive 20 miles to the picnic at an average speed of 35 miles per hour. Approximately how long does Cheryl's entire journey take?

   (1) 34 min
   (2) 48 min
   (3) 1 hr 18 min
   (4) 1 hr 52 min
   (5) Not enough information is given.

<u>Questions 6 through 8</u> refer to the following paragraph and table.

Li leaves Boulder, Colorado, on a car trip to St. Louis at 7:30 in the morning. He plans to make a few stops along the way. He makes his first stop at 8:45 to buy a cup of coffee for the road. He is back on the road by 9:00.

6. Li stops for lunch at 12:10 P.M. How much time has elapsed since he left Boulder?

   (1) 4 hr 30 min
   (2) 4 hr 40 min
   (3) 4 hr 50 min
   (4) 5 hr 5 min
   (5) 5 hr 10 min

7. At 12:40 P.M., Li resumes his trip. Driving at an average speed of 65 mph, how far will he travel in 45 minutes?

   (1) 45.25 mi
   (2) 45.75 mi
   (3) 48.0 mi
   (4) 48.75 mi
   (5) 65.0 mi

8. Li drives the next 100 miles in an hour and a half. What is his average speed in miles per hour?

   (1) 50 mph
   (2) 60.25 mph
   (3) 63.33 mph
   (4) 66.67 mph
   (5) 90 mph

UNIT 2

Questions 9 through 11 refer to the following paragraph and table.

A team of five friends took part in a 20-mile bicycle race to raise money for a local animal shelter. The table below shows their racing times.

ANIMAL SHELTER BENEFIT RACE

TEAM MEMBER	TIME
Hector	1 hr 18 min
Mara	1 hr 15 min
Stacey	1 hr 6 min
Dedrick	1 hr 10 min
Jared	1 hr 30 min

9. Which team member averaged 18 miles per hour for the 20-mile race?

(1) Hector
(2) Mara
(3) Stacey
(4) Dedrick
(5) Jared

10. What team member rode approximately 2 miles per hour faster than Jared?

(1) Hector
(2) Mara
(3) Stacey
(4) Dedrick
(5) Jared

11. If Jared crossed the finish line at 2:38 P.M., at what time did Stacey cross the finish line?

(1) 1:32 P.M.
(2) 1:02 P.M.
(3) 2:14 P.M.
(4) 2:44 P.M.
(5) 3:02 P.M.

Questions 12 through 14 refer to the following paragraph and timetable.

The residents of Midtown and its surrounding towns use the following schedule to plan their commutes from town to town. This part of the bus schedule shows the afternoon departures.

TIMETABLE FOR BUSES LEAVING MIDTOWN

Bus Departure Time

Midtown	Easton	Weston	Northside
12:05	12:22	1:05	1:30
1:35	1:52	2:35	3:00
2:05	2:22	3:05	3:30
3:35	3:52	4:35	5:00
4:05	4:22	5:05	5:30
4:35	4:52	5:35	6:00

12. What is the total travel time between Midtown and Northside?

(1) 1 hr 5 min
(2) 1 hr 25 min
(3) 1 hr 35 min
(4) 2 hr 35 min
(5) 2 hr 55 min

13. If a passenger misses the 2:05 bus to Easton and instead must take the 3:35 bus, what will the wait time plus the travel time be?

(1) 17 min
(2) 30 min
(3) 47 min
(4) 1 hr 30 min
(5) 1 hr 47 min

14. How many miles per hour does the bus average on the trip from Weston to Northside?

(1) 35 mph
(2) 45 mph
(3) 55 mph
(4) 60 mph
(5) Not enough information is given.

Nick runs a 5-mile course in 45 minutes every Monday, Wednesday, and Friday. On Sundays, he runs the same 5-mile course at an average pace of 7 mph.

NICK'S RUNNING STATS			
DAY	DISTANCE	RATE	TIME
Monday	5 mi	?	45 min
Wednesday	5 mi	?	45 min
Friday	5 mi	?	45 min
Sunday	5 mi	7 mph	?

15. How fast does Nick run on Monday, Wednesday, and Friday?

(1) 5.5 mph
(2) 6.0 mph
(3) 6.67 mph
(4) 7.5 mph
(5) 11.11 mph

16. About how long does it take Nick to run the course on Sunday?

(1) about 30 min
(2) about 35 min
(3) about 38 min
(4) about 43 min
(5) about 45 min

17. One Sunday, Nick starts his run at 11:35 A.M. If he maintains his 7 mph rate, what time will he finish?

(1) 12:15 P.M.
(2) 12:18 P.M.
(3) 12:20 P.M.
(4) 12:25 P.M.
(5) 12:42 P.M.

A group of six friends decided to compete in a 25-mile bicycle race for charity. The table below shows their race results.

RESULTS OF CHARITY RACE	
BICYCLIST	TIME
Anna	1 hr 12 min
Emily	1 hr 9 min
Kyle	1 hr 34 min
Hannah	1 hr 4 min
Brian	1 hr 23 min
Tricia	1 hr 17 min

18. What was Anna's average rate of speed?

(1) 17.5 mph
(2) 18.3 mph
(3) 20.8 mph
(4) 21.7 mph
(5) 23.6 mph

19. Hannah's rate of speed was about how much faster than Brian's?

(1) 7.6 mph
(2) 5.4 mph
(3) 4.1 mph
(4) 2.8 mph
(5) 1.9 mph

20. If the race started at 12:30 P.M., at what time did Kyle cross the finish line?

(1) 1:34 P.M.
(2) 1:39 P.M.
(3) 1:47 P.M.
(4) 1:53 P.M.
(5) 2:04 P.M.

UNIT 2

Integers

For use with student book pp. 58-59

① Review the Skill

Integers include positive and negative whole numbers and zero. Use the order of operations to add, subtract, multiply, and divide integers. There are specific rules to follow regarding the signs of integers when performing operations.

② Refine the Skill

To be successful with algebra, you must understand how to solve problems with integers. Understanding order of operations and integer rules are necessary skills for success on the GED Mathematics Test. Examine the table. Then answer the questions that follow.

The table shows the temperature at a weather station at various times during the day.

TEMPERATURE THROUGHOUT THE DAY

TIME	TEMPERATURE (°F)
Ⓐ 6:00 A.M.	68
9:00 A.M.	72
12:00 P.M.	75
3:00 P.M.	78
6:00 P.M.	76
9:00 P.M.	71
Ⓐ 12:00 A.M.	65

Ⓐ Remember that when you are asked to find change, subtract the original temperature from the new temperature. To answer question 1, subtract 68 from 65.

Ⓑ To decide which operation to use, look for key words. In question 2, *dropped* tells you to subtract.

☑ TEST-TAKING TIPS

You can draw a number line to help you visualize situations. To visualize the temperature on a thermometer moving up and down, draw a vertical number line.

80
75
70
65

1. What is the change in temperature between 6:00 A.M. and 12:00 A.M.?

   (1) −3°F
   (2) +3°F
   (3) −4°F
   (4) +4°F
   (5) +5°F

2. If the temperature dropped 4°F between 6:00 P.M. and 8:00 P.M., what would be the temperature at 8:00 P.M.?

   (1) 68°F
   (2) 69°F
   (3) 70°F
   (4) 71°F
   (5) 72°F

Directions: Choose the <u>one best answer</u> to each question.

3. A football team has possession of the ball. On their first play, they gain 8 yards. On their second play, they lose 10 yards. On their third play, they gain 43 yards. How far have they gone?

   (1) 25 yards
   (2) 33 yards
   (3) 41 yards
   (4) 51 yards
   (5) 53 yards

4. The Dow Jones Industrial Average opened trading one morning at 11,498. It closed that day at 11,416. Which integer describes the change?

   (1) +82
   (2) +18
   (3) −18
   (4) −72
   (5) −82

5. A mountain biker begins at the top of a mountain with an elevation of 8,453 feet. She rides 2,508 feet down the mountain before taking a break. She then rides another 584 feet up the mountain. At what elevation is she now?

   (1) 11,545 feet
   (2) 10,961 feet
   (3) 9,037 feet
   (4) 6,529 feet
   (5) 5,945 feet

6. A diver begins at a height of 3 meters above the water on a diving board. In her dive, she reaches a height of 2 meters above the board. From this point, she drops 8 meters. Which integer describes her position at this point, with regard to the surface of the water?

   (1) 3 meters
   (2) 2 meters
   (3) −2 meters
   (4) −3 meters
   (5) −10 meters

7. In a card game, Deshon had −145 points. He then scored 80 points, and then 22 points. What is Deshon's score at this point?

   (1) 225
   (2) 167
   (3) 123
   (4) −43
   (5) −65

8. Anna had $784 in her checking account on Friday. Over the weekend, she wrote checks for $23, $69, and $90. On Monday, she deposited $129. What was her balance after depositing the check?

   (1) $913
   (2) $731
   (3) $692
   (4) $655
   (5) $602

<u>Questions 9 and 10</u> refer to the following table.

Four friends played a game. Each player kept track of the number of points she scored in each round.

	POINTS SCORED EACH ROUND		
PLAYER	ROUND		
	1	2	3
Nikki	0	10	−15
Clara	−15	15	0
Donna	5	−10	−10
Dorothy	15	5	0

9. What was Donna's score after the end of Round 3?

   (1) −25
   (2) −15
   (3) −10
   (4) 0
   (5) 25

10. How many more points did Dorothy score than Nikki?

   (1) 5
   (2) 10
   (3) 15
   (4) 20
   (5) 25

11. A submarine is at 3,290 feet below sea level. It rises 589 feet before dropping another 4,508 feet. Which integer describes its current position with regard to sea level?

(1) 7,209
(2) 1,807
(3) −1,807
(4) −7,209
(5) −8,387

12. A cogwheel train transports skiers to the top of a mountain. There are two stations where skiers can get on and off the train. Station A is 5,993 feet above sea level. Station B is 10,549 feet above sea level. The peak of the mountain is 872 feet above Station B. How tall is the mountain at its highest point?

(1) −16,542 feet
(2) −11,421 feet
(3) 6,865 feet
(4) 11,421 feet
(5) 16,542 feet

13. Jordan had $890 in her bank account. In one week, she withdrew $45 three separate times. What was the balance of her account at the end of the week?

(1) $755
(2) $800
(3) $845
(4) $935
(5) $975

14. A number is multiplied by −2. Then the product is increased by 2. The final result is 0. What is the original number?

(1) −2
(2) −1
(3) 0
(4) 1
(5) 2

15. Four team members each have −120 points. How many points do they have together as a team?

(1) −480
(2) −360
(3) 240
(4) 360
(5) 480

16. A group of rock climbers descended a rock face in three equal phases. They descended the same number of feet each time. If the rock face was 363 feet high, what number describes their change in height in each phase?

(1) −242 feet
(2) −121 feet
(3) 121 feet
(4) 242 feet
(5) 1,089 feet

17. Erik biked 12 miles directly south from his home. He then turned around and biked 8 miles back toward his home before stopping to fix a flat tire. How far from home was he when he was fixing his flat tire?

(1) 4 miles
(2) 8 miles
(3) 12 miles
(4) 16 miles
(5) 20 miles

18. Don played a game. He scored 3 points in the first round. After the second round, his total score was −10. How many points did Don score in the second round?

(1) −13
(2) −7
(3) 5
(4) 7
(5) 13

19. The number –7 is multiplied by –1. The product is then multiplied by –1. Finally, this product is multiplied by –1. What is the final product?

(1) –10
(2) –7
(3) –4
(4) 0
(5) 7

20. Brenda has her health insurance premium of $156 automatically withdrawn from her checking account each month. Which integer describes the change in her bank account due to her health insurance premium in one year?

(1) $1,872
(2) $936
(3) –$156
(4) –$936
(5) –$1,872

21. Karin owes her sister $1,554. She has budgeted an equal amount of money over the next 6 months to pay her sister back. How much money will Karin pay her sister each month?

(1) $257
(2) $258
(3) $259
(4) $260
(5) $261

22. Jumana had $80 in her checking account. She deposited $25 on Monday. She wrote two checks for $75 each on Tuesday. She was charged with a $25 overdraft fee. What is Jumana's account balance?

(1) –$70
(2) –$60
(3) –$50
(4) –$40
(5) –$30

23. Janet visited a skyscraper in Chicago. She entered the elevator on the ground floor and went up 54 floors. After looking at the city from the viewing area, she went back down 22 floors. She realized that she made a mistake and instead should have gotten out of the elevator 5 floors above, so she rides the elevator up. On what floor is Janet now?

(1) 27
(2) 32
(3) 37
(4) 59
(5) 76

24. Cheryl receives $527 per month from her retirement fund. Which integer describes the amount she receives in 6 months?

(1) –$3,689
(2) –$3,162
(3) $2,635
(4) $3,162
(5) $3,689

25. In a year, Connor paid $3,228 for his car loan. He paid the same amount each month. Which integer describes the monthly change in his bank account after paying his monthly car payment?

(1) –$269
(2) –$239
(3) –$229
(4) $239
(5) $269

26. If –10 is subtracted from a number, the result is 6. What is the number?

(1) –16
(2) –4
(3) 0
(4) 4
(5) 16

Algebraic Expressions and Variables
For use with student book pp. 60-61

① Review the Skill

Algebraic expressions translate words into number relationships using numbers, operation signs, and variables. **Variables** are letters that represent numbers. When expressions are simplified, they have the same value. When you evaluate an expression, you substitute values for the variables and then use order of operations to determine the value of the expression.

② Refine the Skill

You must know how to translate word problems into numbers and symbols to succeed on the GED Mathematics Test. You also will use algebra skills to solve problems in areas such as measurement and geometry. Examine the information. Then answer the questions that follow.

☑ TEST-TAKING TIPS

Subtraction and negative signs are entered differently in the calculator. Use the minus sign for subtraction. To enter a negative number, type the number and then press the sign change button: "+/−".

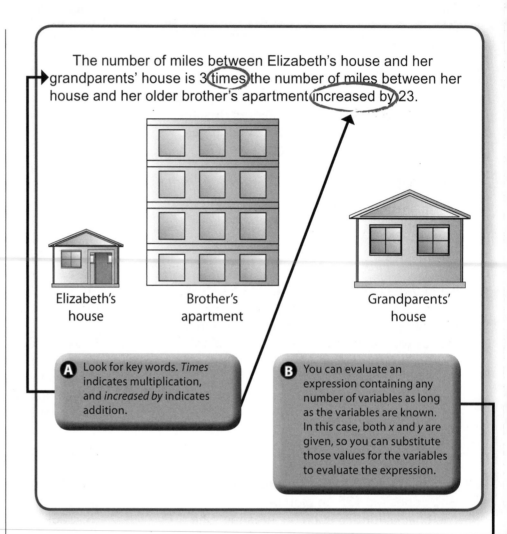

The number of miles between Elizabeth's house and her grandparents' house is 3 times the number of miles between her house and her older brother's apartment increased by 23.

Elizabeth's house   Brother's apartment   Grandparents' house

A Look for key words. *Times* indicates multiplication, and *increased by* indicates addition.

B You can evaluate an expression containing any number of variables as long as the variables are known. In this case, both *x* and *y* are given, so you can substitute those values for the variables to evaluate the expression.

1. If Elizabeth's brother's apartment is 29 miles away from her house, how far away from her house is her grandparents' house?

    (1) 69 miles
    (2) 87 miles
    (3) 110 miles
    (4) 116 miles
    (5) 129 miles

2. If the expression $\frac{4x - y}{5}$ represents the distance between Elizabeth's house and her grandparents' house, and $x = 7$ and $y = 3$, what is the distance from Elizabeth's house to her grandparents' house?

    (1) 5 miles
    (2) 6 miles
    (3) 20 miles
    (4) 25 miles
    (5) 28 miles

Directions: Choose the <u>one best answer</u> to each question.

3. The number of girls that registered to play basketball in a summer league is 15 fewer than twice the number of boys. Which expression describes the number of girls that registered?

   (1) $\dfrac{2b}{15}$

   (2) $\dfrac{1}{2}b + 15$

   (3) $15 + 2b$

   (4) $2b - 15$

   (5) $15 - 2b$

4. A school sold adult tickets and children's tickets to a football game. The number of children's tickets sold was 56 more than one-third the number of adult tickets. Which expression describes the number of children's tickets sold?

   (1) $\dfrac{1}{3}a - 56$

   (2) $\dfrac{a}{3} + 56$

   (3) $\dfrac{56a}{3}$

   (4) $\dfrac{3}{56}a$

   (5) $\dfrac{3}{a} + 56$

5. There are p number of pencils in a pack. There are 50 packs in a box, and 12 boxes in a case. Julia delivers 3 cases to a store. She opens a case to remove 1 pencil to use. Which expression represents the number of pencils that are left?

   (1) $3 + 12 + 50 + p - 1$

   (2) $3(12)(50)p - 1$

   (3) $3(12)\left(\dfrac{50}{p}\right) - 1$

   (4) $3(12)(50)p(1)$

   (5) $3(12)(50)p + 1$

6. Edward drove 4 times as many miles on Tuesday as he did on Wednesday and Thursday combined. Which expression describes the number of miles he drove on Tuesday in terms of the number of miles he drove on Wednesday and Thursday?

   (1) $x + 4y$

   (2) $\dfrac{4}{x + y}$

   (3) $4x + y$

   (4) $\dfrac{x + y}{4}$

   (5) $4(x + y)$

7. The number of students in an incoming freshman class is 3 times the number of students in the sophomore class divided by 4. Which expression describes the number of students in the incoming freshman class?

   (1) $4y + 3$

   (2) $\dfrac{3y}{4}$

   (3) $3y + 4$

   (4) $\dfrac{4}{3y}$

   (5) $3y - 4$

Question 8 refers to the triangle shown below.

8. Which expression represents the perimeter of the triangle?

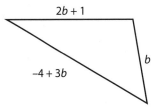

   (1) $5b + 3$
   (2) $6b + 3$
   (3) $6b - 3$
   (4) $-b + 4$
   (5) $3b$

9. The age of Nick's grandfather is 5 years greater than twice the ages of his two grandchildren together. Which expression describes Nick's grandfather's age?

(1) $2(x + y) + 5$

(2) $\dfrac{x + y}{2} + 5$

(3) $\dfrac{2(x + y)}{5}$

(4) $10(x + y)$

(5) $2x + 2y - 5$

10. On Monday, a cyclist rode 20 fewer than 3 times the number of miles he rode on Sunday. If he rode 30 miles on Sunday, how many miles did he ride on Monday?

(1) 30
(2) 40
(3) 60
(4) 70
(5) 90

11. The expression $3(x + 2x)$ represents the distance between two cities. What is the distance if $x = 4$?

(1) 48
(2) 36
(3) 20
(4) 18
(5) Not enough information is given.

12. Leo's age is 2 times the age of his sister decreased by 21. If his sister is 23, how old is Leo?

(1) 2
(2) 21
(3) 25
(4) 46
(5) Not enough information is given.

13. The expression $15a + 25b$ represents the amount of money a theater takes in per night if they sell a amount of $15 seats and b amount of $25 seats. How much money does the theater take in if $a = 207$ and $b = 134$?

(1) $5,115
(2) $5,175
(3) $6,455
(4) $7,185
(5) $7,255

14. A middle school has 374 male students. The number of female students is one-half the number of male students increased by 56. How many female students are in the middle school?

(1) 215
(2) 243
(3) 430
(4) 692
(5) 860

15. A store sells women's and men's shoes. In one day, the number of women's shoes sold was 12 more than 4 times the number of men's shoes sold. How many pairs of women's shoes did the store sell?

(1) 48
(2) 72
(3) 96
(4) 108
(5) Not enough information is given.

16. The height of a triangle is 3 less than 3 times the base. If $b =$ the base of the triangle, which expression represents the area of the triangle?

(1) $3b - 3$

(2) $b(3b - 3)$

(3) $\dfrac{1}{2}b(3b - 3)$

(4) $\dfrac{1}{2}b(b)$

(5) $\dfrac{3b - 3}{2}$

Lesson 2 | Algebraic Expressions and Variables

17. The number of minutes that Erin spent on Project A is 45 less than one-half of her time spent on Project B. Which expression best represents her time spent on Project B, if t equals the number of minutes spent on Project A?

(1) $2t + 90$

(2) $2t - 45$

(3) $\frac{2t}{45}$

(4) $\frac{45}{2t}$

(5) $\frac{1}{2}t - 45$

18. A number is half the value of the sum of a second and third number. Which expression describes the first number?

(1) $2x + 2y$

(2) $\frac{2}{x + y}$

(3) $\frac{x + y}{2}$

(4) $x + y$

(5) $2(x + y)$

19. Sean swam 8 fewer than twice as many laps as Antonio. If Antonio swam 15 laps, how many laps did Sean swim?

(1) 11
(2) 12
(3) 15
(4) 22
(5) 23

20. If $-3 = x$, then what does $4y - 8(3 - 2x)$ equal?

(1) -72
(2) $-68y$
(3) $4y - 24$
(4) $4y + 24$
(5) $4y - 72$

21. The number of students who scored above average on an exam was 34 fewer than twice the number of students who scored at an average level. If 45 students scored at an average level, how many scored above average?

(1) 34
(2) 56
(3) 66
(4) 78
(5) 90

22. Jada wrote a check to pay for gas. The amount of the check was $5 less than one-half the amount that she had deposited into her account that day. If she deposited $84, how much did she pay for gas?

(1) $79
(2) $74
(3) $42
(4) $37
(5) Not enough information is given.

23. A number is 3 times the value of the quotient of a second and third number. Which expression describes the first number?

(1) $\frac{xy}{3}$

(2) $\frac{3}{x + y}$

(3) $\frac{3}{x} + y$

(4) $3(x + y)$

(5) $3\left(\frac{x}{y}\right)$

24. The length of a rectangle is 6 more than two-thirds the width. Which expression represents the perimeter of the rectangle?

(1) $\frac{10}{3}w + 12$

(2) $w\left(6 + \frac{2}{3}\right)w$

(3) $\frac{4}{3}w + 12$

(4) $\frac{10}{3}w + 6$

(5) $\frac{5}{3}w + 6$

Equations

For use with student book pp. 62-63

① Review the Skill

An **equation** is a mathematical statement showing that two quantities are equal. You can solve equations by isolating the variable through performing inverse operations. The formulas used to solve math problems are all equations.

② Refine the Skill

Understanding how to translate word problems into equations and how to solve those equations is a vital skill for the GED Mathematics Test. Examine the information. Then answer the questions that follow.

The menu of a New England restaurant is shown below.

Seafood Heaven Menu

ITEM	PRICE
Lobster Tail	Market Value
Clam Chowder	$8
Atlantic Salmon	$13
Crab Lettuce Wraps	$10
Cup of Lobster Bisque	$8

A There is usually more than one way to write an equation. In question 1, answer choices 3 and 5 are the same, because $\frac{4}{3}$ is the same as $4 \times \frac{1}{3}$.

B For question 2, use the equation $2(8) + 3t = 70$, where t represents the price of one lobster tail.

☑ TEST-TAKING TIPS

When you write an equation to represent a problem, note what your variable represents. The value of the variable in your equation may not necessarily be the answer. Question 2 asks for the cost of the lobster *tails*, not the cost of a single lobster *tail*.

1. If the price of lobster on a given day was $4 more than one-third the price of the crab lettuce wraps, which equation could you use to find the price of lobster that day?

   (1) $3t + 4 = 10$

   (2) $t = \frac{1}{3}(10) + 4$

   (3) $\frac{4}{3}t = 10$

   (4) $4 - 3t = 10$

   (5) $(4)\frac{1}{3}t = 10$

2. Leon and his family ordered 2 cups of lobster bisque and 3 lobster tails. If their bill for these 5 items was $70, what was the cost of the lobster tails?

   (1) $15
   (2) $16
   (3) $18
   (4) $52
   (5) $54

UNIT 3

Directions: Choose the one best answer to each question.

3. One number is 5 times the value of another number. The sum of the numbers is 72. What equation can be used to find the first number?

(1) $\frac{72}{x} = 5$

(2) $\frac{x}{6} = 72$

(3) $\frac{x}{5} = 72$

(4) $5x = 72$

(5) $6x = 72$

4. The amount John spent in restaurants one month is $55 more than twice the amount he spent on groceries. If he spent $228 on groceries, which of the following equations could be solved to find the amount of money he spent in restaurants?

(1) $\frac{r}{2} + 55 = 228$

(2) $\frac{55}{r} - 2 = 228$

(3) $r = 55 + 2(228)$

(4) $55 - 2r = 228$

(5) $\frac{1}{2}r + 55 = 228$

5. Patricia bought a printer. After she paid 6% sales tax, the total was $105.97. Which equation could be solved to find the price p of the printer before tax?

(1) $p + 0.06 = 105.97$

(2) $0.06p = 105.97$

(3) $105.97 + 0.06 = p$

(4) $\frac{105.97}{0.06} = p$

(5) $p + 0.06p = 105.97$

6. The admission to an amusement park for a child under 48 inches tall is $3 less than half the price of an adult ticket. If the admission for a child costs $26, which equation could be used to find the price of an adult's admission?

(1) $2a - 3 = 26$

(2) $\frac{1}{2}a - 3 = 26$

(3) $\frac{a}{2} + 3 = 26$

(4) $3a - 48 = 26$

(5) $\frac{1}{2}a + 26 = 3$

7. Rachel earns twice as much money as her husband. Together, they earn $1,050 each week. Which equation could be used to find Rachel's husband's weekly earnings?

(1) $3h = 1,050$

(2) $2h + 2 = 1,050$

(3) $\frac{1}{2}h = 1,050$

(4) $2h = 1,050$

(5) $\frac{3}{2}h = 1,050$

8. Steven worked 2 more than one-third as many hours this week as he did last week. Last week, he worked 33 hours. How many hours did he work this week?

(1) 11
(2) 13
(3) 17
(4) 21
(5) 35

9. There are 36 inches in one yard. Which equation represents this situation, if i = number of inches, and y = number of yards?

(1) $36i = y$
(2) $36 + i = y$
(3) $36y = i$
(4) $36 - i = y$

(5) $\frac{36}{i} = y$

UNIT 3

10. A barge travels downstream at an average speed of 15 miles per hour. It travels a distance of 60 miles. Which equation can be used to find how many hours the barge traveled?

(1) $\frac{1}{t}(60) = 15 - t$

(2) $15 = 60t$

(3) $\frac{t}{15} = 60$

(4) $\frac{60}{t} = 15 + t$

(5) $60 = 15t$

11. Ben and Brian both rode their bikes long distances on Saturday. Together, they rode 107 miles. If Ben biked 11 more miles than Brian, how many miles did Brian bike?

(1) 32
(2) 37
(3) 48
(4) 59
(5) 96

12. Mrs. Logan ordered 12 new desks and 20 new chairs for her classroom. The total cost of the desks and chairs was $1,260. If each chair cost $30, what was the cost of each desk?

(1) $50
(2) $55
(3) $57
(4) $58
(5) $60

13. A store pays $53.80 for a carton of boxes of cereal. If each box of cereal costs $2.69, how many boxes of cereal are in a carton?

(1) 17
(2) 18
(3) 19
(4) 20
(5) 21

14. One number is two-thirds of another number. The sum of the numbers is 55. What is the greater number?

(1) 22
(2) 23
(3) 30
(4) 32
(5) 33

15. Karleen and her mother went on a vacation. Karleen paid for gas, and her mother paid for lodging. Karleen spent $65.25 more than one-fourth of what her mother spent. If they spent a total of $659, how much did Karleen spend?

(1) $184.00
(2) $181.00
(3) $164.75
(4) $118.75
(5) $53.50

16. Emma purchased 3 bottles of ginger ale for $2.29 per bottle. She also purchased some boxes of crackers for $3.35 per box. Her total bill was $23.62. How many boxes of crackers did she buy?

(1) 4
(2) 5
(3) 6
(4) 7
(5) 8

17. If $y = \frac{1}{2}$, what does x equal when

$4 - 2(3x - y) = 5x - 2\frac{1}{3}$?

(1) $-7\frac{1}{3}$

(2) $-1\frac{1}{3}$

(3) $-\frac{2}{3}$

(4) $\frac{2}{3}$

(5) $1\frac{1}{3}$

18. Myra took her 5 children out for ice cream. Each child ordered a single scoop of ice cream on a cone. The clerk added $0.87 to Myra's bill for sales tax. Myra paid a total of $15.37. If each cone cost the same amount, what was the cost of one cone?

(1) $2.82
(2) $2.87
(3) $2.90
(4) $3.07
(5) $3.25

19. A cell phone at Store A costs $10 less than twice the cost of the same cell phone at Store B. If the phone costs $49.99 at Store B, how much does it cost at Store A?

(1) $89.98
(2) $79.99
(3) $69.99
(4) $59.99
(5) $30.00

20. Tickets to a baseball game are $9 for adults. A child's ticket is $2 more than half the price of an adult's ticket. Melanie buys 4 adult tickets and some children's tickets. If she paid $75 for the tickets, how many children's tickets did she buy?

(1) 3
(2) 4
(3) 5
(4) 6
(5) Not enough information is given.

21. Juan can either earn $200 per week plus 15% commission, or $300 per week plus 10% commission. What do Juan's sales need to be in order for the two earning options to pay the same amount?

(1) $10,000
(2) $2,000
(3) $400
(4) $20
(5) Not enough information is given.

22. A company held a fundraising event for a charity. Andrew contributed $25 less than twice as much as Michael. The sum of their contributions was $200. How much did Andrew contribute?

(1) $25
(2) $75
(3) $125
(4) $150
(5) $175

23. Xavier and Madeleine's ages add up to 28. Xavier is 4 years older than half of Madeleine's age. How old will Xavier be in 2 years?

(1) 12
(2) 14
(3) 15
(4) 16
(5) 18

24. Beth's rent is $74 less than 4 times her student loan payment. The total of these bills is $486. How much is her student loan payment?

(1) $112
(2) $187
(3) $299
(4) $373
(5) $448

25. Ann's weekly salary is $543 less than twice Joe's weekly salary. If Joe earns $874 per week, what is Ann's weekly salary?

(1) $331
(2) $1,174
(3) $1,205
(4) $1,417
(5) $1,748

Exponents and Square Roots

For use with student book pp. 64-65

① Review the Skill

Exponents show how many times a number is multiplied by itself. **Scientific notation** uses exponents and powers of 10 to write very small and very large numbers. The **square root** of a number is a number that when multiplied by itself equals a given number.

② Refine the Skill

When a number is raised to a negative power, write the reciprocal and then change the negative exponent to a positive. For example, $b^{-3} = \frac{1}{b^3}$. Negative exponents do not necessarily mean negative numbers. Examine the information and diagram. Then answer the questions that follow.

The diagram shows the area of Meredith's square garden.

$A = 121$ sq ft

A To answer question 1, remember that a square has four equal sides. To find the area of a square, multiply the length of one side by itself.

B If you use a calculator to perform operations with very large or very small numbers, it may display the result in scientific notation.

☑ TEST-TAKING TIPS

Taking the square root of a number is different from dividing a number by 2. When finding the square root of *x*, think *what number times itself equals x*? When dividing *x* by 2, think *what number plus itself equals x*?

1. Use the formula for the area of a square. What is the length of one side of Meredith's garden?

   (1) 12 ft
   (2) 11 ft
   (3) 10 ft
   (4) 9 ft
   (5) 8 ft

2. Meredith planted 3 packets of broccoli seeds. Each packet contained about 2.3×10^3 seeds. About how many broccoli seeds did she plant?

   (1) 2.3×10^3
   (2) 2.3×10^9
   (3) 6.9×10^9
   (4) 6.9×10^3
   (5) 9.0×10^9

Directions: Choose the <u>one best answer</u> to each question.

3. The North American feather-winged beetle is one of the world's smallest beetles. It is less than 0.0005 meters in length. What is this length written in scientific notation?

   (1) 5.0×10^{-4}
   (2) 5.0×10^{-3}
   (3) 5.0×10^{-2}
   (4) 5.0×10^{3}
   (5) 5.0×10^{4}

4. The Smithsonian Institute has about 3^4 items in its Division of Old World Archeology Collection. About how many items are in this collection?

   (1) 50
   (2) 60
   (3) 70
   (4) 80
   (5) 90

5. A math Web site gives the number of questions in its daily quiz as a square root. Today, there are $\sqrt{144}$ questions. How many questions are there?

   (1) 10
   (2) 11
   (3) 12
   (4) 13
   (5) 14

6. There are 3^4 students in one psychology class and 2^6 students in another psychology class. Which expression represents the total number of students in the two classes?

   (1) 5^{10}
   (2) 6^{10}
   (3) $3^4 + 2^6$
   (4) $34 + 26$
   (5) $3^4 \times 2^6$

Questions 7 and 8 refer to the following table.

The table shows the distances of planets from the sun.

PLANET	DISTANCE FROM THE SUN (km)
Mercury	5.79×10^7
Venus	1.082×10^8
Earth	1.496×10^8
Mars	2.279×10^8
Jupiter	7.786×10^8
Saturn	1.4335×10^9
Uranus	2.8725×10^9
Neptune	4.4951×10^9

7. Find the distance between Saturn and the sun. What is this number written in standard notation?

   (1) 14,335,000 km
   (2) 14,350,000 km
   (3) 143,350,000 km
   (4) 1,433,500,000 km
   (5) 14,335,000,000 km

8. How many kilometers farther from the sun is Jupiter than Venus?

   (1) 6.704×10^7
   (2) 6.704×10^8
   (3) 6.704×10^9
   (4) 6.704×10^{10}
   (5) 6.704×10^{16}

9. Amanda used her calculator to find $\sqrt{7,788}$. What is this number rounded to the nearest hundredth?

   (1) 88.24
   (2) 88.25
   (3) 89.24
   (4) 89.25
   (5) 90.25

UNIT 3

10. The length of a cube is 29 cm. What is the volume of the cube in cubic centimeters?

(1) 87
(2) 841
(3) 24,389
(4) 78,586
(5) 707,281

11. Olivia was asked to write the number of siblings she has using exponents. She wrote 4^0. What is another way to write the number of siblings she has using exponents?

(1) 5^0
(2) 5^1
(3) 4^2
(4) 4^1
(5) 3^1

Questions 12 through 14 refer to the following table.

The table shows the masses of the planets.

PLANET MASSES	
PLANET	MASS (KG)
Mercury	3.3×10^{23}
Venus	4.87×10^{24}
Earth	5.97×10^{24}
Mars	6.42×10^{23}
Jupiter	1.899×10^{27}
Saturn	5.68×10^{26}
Uranus	8.68×10^{25}
Neptune	1.02×10^{26}

12. Which of the following planets has the greatest mass?

(1) Venus
(2) Earth
(3) Jupiter
(4) Uranus
(5) Neptune

13. Which of the following planets has the least mass?

(1) Mercury
(2) Venus
(3) Earth
(4) Mars
(5) Jupiter

14. About how many times greater is the mass of Jupiter than the mass of Mars?

(1) 3×10^3
(2) 3×10^4
(3) 3×10^5
(4) 3×10^6
(5) 3×10^7

15. The expression $4x(x^2 + 2y)$ is equal to which of the following expressions?

(1) $4x^3 + 2y$
(2) $4x^2 + 8xy$
(3) $4x^2 + 2xy$
(4) $4x^3 + 8xy$
(5) $4x^3 + 8y$

16. The approximate number of people who visited an amusement park in July can be written as 10^5. About how many people attended the park in July?

(1) 1,000
(2) 10,000
(3) 100,000
(4) 1,000,000
(5) 10,000,000

17. Which expression is equivalent to b^{-4}?

(1) b^4

(2) $\dfrac{1}{b^4}$

(3) $-b^4$

(4) $\dfrac{1}{b^{-4}}$

(5) $-b(-b)(-b)(-b)$

Lesson 4 | Exponents and Square Roots

18. The area of a square is 6.7 sq ft. What is the length of a side of the square to the nearest tenth of a foot?

    (1) 2.5
    (2) 2.6
    (3) 2.9
    (4) 3.3
    (5) 3.4

19. One of the largest genomes is that of the marbled lungfish. Even so, the genome is only 1.3283×10^{-10} grams. What is this number expressed in standard notation?

    (1) 0.000013283
    (2) 0.0000013283
    (3) 0.00000013283
    (4) 0.000000013283
    (5) 0.00000000013283

20. The square root of 33 is between which two numbers?

    (1) 4 and 5
    (2) 5 and 6
    (3) 6 and 7
    (4) 7 and 8
    (5) 8 and 9

21. The perihelion of Pluto is 4,435,000,000 km. What is this distance written in scientific notation?

    (1) 4.435×10^7
    (2) 4.435×10^8
    (3) 4.435×10^9
    (4) 4.435×10^{10}
    (5) 4.435×10^{11}

22. Which has the same value as 4.404×10^9?

    (1) 0.4404×10^8
    (2) 0.4404×10^9
    (3) 0.4404×10^{10}
    (4) 44.04×10^9
    (5) 44.04×10^{10}

23. If $3^x = 81$, what is the value of x?

    (1) 1
    (2) 2
    (3) 3
    (4) 4
    (5) 5

24. The side of a square is 7.8 in. What is the area of the square?

    (1) 15.6 sq in.
    (2) 49.00 sq in.
    (3) 60.84 sq in.
    (4) 62.41 sq in.
    (5) 64.00 sq in.

25. The number of students who attend Shadyside High School can be written as 2^9. Sunnyside High School has 3 times the amount of students as Shadyside. How many students attend Sunnyside High School?

    (1) 171
    (2) 515
    (3) 1,536
    (4) 4,096
    (5) Not enough information is given.

26. The side of a cube is 15 cm. What is the volume of the cube?

    (1) 50,625 cm^3
    (2) 3,375 cm^3
    (3) 675 cm^3
    (4) 225 cm^3
    (5) 45 cm^3

27. Which statement is true about the following expression?

    $(-5)^x$

    (1) If x equals an even number, the answer will be negative.
    (2) If x equals an even number, the answer will be positive.
    (3) If x equals an odd number, the answer will be positive.
    (4) If x equals zero, the answer will be zero.
    (5) If x equals an even number, the answer could be positive or negative.

Patterns and Functions

For use with student book pp. 66-67

① Review the Skill

A **mathematical pattern** is an arrangement of numbers or terms in a particular order. The order of the arrangement follows a specific rule. You can identify the rule by describing what you would do to one term to get the next term. A function can be written as an algebraic rule.

② Refine the Skill

Identifying and extending patterns is an important part of algebra and succeeding on the GED Mathematics Test. You will extend this knowledge to working with functions and function tables. Examine the information and function table. Then answer the questions that follow.

The distance of a train from Station A was measured at different times as the train traveled to Station B. A record of the train's position and time is shown in the table below.

DISTANCE OF A TRAIN FROM STATION A					
TIME (t) IN HOURS	1	2	3	4	5
DISTANCE FROM STATION IN KM (d)	80	140	200	260	

A Substitute 5 for t in the equation and solve to find the train's distance after 5 hours to answer question 1.

B The train is traveling 60 km each hour. However, after 1 hour, it is 80 km from Station A. This is because when it began its journey, it was already 20 km from Station A. This is shown as "+ 20" in the equation.

☑ TEST-TAKING TIPS

You can use the answer choices to help you solve the problem. Instead of determining the rule from the table, you can try each one to see if it works. Note that other variables can be substituted for x and y; the table only lists a few pairs.

1. How many kilometers from the station will the train be after 5 hours?

   (1) 290
   (2) 300
   (3) 310
   (4) 320
   (5) 330

2. How many kilometers from the station was the train when it began its trip?

   (1) 20
   (2) 30
   (3) 50
   (4) 60
   (5) Not enough information is given.

Directions: Choose the one best answer to each question.

Questions 3 and 4 refer to the function table below.

x	−2	0	2	4	6
y	−8	−2	4	10	

3. Which of the following equations expresses the relationship between x and y?

   (1) $y = 3x − 2$

   (2) $y = \frac{1}{4}x$

   (3) $y = 2x + 3$

   (4) $y = \frac{2}{3}x$

   (5) $y = 4x$

4. What number is missing from the table?

   (1) 12
   (2) 14
   (3) 16
   (4) 18
   (5) 20

5. Which of the following rules can be used to extend the following sequence?

   $$2, 4, 8, 16, 32, \ldots$$

   (1) Add 4.
   (2) Subtract 8.
   (3) Multiply by 2.
   (4) Divide by 2.
   (5) Multiply by 8.

6. What is the sixth term in the sequence?

   $$1, 3, 9, 27, \ldots$$

   (1) 729
   (2) 243
   (3) 81
   (4) 9
   (5) 3

7. Solomon is following a pattern as he stacks the blocks shown below. How many blocks will he stack in the next figure in his sequence?

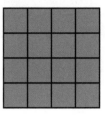

   (1) 18
   (2) 25
   (3) 32
   (4) 42
   (5) 64

8. What is the next term in the sequence below?

   $$−5, −10, −20, −40, −80, \ldots$$

   (1) −160
   (2) −140
   (3) −120
   (4) −100
   (5) −90

9. The function $f(x) = 50 − x^2$ was used to create the following function table. Which number is missing from the table?

x	−2	−1	0	1	2
f(x)	46	49	50		46

   (1) 54
   (2) 51
   (3) 50
   (4) 49
   (5) 46

10. Which value for x for the function $f(x) = \frac{1}{2}x$ results in a value of f(x) that is equal to 1?

   (1) −2
   (2) −1
   (3) 0
   (4) 1
   (5) 2

UNIT 3

11. What term in the sequence will have only one circle?

(1) fourth
(2) fifth
(3) sixth
(4) seventh
(5) eighth

12. What is the seventh term in the sequence?

$$-3, -6, -9, -12, -15, \ldots$$

(1) −18
(2) −21
(3) −24
(4) −27
(5) −30

13. For the function $f(x) = \frac{8}{x}$, which of the following values for x results in a value of $f(x)$ that is less than 1?

(1) 5
(2) 6
(3) 7
(4) 8
(5) 9

14. How many triangles will the next term of the sequence have?

(1) 13
(2) 14
(3) 16
(4) 17
(5) 18

15. The formula $I = (1,000)(r)(5)$ shows the amount of interest earned on a $1,000 investment over 5 years with a certain interest rate. What must the interest rate be to earn $250 interest on the investment in 5 years?

(1) 2%
(2) 3%
(3) 4%
(4) 5%
(5) 6%

16. The function $d = 55t$ describes the distance d a car will travel at a constant speed of 55 miles per hour in a certain amount of time t. For which of the following values of t is the value of d equal to 220?

(1) 2.0
(2) 2.5
(3) 3.0
(4) 3.5
(5) 4.0

17. The increase in a population that grows annually at 1% can be described by the function $I = 0.01N$, where I is the increase and N is the initial population size. By what number does the population increase in a year if the initial population is 5,000?

(1) 5
(2) 10
(3) 25
(4) 50
(5) 55

18. $F = \frac{9}{5}C + 32$ describes the relationship between degrees Fahrenheit (F) and degrees Celsius (C). For which of the following Celsius temperatures is the equivalent Fahrenheit temperature 80°?

(1) 176.0°C
(2) 62.2°C
(3) 86.4°C
(4) 44.5°C
(5) 26.7°C

Lesson 5 | Patterns and Functions

Questions 19 and 20 refer to the function table below.

An archer shot an arrow at an angle of 45 degrees. The distance and height of the arrow along its path were recorded at several points. The data is shown in the table below.

DISTANCE (d) in METERS	1	2	3	4	5
HEIGHT (h) in METERS	0.8	1.2	1.2	0.8	

19. Which of the following equations expresses the relationship between h and d?

   (1) $h = d + 0.2d$
   (2) $h = d^2$
   (3) $h = d - 0.2$
   (4) $h = d - 0.2d^2$
   (5) $h = d^2 - 0.2d^2$

20. What is the height of the arrow when it has traveled a distance of 5 meters?

   (1) 1.8 meters
   (2) 1.6 meters
   (3) 1.2 meters
   (4) 0.8 meters
   (5) 0 meters

21. Kara substituted 1 for x into the function $f(x) = 3x^2 + 1$. Henry substituted a different value for x but found the same output. Which value of x would give the same output?

   (1) 4
   (2) 2
   (3) 0
   (4) −1
   (5) −2

22. For the function $y = x^3$, which of the following values for x results in a value for y that is equal to the value for x?

   (1) 1
   (2) 2
   (3) 4
   (4) 8
   (5) 16

23. What is the eighth term in the sequence?

   $$2, -4, 8, -16, 32, \ldots$$

   (1) −512
   (2) −256
   (3) −128
   (4) 128
   (5) 256

24. The function $y = x^2$ was used to create the following function table. Which number is missing from the table?

x	−5	−1	0	$\frac{1}{2}$	
y	25	1	0	$\frac{1}{4}$	4

   (1) −4
   (2) −1
   (3) 0
   (4) 1
   (5) 2

Question 25 refers to the following table.

As you move below sea level, the pressure increases. Pressure at different levels below sea level are shown in the table.

DISTANCE (d) in METERS BELOW SEA LEVEL	0	10	20	30	40
PRESSURE (p) in POUNDS PER SQUARE INCH	14.7	29.4	44.1	58.8	

25. Which of the following equations expresses the relationship between d and p?

   (1) $p = \dfrac{d}{10} + 14.7$

   (2) $p = \dfrac{d}{10}(14.7) + 14.7$

   (3) $p = 10d + 14.7$

   (4) $p = \dfrac{d}{10}(14.7)$

   (5) $p = 10d\,(14.7)$

Factoring

For use with student book pp. 68-69

① **Review the Skill**

Factors of an expression are the expressions that are multiplied together to get the original expression. You can multiply these factors together using the FOIL method, in which you multiply the *First*, *Inner*, *Outer*, and *Last* terms in that order.

② **Refine the Skill**

Understanding how to write and solve equations using factors and factoring will help you to solve problems successfully on the GED Mathematics Test. Examine the information and diagram. Then answer the questions that follow.

☑ TEST-TAKING TIPS

It is important to know when and why to use the FOIL method. For example, the FOIL method can be used to simplify $(4 + x)(3 - x)$, but it is not needed to simplify $(4x)(3x)$. The expression $(4x)(3x)$ means $4x$ times $3x$, which equals $12x^2$.

A rectangular area rug is shown in the diagram. The length of the rug is 2 feet less than the width. The area of the rug is 48 square feet.

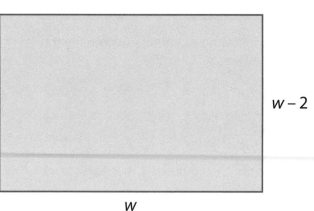

$w - 2$

w

A The equation for the area of the rug is a quadratic equation. Set it equal to zero to solve.

B The solutions for w are 8 and −6. The width of a rug cannot be negative, so $w = 8$ feet.

1. Which equation represents the area of the rug?

    (1) $w^2 = 48$
    (2) $w^2 - 2w = 48$
    (3) $2w - 2 = 48$
    (4) $w^2 + 2w = 48$
    (5) $2w + 2 = 48$

2. What is the width in feet of the rug?

    (1) −8
    (2) −6
    (3) 6
    (4) 8
    (5) 14

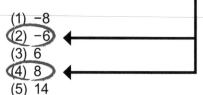

UNIT 3

Directions: Choose the <u>one best answer</u> to each question.

3. What is the product of $(x + 5)(x - 4)$?

(1) $x^2 + x + 20$
(2) $x^2 + 9x - 20$
(3) $x^2 + x - 20$
(4) $x^2 - x - 20$
(5) $x^2 - 9x + 20$

4. The side of a square is represented by $x - 4$. What expression represents the area of the square?

(1) $x^2 + 16$
(2) $x^2 - 16$
(3) $x^2 - 8x - 16$
(4) $x^2 - 8x + 16$
(5) $x^2 + 4x + 16$

5. The number of students in a classroom is 5 less than the number of pencils each student has. Which expression represents the total number of pencils?

(1) $x^2 - 5$
(2) $x^2 - 5x$
(3) $x - 5$
(4) $25 - x$
(5) $x^2 - 25$

6. Which expression is the same as $x^2 - 4x - 21$?

(1) $(x + 3)(x - 7)$
(2) $(x - 3)(x + 7)$
(3) $(x + 1)(x - 21)$
(4) $(x - 1)(x + 21)$
(5) $(x - 3)(x - 7)$

7. In the equation $x^2 + 8x - 20 = 0$, which of the following is a possible value of x?

(1) 10
(2) 8
(3) 0
(4) −8
(5) −10

8. If $x^2 - 5x - 6 = 0$, what is one possible value for x?

(1) −1
(2) −3
(3) −5
(4) −7
(5) −9

9. What are the solutions of the quadratic equation $x^2 - 7x - 30 = 0$?

(1) −6 and 5
(2) −3 and 10
(3) −5 and 6
(4) −10 and 3
(5) −3 and 4

10. The length of a rectangle is represented by $x + 2$ and the width of the rectangle is represented by $x - 5$. Which expression represents the area of the rectangle?

(1) $x^2 - 3x - 10$
(2) $x^2 - 10x - 3$
(3) $x^2 + 3x - 10$
(4) $x^2 + 3x + 10$
(5) $x^2 + 10x - 3$

11. Which pair of solutions makes the quadratic equation $x^2 - 16 = 0$ true?

(1) −4 and 2
(2) 2 and −8
(3) −4 and 1
(4) −4 and 4
(5) −2 and 8

12. If the area of a square is represented by $x^2 + 6x + 9$, which expression represents the side of the square?

(1) $x + 1$
(2) $x + 3$
(3) $x + 6$
(4) $x + 9$
(5) $x + 15$

13. The product of two consecutive integers is 42. Which quadratic equation could be solved to find the value of the first integer?

   (1) $x^2 + 2x - 42 = 0$
   (2) $x^2 + x - 42 = 0$
   (3) $x^2 - 42x = 0$
   (4) $x^2 - x + 42 = 0$
   (5) $x^2 - 2x + 42 = 0$

14. The area of the square shown below is 49 square feet. What is the value of x?

$x + 4$

   (1) −11
   (2) −3
   (3) 0
   (4) 3
   (5) 11

15. The sum of the squares of two consecutive integers is 113. What are the two integers?

   (1) 4 and 5
   (2) 5 and 6
   (3) 6 and 7
   (4) 7 and 8
   (5) 8 and 9

16. The product of two consecutive odd integers is 35. What is the second integer?

   (1) 1
   (2) 3
   (3) 5
   (4) 7
   (5) 9

17. The length of the side of a square is $x - 3$. The area of the square is 81 square meters. What is the value of x?

   (1) 9
   (2) 11
   (3) 12
   (4) 13
   (5) 15

Questions 18 and 19 refer to the figure below.

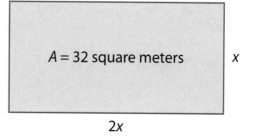

$A = 32$ square meters x

$2x$

18. Which of the following equations could be used to find the value of x?

   (1) $2x^2 - 32 = 0$
   (2) $2x - 16 = 0$
   (3) $x^2 - 32 = 0$
   (4) $2(x^2 - 4) = 0$
   (5) $2x - 32 = 0$

19. What is the length of the longer side of the rectangle?

   (1) 2 m
   (2) 4 m
   (3) 6 m
   (4) 8 m
   (5) 10 m

20. Hank is standing on a hotel balcony. He throws a ball to his friend on the street. The equation for the ball's height h at time t seconds after being thrown is $h = t^2 - 2t - 8$. How many seconds does it take the ball to reach the ground, or a height of 0?

   (1) 1
   (2) 2
   (3) 3
   (4) 4
   (5) 5

21. The product of two consecutive integers is 110. What are the two integers?

   (1) −12 and −11
   (2) −11 and −10
   (3) 9 and 10
   (4) 10 and 12
   (5) 11 and 12

UNIT 3

22. What is the difference of
    $(x + 7)(x – 8) – 4(x – 1)$?

    (1) $x^2 – 5x – 52$
    (2) $x^2 – 4x – 52$
    (3) $x^2 – 4x + 60$
    (4) $x^2 – 3x – 52$
    (5) $x^2 – 3x – 60$

23. The product of two consecutive even integers
    is 10 more than 5 times their sum. What are the
    two integers?

    (1) 4 and 6
    (2) 6 and 8
    (3) 7 and 8
    (4) 10 and 12
    (5) 14 and 16

24. Joann drew a sketch of the garden she'd like to
    have. If she would like her garden to have an
    area of 160 square feet, how long should the
    shorter side of the garden be?

    x

    $2x + 4$

    (1) 8
    (2) 9
    (3) 10
    (4) 11
    (5) 12

25. The product of two consecutive even positive
    integers is 48. Which quadratic equation could
    be solved to find the value of the first integer?

    (1) $x^2 + 4x – 48 = 0$
    (2) $x^2 + x – 48 = 0$
    (3) $x^2 – 48x = 0$
    (4) $x^2 + 2x – 48 = 0$
    (5) $x^2 – x + 48 = 0$

26. Two consecutive integers have a product of 12.
    What are the two integers?

    (1) –2 and 3
    (2) –3 and –3
    (3) –3 and 4
    (4) –3 and –4
    (5) –4 and –5

27. In the quadratic equation $2x^2 – 8x – 10 = 0$,
    which of the following is a possible value of x?

    (1) 1
    (2) 2
    (3) 5
    (4) 7
    (5) 10

28. The area of a square is 64 square meters. If
    each side is $x – 2$, what is the value of x?

    (1) 10
    (2) 9
    (3) 8
    (4) 7
    (5) 6

Questions 29 and 30 refer to the rectangle below.

The area of the rectangle is 84 square feet.

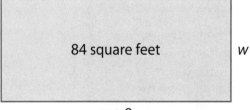

84 square feet

w

$w + 8$

29. What is the width of the rectangle?

    (1) 6
    (2) 8
    (3) 14
    (4) 16
    (5) 20

30. What is the length of the rectangle?

    (1) 8
    (2) 12
    (3) 14
    (4) 16
    (5) 18

Solving and Graphing Inequalities
For use with student book pp. 70-71

① Review the Skill

An **inequality** is a statement in which two algebraic expressions are unequal. The expressions are separated by one of four symbols: >, <, ≥, or ≤. Inequalities are solved like equations.

② Refine the Skill

As you translate words into inequalities, remember that the inequality symbols always point to the lesser amount. Examine the information and diagram. Then answer the questions that follow.

☑ TEST-TAKING TIPS

After a solution is graphed on a number line, check your solution by substituting values for the variable. For example, if 3 is shaded on the number line, $x = 3$ should make the inequality true.

Alex is using a rectangular piece of plywood to build a workbench. He wants the area of the workbench to be at least 100 square feet. The length of the plywood is 25 feet.

$$A ≥ 100 \text{ square feet}$$

25 feet

Ⓐ The formula for area is $A = l × w$. Since the area must be at least 100 square feet, $l × w$ can be greater than or equal to 100.

Ⓑ The smallest width the plywood could have is the solution of the inequality.

Ⓐ

1. Which inequality could be solved to find the minimum width of the plywood?

   (1) $25 - w ≤ 100$
   (2) $25 + w ≥ 100$
   (3) $100 - 25 ≤ w$
   (4) $25w ≤ 100$
   (5) $25w ≥ 100$

2. What is the solution to the inequality?

   (1) $w ≤ 4$
   (2) $w > 4$
   (3) $w ≥ 4$
   (4) $w = 4$
   (5) $w < 4$

Directions: Choose the <u>one best answer</u> to each question.

3. Which of the following inequalities is shown on the number line?

(1) $x \geq 3$
(2) $x \geq -3$
(3) $x \leq 3$
(4) $x \leq -3$
(5) $x > -3$

4. What is the solution to the inequality $x + 5 < 14$?

(1) $x < -9$
(2) $x \geq 19$
(3) $x \leq 19$
(4) $x > 9$
(5) $x < 9$

5. Which of the following inequalities is graphed on a number line using a closed circle?

(1) $x < 5$
(2) $x > -4$
(3) $x \geq -3$
(4) $x < -2$
(5) $x > 0$

6. Which of the following shows the solution to the inequality $4(x - 1) \geq 8$?

(1)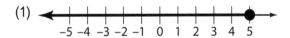

(2)

(3)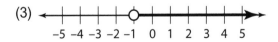

(4)

(5)

7. What is the solution to the inequality $2x + 3 \geq 5x + 4$?

(1) $x < -\frac{1}{3}$

(2) $x \leq -\frac{1}{3}$

(3) $x \geq \frac{1}{3}$

(4) $x \geq -3$

(5) $x < 3$

8. Which inequality is shown on the number line?

(1) $x > 1$
(2) $x \geq -1$
(3) $x < -1$
(4) $x \leq 1$
(5) $x \leq -1$

9. What is the solution to the inequality $2x - 7 \geq 15$?

(1) $x \geq 11$
(2) $x \geq 22$
(3) $x \leq 11$
(4) $x \leq 22$
(5) $x > 11$

10. When 4 times a number is added to 3, the result is greater than 2 less than 5 times that same number. Which of the following is the inequality?

(1) $4x + 3 > 5x - 2$
(2) $4x + 3 \geq 2 - 5x$
(3) $4x + 12 > 5x - 2$
(4) $4x + 3 \geq 5x - 10$
(5) $4(x + 3) > 5(x - 2)$

UNIT 3

11. Stacy pays $12 a month for basic cell phone service. Each minute she talks is an additional $.10. If she budgets $25 a month for her cell phone bill, what is the maximum number of minutes she can talk each month?

(1) 12
(2) 120
(3) 130
(4) 1,330
(5) 1,300

12. Lydia purchased 3 gallons of milk. Her total was more than $9. What was the lowest possible price of 1 gallon of milk?

(1) $2.00
(2) $2.50
(3) $3.01
(4) $3.50
(5) $4.00

13. Brit scored 45, 38, and 47 on her first three math quizzes. What is the minimum score she must earn on the fourth quiz to have an average quiz score of at least 44?

(1) 43
(2) 44
(3) 45
(4) 46
(5) 47

14. Colin earned $450 one week and $550 the next week. How much must he earn the third week to average $600 or more per week?

(1) $600
(2) $650
(3) $700
(4) $750
(5) $800

15. Admission to a park is $15. Each game in the park costs $.75. Cole takes $25 to the park. Which inequality represents the possible number of games that he can play?

(1) $25 - 15 \le 0.75x$
(2) $15 + 0.75x \le 25$
(3) $0.75x - 15 \ge 25$
(4) $15 - 0.75 \le 25$
(5) $25 + 0.75x \ge 15$

16. A store sold 156 football T-shirts. If the store has fewer than 34 of the T-shirts left, which expresses how many T-shirts the store had originally in terms of x?

(1) $x \ge 190$
(2) $x \le 190$
(3) $x = 190$
(4) $x > 190$
(5) $x < 190$

17. Gabe makes a base salary of $1,500 per month. He also earns a 3% commission on all of his sales. What must the amount of his monthly sales be for him to earn at least $3,000 per month?

(1) $50
(2) $500
(3) $5,000
(4) $50,000
(5) $500,000

18. Sara sold $14,000 worth of computer equipment in January. She sold $9,000 of computer equipment in February. What is the least amount of computer equipment Sara must sell in March to have average monthly sales greater than $10,000 for the first quarter?

(1) $5,001
(2) $7,001
(3) $9,001
(4) $12,001
(5) $26,001

19. A grocery store has spaghetti noodles on sale. The first box of noodles is $1.60. Each additional box is only $.95. What is the maximum number of boxes of noodles Jax can buy with $4.50?

(1) 1
(2) 2
(3) 3
(4) 4
(5) 5

20. Alia wants to buy a new winter jacket and boots. The jacket costs $2\frac{1}{2}$ times more than the boots. If Alia cannot spend more than $157.50, what is the most she can spend on the boots?

(1) $37.50
(2) $45.00
(3) $75.50
(4) $90.00
(5) $112.50

21. The number of yards Michael swam on Tuesday was 400 less than 3 times the number of yards he swam on Monday. The number of yards he swam over the two days was less than 2,000. Which could be the number of yards Michael swam on Monday?

(1) 500
(2) 600
(3) 800
(4) 1,000
(5) 1,400

22. Jose's batting average last year was .266. Provided Jose has the same number of at-bats, what is the minimum batting average he can have this year to finish with a combined average of at least .300 over the two years?

(1) .044
(2) .144
(3) .334
(4) .366
(5) .444

23. The number of students who are enrolled in first-semester biology at a university is 30 fewer than twice as many as last year. If the enrollment for the class cannot exceed 100 students, what was the maximum number of students enrolled in the class last year?

(1) 30
(2) 35
(3) 65
(4) 70
(5) 100

24. In the second round of a card game, Allen scored less than 2 times the number of points that he scored in the first round. If he scored 10 points in the first round, which inequality shows the number of points that he could have scored in the second round?

(1) $y < 20$
(2) $y > 10$
(3) $y \leq 20$
(4) $y \geq 20$
(5) $y < -20$

25. A restaurant bill was less than $45. Three friends split the bill evenly. What is the greatest amount each friend could have paid?

(1) $11.99
(2) $12.99
(3) $13.99
(4) $14.99
(5) $15.99

26. In an English class, students must earn an average score of 80% or above on their written papers to earn at least a B in the class. Leah's scores on her first four papers are shown below.

LEAH'S ENGLISH PAPER SCORES	
PAPER	SCORE (%)
1	78
2	85
3	82
4	74
5	?

What is the minimum score Leah needs on her fifth and final paper to earn a B in the class?

(1) 78
(2) 79
(3) 80
(4) 81
(5) 82

The Coordinate Grid

For use with student book pp. 72-73

① Review the Skill

Coordinate grids are used to plot points, draw line segments and figures, and perform transformations. Plot points by plotting the *x*-coordinate and *y*-coordinate of the ordered pair. Transformations to figures include *translations, reflections, rotations,* and *dilations.*

② Refine the Skill

You must understand how to work with coordinate grids to solve problems on the GED Mathematics Test. Knowledge of how to plot points, draw line segments, and identify transformations will help you solve these problems successfully. Examine the grid. Then answer the questions that follow.

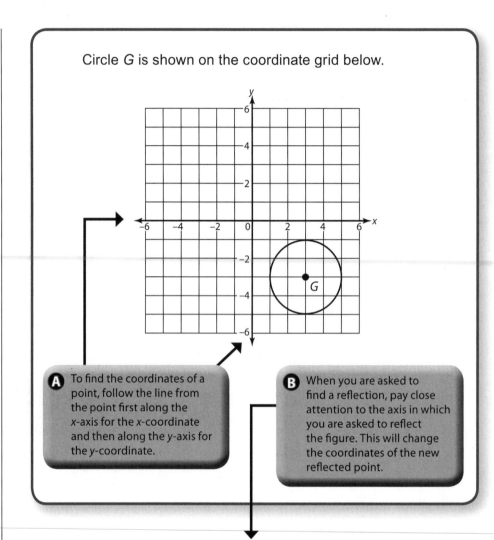

Circle *G* is shown on the coordinate grid below.

A To find the coordinates of a point, follow the line from the point first along the *x*-axis for the *x*-coordinate and then along the *y*-axis for the *y*-coordinate.

B When you are asked to find a reflection, pay close attention to the axis in which you are asked to reflect the figure. This will change the coordinates of the new reflected point.

☑ TEST-TAKING TIPS

Remember that the *x*-coordinate of an ordered pair is always written first. Also, remember that *negative* means *left* or *down*, and *positive* means *right* or *up*.

---

1. What are the coordinates of point *G*?

   (1) (3, −4)
   (2) (4, −3)
   (3) (−3, 3)
   (4) (3, −3)
   (5) (4, −4)

B 2. If circle *G* and its center were reflected in the *x*-axis, what would be the new location of point *G*?

   (1) (−4, −3)
   (2) (−3, −3)
   (3) (−3, 3)
   (4) (3, 3)
   (5) (3, −4)

Directions: Choose the <u>one best answer</u> to each question.

<u>Questions 3 through 7</u> refer to the following coordinate grid.

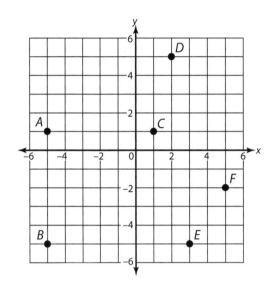

3. Which of the following ordered pairs identifies the location of point *D*?

   (1) (−5, 2)
   (2) (−2, −5)
   (3) (−2, 5)
   (4) (5, −2)
   (5) (2, 5)

4. Points *A*, *B*, and *C* mark three corners of a square. What is the location of the fourth corner needed to complete the square?

   (1) (−5, 1)
   (2) (1, −5)
   (3) (−5, −1)
   (4) (−1, −5)
   (5) (1, 5)

5. Points *C*, *F*, and *E* mark the corners of a rectangle. What is the location of the fourth corner needed to complete the rectangle?

   (1) (−1, −3)
   (2) (−1, −2)
   (3) (−2, −1)
   (4) (0, −2)
   (5) (−2, −2)

6. What is the new location of point *D* if it is translated 5 units down and 2 units to the right?

   (1) (4, 0)
   (2) (0, 4)
   (3) (0, 0)
   (4) (−3, 3)
   (5) (3, −3)

7. If point *C* were the center of a circle and the circle were reflected in the *x*-axis, what would be the new location of point *C*?

   (1) (−1, 0)
   (2) (0, −1)
   (3) (0, 1)
   (4) (1, 1)
   (5) (1, −1)

8. Which of the following points is found in quadrant 2 of the coordinate grid?

   (1) (2, 3)
   (2) (−4, −3)
   (3) (−2, 5)
   (4) (1, −6)
   (5) (−4, −5)

9. Frank started at point (4, −3). He then moved down 1 and right 2. At which point did he land?

   (1) (6, −4)
   (2) (3, −1)
   (3) (−1, 3)
   (4) (−4, 6)
   (5) (−6, 4)

10. If point (*x*, −6) is translated 3 units down, what would be the new coordinates?

   (1) (*x* − 3, −6)
   (2) (*x* − 3, −9)
   (3) (*x*, −9)
   (4) (*x*, −3)
   (5) Not enough information is given.

Questions 11 through 13 refer to the coordinate grid below.

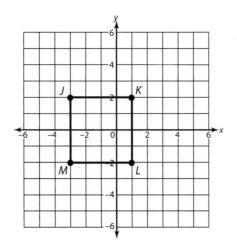

Questions 14 through 16 refer to the following coordinate grid.

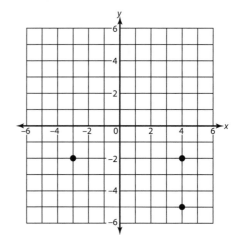

11. When square *JKLM* is translated 2 units up and 3 units to the right, the new location of point *J* is (0, 4). Which shows the new location of point *M*?

(1) (−1, 1)
(2) (0, 0)
(3) (0, −1)
(4) (0, −5)
(5) (1, 5)

12. Under a translation, the new point *M*, which is represented by *M'*, is in the same location as the original point *K*. Which of the following describes the translation?

(1) 2 units up and 3 units to the right
(2) 3 units up and 3 units to the right
(3) 4 units up and 4 units to the right
(4) 4 units up and 3 units to the right
(5) 5 units up and 4 units to the right

13. When square *JKLM* is reflected across the *y*-axis, the new location of point *J* is (3, 2). What is the new location of point *K*?

(1) (0, −1)
(2) (−1, 0)
(3) (−1, 2)
(4) (1, 2)
(5) (2, −1)

14. Which of the following ordered pairs describes the location of a point that lies in the third quadrant?

(1) (3, 2)
(2) (2, 3)
(3) (−2, 3)
(4) (−3, −2)
(5) (5, −2)

15. The three points on the coordinate grid mark the corners of a rectangle. What is the location of the fourth corner needed to complete the figure?

(1) (−3, −5)
(2) (−3, −4)
(3) (5, −3)
(4) (4, −3)
(5) (3, 5)

16. If you drew line segments to connect the three existing points on the coordinate grid, what figure would you draw?

(1) an equilateral triangle
(2) an obtuse triangle
(3) an equiangular triangle
(4) an isosceles triangle
(5) a right triangle

Lesson 8 | The Coordinate Grid

Questions 17 through 19 refer to the following coordinate grid.

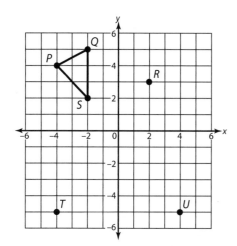

Questions 20 and 21 refer to the following coordinate grid.

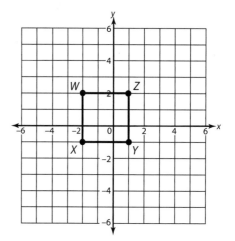

17. If triangle *PQS* were rotated a half turn, or 180°, about point *S*, what would be the new location of point *P*?

(1) (−2, 2)
(2) (−1, 2)
(3) (2, −2)
(4) (0, 1)
(5) (0, 0)

18. If triangle *PQS* were translated 4 units down, which of the following ordered pairs would describe the location of *P'*?

(1) (4, −1)
(2) (−4, −4)
(3) (−4, −1)
(4) (0, −4)
(5) (−4, 0)

19. If point (5, −2) were reflected across the y-axis, what would its new location be?

(1) (5, 2)
(2) (−5, 2)
(3) (−5, −2)
(4) (5, 0)
(5) (−2, −2)

20. When square *WXYZ* is dilated by a factor of 2 using point *W* as the center of dilation, the location of point *W* remains the same. The new location of the other points is found by drawing a ray from *W* through the other points and marking a point 2 times the distance from *W* to the point. For example, the new location of point *X* would be (−2, −4).

Which point is *Z'*, the new location of point *Z*, under the same dilation?

(1) (4, 2)
(2) (4, 3)
(3) (5, 1)
(4) (4, −4)
(5) (3, 2)

21. If square *WXYZ* is dilated by a factor of $\frac{1}{3}$ using point *Z* as the center of dilation, what is the new location of point *Y*?

(1) (−1, 1)
(2) (1, 1)
(3) (1, 2)
(4) (1, 3)
(5) (1, 4)

Graphing Equations

For use with student book pp. 74-75

UNIT 3

① Review the Skill

You can graph an equation that has two variables. For each *x*-value, there is a unique *y*-value. These values can be written as ordered pairs and plotted on a grid. A **linear equation** forms a straight line on a graph. A line can be drawn for the equation when two points have been identified.

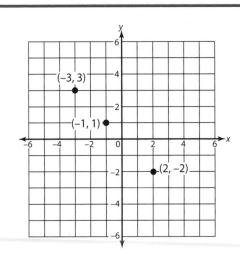

② Refine the Skill

You can count spaces to determine the distance between two points on a vertical or horizontal line. However, for any other kind of line, use the distance formula. Examine the grid. Then answer the questions that follow.

Ⓐ To answer question 1, determine the equation that is graphed. Then substitute each answer choice into the equation to find one that makes the equation true.

Ⓑ To answer question 2, use the following formula :
distance $= \sqrt{(x_2 - x_1)^2 + (y_2 - y_1)^2}$,
where one point is (x_1, y_1) and the other is (x_2, y_2).

☑ **TEST-TAKING TIPS**

It can be helpful to work backward from the answer choices. To answer question 1, work backward by substituting the *x*- and *y*-values of one point into each equation to see if they make the equation true. Eliminate answer choices. Then try a second point in each remaining equation.

1. The points graphed on the grid above satisfy which of the following equations?

   (1) $x - y = 1$
   (2) $x + y = 0$
   (3) $x - y = -1$
   (4) $x - y = 0$
   (5) $x + y = 1$

2. A line is drawn from point $(-3, 3)$ to point $(2, -2)$. What is the length of the line to the nearest tenth?

   (1) 6.9
   (2) 7.0
   (3) 7.1
   (4) 7.2
   (5) 7.3

Directions: Choose the <u>one best answer</u> to each question.

3. Which ordered pair is a solution of $y = \frac{1}{2}x$?

   (1) (4, 8)
   (2) (1, 3)
   (3) (4, 2)
   (4) (4, 1)
   (5) (1, 2)

4. What is the missing y-value if $(2, y)$ is a solution of $-x = y + 1$?

   (1) −3
   (2) −2
   (3) −1
   (4) 0
   (5) 1

5. What is the missing x-value if $(x, -3)$ is a solution of $2x + 2y = -8$?

   (1) −3
   (2) −1
   (3) −0
   (4) 1
   (5) 3

6. The graph of the equation $y = 4 - 3x$ would pass through which of the following points on the coordinate grid?

   (1) (1, −1)
   (2) (3, 3)
   (3) (4, 8)
   (4) (3, 1)
   (5) (2, −2)

7. What is the missing x-value if $(x, 1)$ is a solution of $3x - y = 5$?

   (1) 2
   (2) 3
   (3) 6
   (4) 7
   (5) 9

8. Which of the following shows the graph of the equation $x + 2y = 2$?

   (1)
   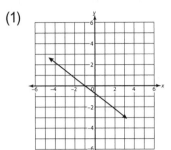

   (2)
   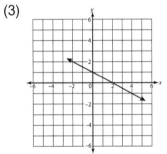

   (3)
   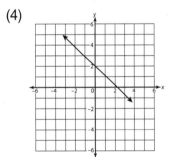

   (4)
   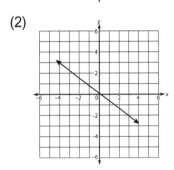

   (5)
   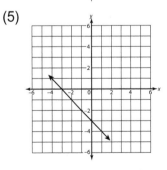

9. Point B is located at (4, 7) on a coordinate grid. If a line were drawn directly from the point to the origin, what would be the length of the line to the nearest tenth?

(1) 3.0
(2) 7.9
(3) 8.0
(4) 8.1
(5) 8.2

10. The points graphed on the grid below satisfy which of the following equations?

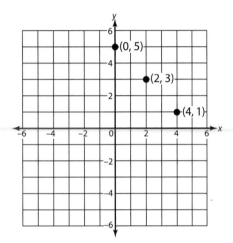

(1) $x + y = -3$
(2) $y - x = 5$
(3) $x + y = 2$
(4) $x - y = -1$
(5) $x + y = 5$

11. Two points are located at (−2, −5) and (−3, −8). What is the distance between these two points?

(1) 3.2
(2) 4.6
(3) 5.8
(4) 8.1
(5) 13.9

12. The graph of the equation $y = -2x - 1$ passes through which of the following points?

(1) (1, −3)
(2) (1, −2)
(3) (0, 1)
(4) (0, 2)
(5) (−1, 2)

Questions 13 through 15 refer to the grid below.

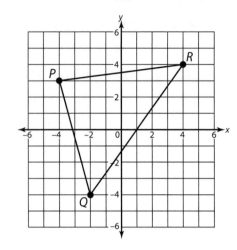

13. What is the length of side PQ to the nearest tenth?

(1) 6.4
(2) 7.1
(3) 7.3
(4) 8.1
(5) 9.2

14. What is the length of side PR to the nearest tenth?

(1) 6.4
(2) 7.3
(3) 8.1
(4) 9.2
(5) 10.0

15. What is the perimeter of triangle PRQ to the nearest tenth?

(1) 10.0
(2) 12.5
(3) 15.2
(4) 25.4
(5) 30.4

16. Which ordered pair is a solution of $2x - 3 = y$?

   (1) (0, 3)
   (2) (1, 1)
   (3) (−2, 1)
   (4) (3, −3)
   (5) (4, 5)

17. Which equation of a line is shown on the graph?

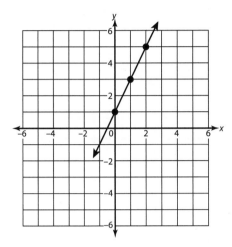

   (1) $2x - y = 1$

   (2) $\frac{1}{2}x = y$

   (3) $2x + 1 = y$

   (4) $\frac{1}{2}x + 1 = y$

   (5) $2y - 1 = x$

18. Which of the following points is found on the graph of $y = 4 - 2x$?

   (1) (−2, 3)
   (2) (4, 0)
   (3) (−2, 0)
   (4) (0, −4)
   (5) (3, −2)

Questions 19 and 20 refer to the grid and information below.

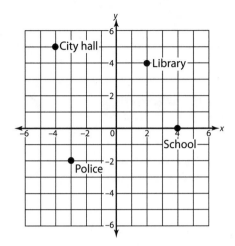

Jack sketched out a map of his city using a coordinate grid. Each unit on the grid represents 1 mile.

19. A bike path was made that goes straight from the library to the school. How many miles long is the bike path to the nearest tenth of a mile?

   (1) 2.7
   (2) 3.2
   (3) 4.5
   (4) 5.7
   (5) 7.0

20. A police officer drove from the police station to city hall by driving 1 mile straight west and then driving straight north. How many miles straight north did the officer drive?

   (1) 4
   (2) 5
   (3) 6
   (4) 7
   (5) 8

21. What is the distance, to the nearest tenth, between two points on a graph that are located at (−5, 1) and (5, 5)?

   (1) 6.4
   (2) 10.8
   (3) 11.0
   (4) 11.7
   (5) 12.8

(S)lope

For use with student book pp. 76-77

① Review the Skill

Slope is a number that describes the steepness of a line. Determine the slope between two points (x_1, y_1) and (x_2, y_2) by using the formula $m = \frac{y_2 - y_1}{x_2 - x_1}$. Use the slope-intercept form of a line $(y = mx + b)$ to find the equation of a line. In the slope-intercept form of a line, $y = mx + b$, m = slope and b = y-intercept.

② Refine the Skill

You must be able to find the slope of a line and the equation of a line to solve problems on the GED Mathematics Test. Examine the grid. Then answer the questions that follow.

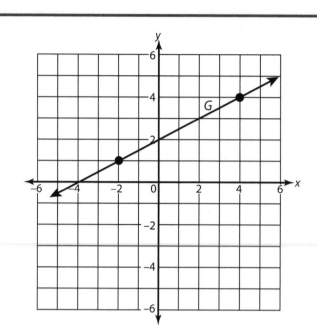

Ⓐ When you count grids to find slope, be sure to identify whether the slope is positive or negative. To get from the lower to upper point on line G, you must go up 3 and right 6. Write $\frac{3}{6}$ and simplify.

Ⓑ Use the slope-intercept form of a line to find the equation of a line. Substitute the slope for m and the y-intercept for b. Be sure to include the sign for each number.

☑ TEST-TAKING TIPS

If you are given a point and a slope of a line, you can substitute the slope, x-value, and y-value into $y = mx + b$ to find the y-intercept. Then you can use the slope and y-intercept to write an equation for the line.

1. What is the slope of line G?

   (1) −1

   (2) $-\frac{1}{2}$

   (3) 0

   (4) $\frac{1}{2}$

   (5) 1

2. What is the equation of line G?

   (1) $y = -\frac{1}{2}x - 2$

   (2) $y = 2x + 1$

   (3) $y = \frac{1}{2}x + 2$

   (4) $y = -\frac{1}{2}x + 2$

   (5) $y = x + \frac{1}{2}$

UNIT 3

Directions: Choose the <u>one best answer</u> to each question.

3. The points $(-4, 4)$ and $(2, 3)$ lie on line H. What is the slope of line H?

(1) $-\dfrac{1}{6}$

(2) $-\dfrac{1}{3}$

(3) $-\dfrac{1}{2}$

(4) 2

(5) 6

4. What is the slope of a line that passes through points $(-1, -2)$ and $(-3, -4)$?

(1) 1

(2) $\dfrac{1}{2}$

(3) 0

(4) $-\dfrac{1}{2}$

(5) -2

5. A linear equation is represented by $y = \dfrac{1}{2}x + 3$. The graph of which of the following equations would be parallel to that of the equation above?

(1) $y = -\dfrac{1}{3}x + 2$

(2) $y = \dfrac{1}{2}x - 3$

(3) $y = 2x + 3$

(4) $y = x - 3$

(5) $y = x + 3$

6. Line B has a slope of -1. It passes through point K at $(4, -2)$, and it passes through point L, which has an x-coordinate of 2. What are the coordinates of point L?

(1) $(2, -2)$
(2) $(0, 2)$
(3) $(2, 0)$
(4) $(-2, 0)$
(5) Not enough information is given.

<u>Question 7</u> refers to the following grid.

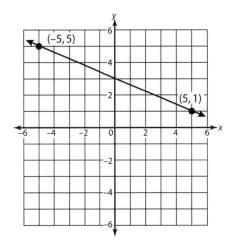

7. What is the equation of the line shown in the grid?

(1) $y = -\dfrac{2}{5}x + 3$

(2) $y = -\dfrac{1}{3}x + 3$

(3) $y = \dfrac{2}{5}x + 3$

(4) $y = \dfrac{1}{3}x + 3$

(5) $y = 3x + 3$

8. Which of the following equations shows the slope-intercept form for a line with a slope of 2 that passes through point $(4, 1)$?

(1) $y = -2x + 5$
(2) $y = 2x - 4$
(3) $y = 2x + 3$
(4) $y = 2x + 1$
(5) $y = 2x - 7$

9. Andrea paid an initial fee of $20 to set up her cell phone. Now she pays $30 per month for service. The amount she pays for cell phone service for a certain number of months can be graphed in the first quadrant of a coordinate grid.

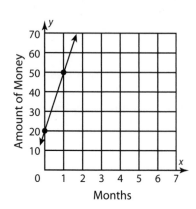

Months

Which of the following is the equation of the line on the graph?

(1) $y = 30x - 20$

(2) $y = \frac{1}{3}x + 20$

(3) $y = 20x + 30$

(4) $y = 30x + 20$

(5) $y = 20x - 30$

10. What is the slope of line T?

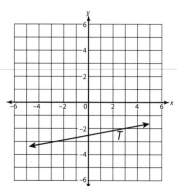

(1) $-\frac{1}{6}$

(2) $\frac{1}{6}$

(3) $\frac{1}{3}$

(4) $-\frac{1}{3}$

(5) $\frac{2}{3}$

Question 11 refers to the information and figure below.

The slope of the roof shown on the house is $\frac{1}{3}$.

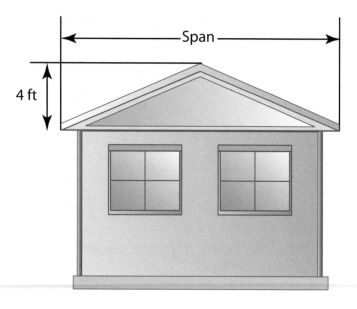

11. What is the span of the roof?

(1) 4 ft
(2) 12 ft
(3) 18 ft
(4) 24 ft
(5) 30 ft

12. Line J has a slope of $-\frac{1}{2}$. It passes through point Q at $(-4, -3)$ and through point R, which has an x-coordinate of 0. What is the equation of line J?

(1) $y = -\frac{1}{2}x - 5$

(2) $y = -\frac{1}{2}x - 4$

(3) $y = -\frac{1}{2}x - 3$

(4) $y = -\frac{1}{2}x + 4$

(5) $y = -\frac{1}{2}x + 5$

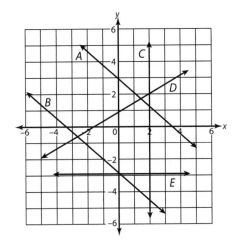

13. Which of the lines has a positive slope?

(1) line A
(2) line B
(3) line C
(4) line D
(5) line E

14. Which of the lines has a slope of zero?

(1) line A
(2) line B
(3) line C
(4) line D
(5) line E

15. Which of the lines has no slope?

(1) line A
(2) line B
(3) line C
(4) line D
(5) line E

16. Which two lines are parallel to each other?

(1) line A and line B
(2) line B and line C
(3) line C and line D
(4) line D and line E
(5) line E and line A

17. What would be the slope of a line drawn through points M and N?

(1) -3

(2) $-\frac{1}{3}$

(3) 1

(4) $\frac{1}{3}$

(5) 3

18. Which of the following could be the equation of a line that is parallel to a line drawn through points N and P?

(1) $y = \frac{5}{4}x + 4$

(2) $y = -\frac{1}{5}x + 4$

(3) $y = -4x + 3$

(4) $y = 4x + 2$

(5) $y = \frac{4}{5}x - 2$

19. What would be the slope of a line that is parallel to a line drawn through points M and P?

(1) 2

(2) $-\frac{1}{2}$

(3) $-\frac{1}{7}$

(4) $-\frac{2}{7}$

(5) -2

LESSON 1 FOCUS ON...

Lines and Angles

For use with student book pp. 86-87

① Review the Skill

An **angle** is formed when two rays have the same endpoint. The endpoint shared by the two rays is called the **vertex**. A **right angle** is a 90° angle. Two angles whose sum is 90° are **complementary**. Two angles whose sum is 180° are **supplementary**.

② Refine the Skill

You can often find the measure of an unknown angle by using the measures of known angles. Read the text and examine the figure. Then answer the questions that follow.

The figure below shows several rays with a common endpoint, the vertex *K*. The figure also gives you information about the measure of two angles.

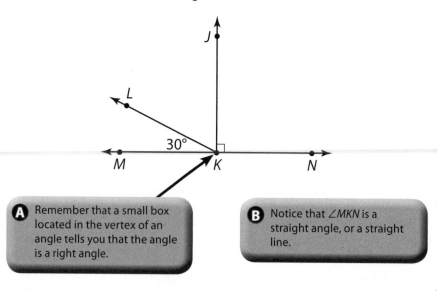

A Remember that a small box located in the vertex of an angle tells you that the angle is a right angle.

B Notice that ∠*MKN* is a straight angle, or a straight line.

1. What is the measure of ∠*JKL*?

   (1) 30°
   (2) 45°
   (3) 60°
   (4) 90°
   (5) 120°

2. What is the measure of ∠*MKN*?

   (1) 0°
   (2) 90°
   (3) 120°
   (4) 180°
   (5) 360°

UNIT 4

③ **Master the Skill**

Directions: Choose the <u>one best answer</u> to each question.

Questions 3 through 5 refer to the following figure.

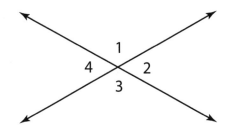

3. If ∠2 measures 55°, what is the measure of ∠4?

   (1) 35°
   (2) 55°
   (3) 110°
   (4) 125°
   (5) 180°

4. What kind of angles are ∠1 and ∠3?

   (1) right
   (2) supplementary
   (3) complementary
   (4) adjacent
   (5) vertical

5. If angle 4 has a measure of 52°, then what is the measure of angle 3?

   (1) 38°
   (2) 48°
   (3) 52°
   (4) 128°
   (5) 138°

6. Two angles are congruent and complementary. What is the measure of the supplement of one of the angles?

   (1) 45°
   (2) 90°
   (3) 125°
   (4) 135°
   (5) Not enough information is given.

Questions 7 through 9 refer to the following figure.

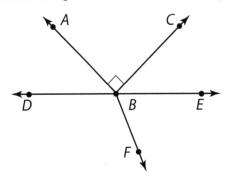

7. If ∠DBF measures 115°, what is the measure of ∠EBF?

   (1) 45°
   (2) 65°
   (3) 70°
   (4) 75°
   (5) Not enough information is given.

8. If ∠CBE and ∠ABD are congruent, what is the measure of each angle?

   (1) 15°
   (2) 25°
   (3) 45°
   (4) 55°
   (5) 90°

9. If ∠CBE and ∠ABD are congruent, what is the measure of ∠CBD?

   (1) 45°
   (2) 90°
   (3) 100°
   (4) 135°
   (5) 155°

10. Two angles are supplementary. Angle A is 20 degrees larger than three times the size of angle B. What is the measure of angle A?

   (1) 40°
   (2) 60°
   (3) 120°
   (4) 140°
   (5) 180°

Questions 11 through 14 refer to the following text and figure.

The figure shows two parallel lines intersected by a third line.

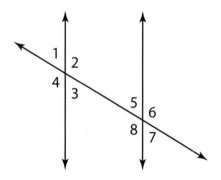

11. Which two angles are both adjacent and supplementary?

(1) ∠1 and ∠3
(2) ∠3 and ∠6
(3) ∠4 and ∠5
(4) ∠2 and ∠3
(5) ∠4 and ∠7

12. If ∠7 measures 60°, what is the measure of ∠8?

(1) 60°
(2) 90°
(3) 120°
(4) 180°
(5) Not enough information is known.

13. Which angle is alternate exterior to ∠4?

(1) ∠1
(2) ∠2
(3) ∠6
(4) ∠7
(5) ∠8

14. Which angles are corresponding angles?

(1) ∠1 and ∠3
(2) ∠4 and ∠6
(3) ∠2 and ∠5
(4) ∠1 and ∠6
(5) ∠3 and ∠7

Questions 15 and 16 refer to the following text and figure.

The figure shows several rays with vertex E in common.

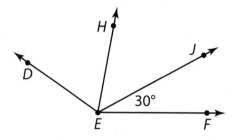

15. Which angle has a 30° measure?

(1) ∠JEF
(2) ∠FEH
(3) ∠DEJ
(4) ∠HED
(5) ∠JEH

16. What is the measure of ∠HED?

(1) 30°
(2) 45°
(3) 60°
(4) 90°
(5) Not enough information is given.

Question 17 refers to the following text and figure.

The figure shows three rays that have a common endpoint.

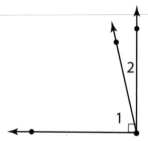

17. What kind of relationship do ∠1 and ∠2 have?

(1) vertical
(2) complementary
(3) congruent
(4) supplementary
(5) straight

Questions 18 through 20 refer to the following figure.

Questions 22 through 24 refer to figures A through E.

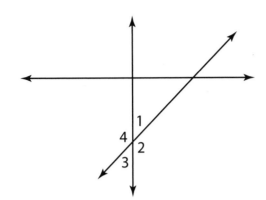

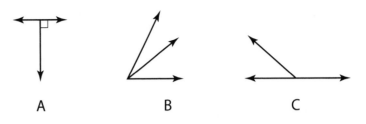

A   B   C

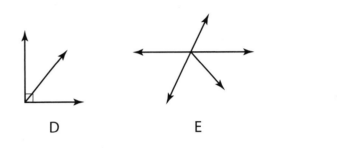

D   E

18. If ∠1 has a measure of 35°, what is the sum of the measures of ∠2 and ∠4?

(1) 70°
(2) 145°
(3) 180°
(4) 290°
(5) Not enough information is given.

19. What is the sum of the measures of ∠1, ∠2, ∠3, and ∠4?

(1) 140°
(2) 180°
(3) 270°
(4) 360°
(5) Not enough information is given.

20. If ∠4 has a measure of 30°, then what is the measure of ∠3?

(1) 30°
(2) 60°
(3) 90°
(4) 150°
(5) 180°

21. Perpendicular lines are lines that meet at right angles. What is the sum of the measures of any two adjacent angles formed when two perpendicular lines intersect?

(1) 45°
(2) 90°
(3) 180°
(4) 360°
(5) Not enough information is given.

22. Which figure shows two congruent and supplementary angles?

(1) A
(2) B
(3) C
(4) D
(5) E

23. Which figure contains complementary angles?

(1) A
(2) B
(3) C
(4) D
(5) E

24. Which figure includes a pair of vertical angles?

(1) A
(2) B
(3) C
(4) D
(5) E

Triangles and Quadrilaterals

For use with student book pp. 88-89

① Review the Skill

All **triangles** have three sides and three angles. The angles are right angles (90°), acute angles (less than 90°), and obtuse angles (more than 90°). The sum of the three angles is always 180°. Here's how to find an unknown angle:

Unknown ∠ = 180° − Known ∠ − Known ∠

Rectangles, parallelograms, and trapezoids are **quadrilaterals**, or four-sided figures. Sometimes, you can use the measures of known angles to find the measure of an unknown angle in a quadrilateral.

② Refine the Skill

The relationships of angles, such as interior and exterior angles, and the characteristics of different quadrilaterals also can help you find the unknown measure of an angle in a quadrilateral. Read the text and examine the figure. Then answer the questions that follow.

☑ TEST-TAKING TIPS

Knowing the traits of quadrilaterals can help you to answer questions. For example, the sum of the four angles in a quadrilateral is always 360°.

The figure shows two transversals intersecting two parallel lines to form a trapezoid.

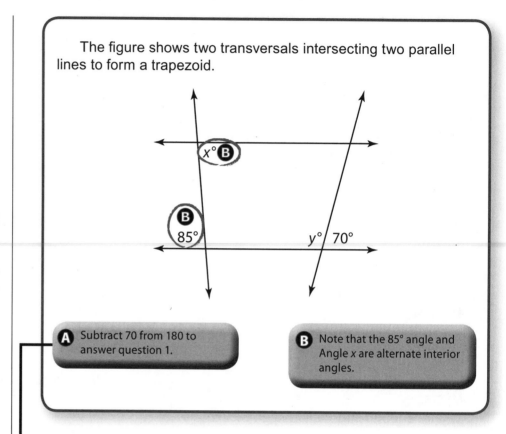

A Subtract 70 from 180 to answer question 1.

B Note that the 85° angle and Angle x are alternate interior angles.

1. What is the value of y?

  (1) 70°
  (2) 90°
  (3) 110°
  (4) 155°
  (5) 180°

2. What is the value of x?

  (1) 70°
  (2) 85°
  (3) 95°
  (4) 140°
  (5) 155°

UNIT 4

③ *Master the Skill*

Directions: Choose the <u>one best answer</u> to each question.

<u>Questions 3 through 5</u> refer to the following text and figure.

The figure shows two transversals intersecting two parallel lines to form a parallelogram.

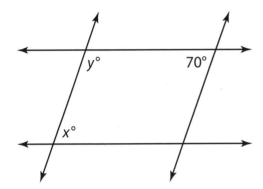

3. What is the measure of ∠x?

   (1) 20°
   (2) 70°
   (3) 90°
   (4) 110°
   (5) Not enough information is given.

4. What is the measure of ∠y?

   (1) 70°
   (2) 90°
   (3) 110°
   (4) 140°
   (5) Not enough information is given.

5. What is the measure of the missing angle in the parallelogram?

   (1) 110°
   (2) 90°
   (3) 70°
   (4) 20°
   (5) 10°

<u>Questions 6 through 8</u> refer to following text and figure.

An architect is designing a triangular eating area beside an outdoor pool.

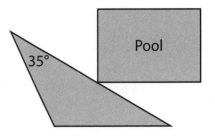

6. If the other acute angle of the eating area is 45°, what is the measure of the obtuse angle?

   (1) 45°
   (2) 80°
   (3) 90°
   (4) 100°
   (5) Not enough information is given.

7. If the shape of the pool is a rectangle, what is the measure of each angle?

   (1) 35°
   (2) 90°
   (3) 180°
   (4) 360°
   (5) Not enough information is given.

8. If the two acute angles of the eating area are congruent, what is the measure of the obtuse angle?

   (1) 55°
   (2) 73°
   (3) 110°
   (4) 145°
   (5) 180°

9. An acute angle in a right triangle has a measure of 40°. What is the measure of the other acute angle in the triangle?

   (1) 40°
   (2) 50°
   (3) 90°
   (4) 140°
   (5) Not enough information is given.

10. In a certain right triangle, one acute angle is one-half the measure of the right angle. What is the measure of the other acute angle?

(1) 35°
(2) 45°
(3) 60°
(4) 90°
(5) Not enough information is given.

Questions 11 and 12 refer to the following text and figure.

A section of a square park has been roped off so that the park attendants can plant grass seed. The roped-off area forms △XYZ.

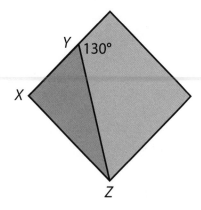

11. What is the measure of the larger of the two acute angles of the triangle?

(1) 30°
(2) 40°
(3) 50°
(4) 90°
(5) Not enough information is given.

12. What is the measure of the angle that is complementary to ∠YZX?

(1) 35°
(2) 40°
(3) 45°
(4) 50°
(5) Not enough information is given.

Questions 13 and 14 refer to the following text and figure.

Quadrilateral HIJK is a trapezoid. Quadrilateral HIJL is a parallelogram.

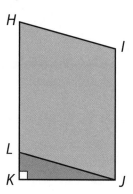

13. If ∠L of △JKL measures 60°, what is the measure of the other acute angle in the triangle?

(1) 30°
(2) 35°
(3) 45°
(4) 60°
(5) Not enough information is given.

14. If ∠L of △JKL measures 60°, what is the measure of ∠H in quadrilateral HIJK?

(1) 30°
(2) 35°
(3) 45°
(4) 55°
(5) 60°

Question 15 refers to the following figure.

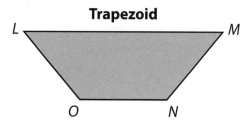

Trapezoid

15. Which two sides of this quadrilateral are parallel?

(1) $\overline{LM}$ and $\overline{MN}$
(2) $\overline{NO}$ and $\overline{OL}$
(3) $\overline{OL}$ and $\overline{MN}$
(4) $\overline{LM}$ and $\overline{NO}$
(5) $\overline{OL}$ and $\overline{NO}$

Questions 16 and 17 refer to the following text and figure.

Quadrilateral *QRST* is a trapezoid. The measures of ∠*T* and ∠*S* are equal. The measures of ∠*Q* and ∠*R* are equal.

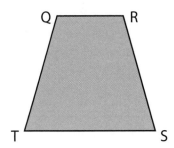

16. What is the sum of angles *Q*, *R*, *S*, and *T*?

    (1) 90°
    (2) 180°
    (3) 270°
    (4) 360°
    (5) Not enough information is given.

17. If the measure of ∠*R* is 105°, what is the measure of ∠*S*?

    (1) 37.5°
    (2) 52.5°
    (3) 75°
    (4) 150°
    (5) Not enough information is given.

18. What kind of angle would represent the sum of the interior angles of a triangle?

    (1) right angle
    (2) straight angle
    (3) acute angle
    (4) obtuse angle
    (5) Not enough information is given.

19. What is the measure of one acute angle in an isosceles right triangle?

    (1) 30°
    (2) 45°
    (3) 60°
    (4) 90°
    (5) Not enough information is given.

Questions 20 through 22 refer to the following text and figure.

The figure shows △*BCD*, △*BFE* and quadrilateral *CDEF*. Segments *EF* and *DC* are parallel.

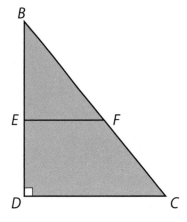

20. Which angle is congruent to ∠*BDC*?

    (1) ∠*BEF*
    (2) ∠*BCD*
    (3) ∠*DCF*
    (4) ∠*BFE*
    (5) ∠*EFB*

21. If the measure of ∠*FCD* is 60°, what is the measure of ∠*BFE*?

    (1) 30°
    (2) 60°
    (3) 90°
    (4) 120°
    (5) Not enough information is given.

22. If the measure of ∠*B* is 30°, what is the measure of the obtuse angle in quadrilateral *CDEF*?

    (1) 180°
    (2) 150°
    (3) 145°
    (4) 120°
    (5) Not enough information is given.

UNIT 4

Congruent and Similar Figures

For use with student book pp. 90-91

① Review the Skill

When corresponding angles and corresponding sides of two figures are equal, the figures are exactly the same shape and size. These are **congruent figures**. When corresponding angles of two figures are equal but the lengths of their corresponding sides are proportional, the figures are the same shape but not the same size. These are **similar figures**.

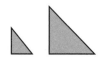

Congruent Figures   **Similar Figures**

② Refine the Skill

The known measures of sides and angles of one figure can help you find the unknown measure of a side or angle of a congruent or similar figure. Read the text and examine the figures. Then answer the questions that follow.

> **☑ TEST-TAKING TIPS**
>
> Knowing math vocabulary and symbols is essential to succeeding on the GED Mathematics Test. Learn the vocabulary and symbols that you use in each lesson.

Quadrilateral *JKLM* and quadrilateral *TUVW* are congruent figures.

A The symbol ≅ means "is congruent to." The symbol ~ means "is similar to." A line above two letters means "line segment."

B The word *corresponding* means "in the same place." The corresponding angles or lines of one figure are in the same place within the figure as they are in another figure.

---

1. Which of the following conditions is true about the two parallelograms?

   (1) $\overline{JK} \cong \overline{TU}$
   (2) $\angle M \cong \angle T$
   (3) $\overline{KL} \cong \overline{WV}$
   (4) $\angle L \cong \angle U$
   (5) $\angle K \cong \angle V$

2. If the length of $\overline{JK}$ is 12 centimeters and the length of $\overline{KL}$ is 4 centimeters, what is the length of $\overline{VW}$?

   (1) 4 cm
   (2) 8 cm
   (3) 12 cm
   (4) 16 cm
   (5) 24 cm

UNIT 4

Directions: Choose the one best answer to each question.

Questions 3 through 5 refer to the following information and figures.

The corresponding angles and sides of quadrilateral *CDEF* and quadrilateral *MJKL* are congruent. $\overline{CD}$ and $\overline{FE}$ are parallel. Angle *F* and angle *E* are congruent.

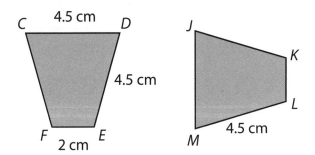

3. Which statement about the two figures is true?

    (1) Angle *L* is congruent to angle *F*.
    (2) $\overline{CD}$ is congruent to $\overline{KL}$.
    (3) Angle *F* is congruent to angle *J*.
    (4) $\overline{DE}$ is perpendicular to $\overline{JM}$.
    (5) Angle *K* is similar to angle *C*.

4. Which segment corresponds to $\overline{ML}$?

    (1) $\overline{FE}$
    (2) $\overline{CD}$
    (3) $\overline{DC}$
    (4) $\overline{CF}$
    (5) $\overline{DE}$

5. What is the perimeter of quadrilateral *JKLM*?

    (1) 9 cm
    (2) 11 cm
    (3) 13.5 cm
    (4) 15.5 cm
    (5) Not enough information is given.

Questions 6 through 8 refer to following information and figures.

The following right triangles are similar. $\overline{CB}$ corresponds to $\overline{GF}$.

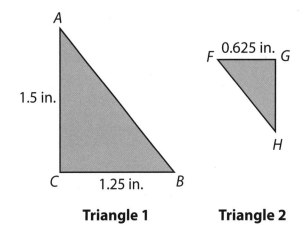

Triangle 1   **Triangle 2**

6. Which condition is true about the two figures?

    (1) $\angle C \cong \angle H$
    (2) $\overline{CB} \cong \overline{FH}$
    (3) $\angle A \cong \angle H$
    (4) $\overline{AC} \cong \overline{HF}$
    (5) $\overline{AB} \cong \overline{FH}$

7. What is the length of the side of Triangle 2 that corresponds to $\overline{AC}$ of Triangle 1?

    (1) 0.5 in.
    (2) 0.75 in.
    (3) 1.25 in.
    (4) 1.5 in.
    (5) Not enough information is given.

8. What is the length of the side of Triangle 2 that corresponds to $\overline{AB}$ of Triangle 1?

    (1) 0.5 in.
    (2) 0.625 in.
    (3) 0.75 in.
    (4) 1 in.
    (5) Not enough information is given.

Questions 9 and 10 refer to the following information and figures.

The two triangles are similar. The corresponding angles and sides of the two trapezoids are congruent.

Questions 12 through 14 refer to the following information and figures.

The corresponding angles of these two triangles are congruent. The corresponding sides of △GIH are twice the length of the sides of △BCD.

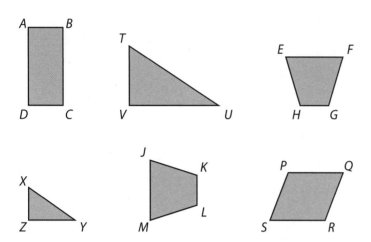

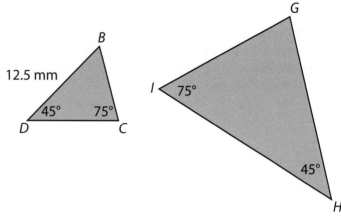

9. Which statement about the figures is true?

(1) △XYZ ≅ △TUV
(2) quadrilateral EFGH ~ quadrilateral PQRS
(3) △TUV ~ △XYZ
(4) quadrilateral PQRS ~ quadrilateral ABCD
(5) quadrilateral JKLM ~ △XYZ

10. Which condition is true about △TUV and △XYZ?

(1) ∠Y ~ ∠V
(2) $\overline{TU} \cong \overline{XY}$
(3) $\overline{VU} \cong \overline{XZ}$
(4) ∠Z ≅ ∠V
(5) $\overline{TV} \cong \overline{XY}$

11. Which statement is true?

(1) A right triangle can be similar to an equilateral triangle.
(2) A scalene triangle cannot be congruent to a right triangle.
(3) An obtuse triangle cannot be congruent to a right triangle.
(4) A quadrilateral cannot be congruent to a square.
(5) A triangle can be similar to a rectangle.

12. What is the measure of ∠G in △GIH?

(1) 45°
(2) 60°
(3) 65°
(4) 70°
(5) 75°

13. What is the measure of the angle in △GIH that corresponds to ∠C in △BCD?

(1) 45°
(2) 60°
(3) 75°
(4) 90°
(5) Not enough information is given.

14. What is the length of $\overline{GI}$ in △GIH?

(1) 6.4 mm
(2) 12 mm
(3) 12.8 mm
(4) 25.6 mm
(5) Not enough information is given.

UNIT 4

Questions 15 through 17 refer to the following information and figures.

A sculptor's design consists of two identical steel triangles shown below. However, the plans provided by the sculptor are incomplete. The manager of the foundry at which the sculpture is being cast knows, however, that the pieces are to be identical and that the sides of the triangles are congruent.

SCULPTURE PLANS

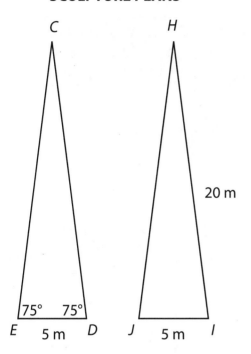

Triangle 1   Triangle 2

15. What is the length of the side of Triangle 1 that corresponds to $\overline{HI}$ of Triangle 2?

(1) 5 m
(2) 10 m
(3) 20 m
(4) 25 m
(5) Not enough information is given.

16. What is the measure of ∠H?

(1) 15°
(2) 30°
(3) 75°
(4) 105°
(5) Not enough information is given.

17. What is the perimeter of each triangular sculpture?

(1) 25 m
(2) 40 m
(3) 45 m
(4) 90 m
(5) Not enough information is given.

Questions 18 and 19 refer to the following information and figures.

A carpet company makes two sizes of a popular carpet. The sides of the smaller carpet will be two-thirds the length of the larger carpet's sides. This illustration shows the smaller carpet lying over top of the larger carpet.

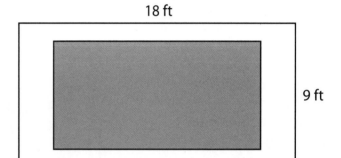

18. The larger carpet is 18 feet long. What is the length of the smaller carpet?

(1) 5 ft
(2) 6 ft
(3) 10 ft
(4) 12 ft
(5) Not enough information is given.

19. What is the difference between the areas of the two carpets?

(1) 90 ft²
(2) 120 ft²
(3) 162 ft²
(4) 234 ft²
(5) Not enough information is given.

Indirect Measurement and Proportion

For use with student book pp. 92-93

1 Review the Skill

Use **indirect measurement** to find a measurement that you cannot find directly. Set up a **proportion** using corresponding parts and then solve. Indirect measurement problems include those related to scale drawings and shadows.

2 Refine the Skill

Understanding indirect measurement will help you solve many real-world problems, including those found on the GED Mathematics Test. Examine the floor plan. Then answer the questions that follow.

UNIT 4

☑ TEST-TAKING TIPS

Use common knowledge to determine whether your answer makes sense. For example, it would be reasonable for a room to be 12 feet wide and 8 feet long. It would not reasonable for a room to be 12 inches wide or 12 inches long.

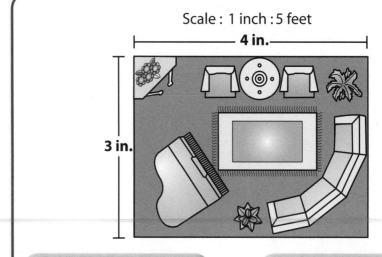

Scale : 1 inch : 5 feet

4 in.

3 in.

A Read the question carefully to understand which part of the proportion is unknown. Here, you know the length of the actual object and need to find its length in the floor plan.

B This is a multi-step problem. First, find the dimensions of the living room. Then use the dimensions to solve for the area.

1. The length of the area rug in the actual living room is 8 feet. How many inches long is the area rug in the floor plan?

   (1) 0.625
   (2) 0.975
   (3) 1.6
   (4) 5.8
   (5) 40

2. The homeowners want to replace the living room carpet. How many square feet of carpet will they need for the living room?

   (1) 35
   (2) 180
   (3) 250
   (4) 300
   (5) 600

③ Master the Skill

Directions: Choose the <u>one best answer</u> to each question.

<u>Question 3</u> refers to the following information and diagram.

A 4-inch by 6-inch photograph is enlarged proportionally to make the shorter side 12 inches, as shown in the diagram.

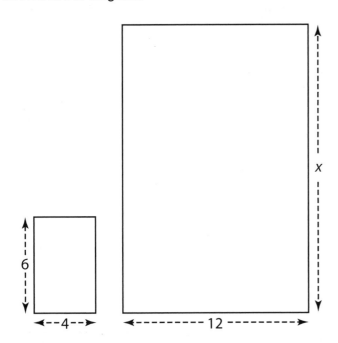

3. What is the measure, in inches, of the longer side in the enlargement?

(1) 9
(2) 12
(3) 15
(4) 18
(5) 21

4. Two towns on a map are 3.5 inches apart. The map scale is 1 inch : 5.5 miles. What is the actual distance in miles between the two towns?

(1) 2.25
(2) 7.25
(3) 9.25
(4) 11.25
(5) 19.25

5. Lake Superior is 350 miles in length. If the map scale is 1 inch : 25 miles, how many inches long is Lake Superior on the map?

(1) 14
(2) 16
(3) 325
(4) 1,050
(5) 10,500

<u>Questions 6 and 7</u> refer to following information and map.

On the map below, 2 centimeters represent 6.5 kilometers in actuality.

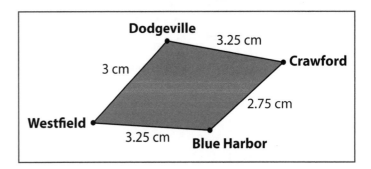

6. What is the actual distance in kilometers between Dodgeville and Crawford?

(1) 1.1
(2) 4.0
(3) 9.8
(4) 10.6
(5) 12.2

7. About how many more kilometers would you drive from Blue Harbor to Dodgeville through Westfield than from Blue Harbor to Dodgeville through Crawford?

(1) 0.1
(2) 0.3
(3) 0.4
(4) 0.6
(5) 0.8

Questions 8 through 10 refer to the following floor plan.

In this floor plan, the scale is $\frac{1}{2}$ inch = 5 feet.

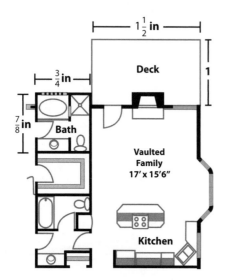

8. What are the dimensions of the actual deck?

(1) 1.5 feet by 5 feet
(2) 5.5 feet by 10 feet
(3) 5 feet by 7.5 feet
(4) 10 feet by 15 feet
(5) 12 feet by 18 feet

9. What is the actual length of the longer side of the bathroom?

(1) $8\frac{3}{4}$ ft

(2) $8\frac{1}{2}$ ft

(3) 8 ft

(4) $7\frac{1}{2}$ ft

(5) $4\frac{3}{8}$ ft

10. What are the dimensions of the actual bath?

(1) $7\frac{1}{2}$ feet by $8\frac{3}{4}$ feet

(2) $5\frac{1}{2}$ feet by $8\frac{1}{2}$ feet

(3) 5 feet by 8 feet

(4) 5 feet by $7\frac{1}{2}$ feet

(5) $3\frac{3}{4}$ feet by $4\frac{3}{8}$ feet

11. Peri biked 19.2 miles. She drew a map of her route for a friend using a scale of 2 inches = 3.2 miles. How many inches long is Peri's route on the map she drew?

(1) 8
(2) 10
(3) 12
(4) 14
(5) 16

12. Bloomington is 48 km from Orchard Point. On a map, these towns are 4 cm apart. What is the scale of this map?

(1) 1 cm = 16 km
(2) 1 cm = 12 km
(3) 1 cm = 8 km
(4) 1 cm = 4.5 km
(5) 1 cm = 0.5 km

13. A 22-foot pole casts a shadow that is 31.9 feet long. At the same time of day, how many feet long would a 55-foot building's shadow be?

(1) 12.8
(2) 31.9
(3) 37.9
(4) 64.9
(5) 79.8

14. An animal that is 4.2 feet tall casts a shadow that is 3.8 feet long. At the same time of day, a second animal casts a shadow that is 6.8 feet long. How tall is the second animal?

(1) 7.5 ft
(2) 7.2 ft
(3) 6.4 ft
(4) 6.2 ft
(5) 2.3 ft

15. A model car was built using the scale 1 in. :
32 in. If the length of the bumper of the actual
car is 108.8 in., how many inches long is the
bumper on the model car?

(1) 3.1 in.
(2) 3.3 in.
(3) 3.4 in.
(4) 3.6 in.
(5) 3.7 in.

16. A rectangular floor plan is drawn to a scale of
1 in. : 6 ft. The dimensions of a living room on
the plan are $2\frac{1}{4}$ in. by $3\frac{1}{8}$ in. What is the actual
area of the living room?

(1) $64\frac{1}{2}$ square feet

(2) $213\frac{1}{8}$ square feet

(3) $233\frac{1}{4}$ square feet

(4) $243\frac{1}{8}$ square feet

(5) $253\frac{1}{8}$ square feet

17. A map scale is 3 cm : 18.6 km. Two cities are
10 cm apart on the map. If Stacey drives at an
average speed of 90 km/hr from one city to the
other, about how long will it take her?

(1) 20 minutes
(2) 40 minutes
(3) 1 hour
(4) 1 hour 10 minutes
(5) 1 hour 20 minutes

18. A scale drawing of a square lot has a perimeter
of 22 cm. The scale of the drawing is 2 cm : 5
yards. How long is one side of the square in
actuality?

(1) 2.2 yd
(2) 5.5 yd
(3) 8.5 yd
(4) 13.75 yd
(5) 55 yd

Questions 19 and 20 refer to the following
information and map.

Michael had to submit the map below with his
application for a permit to build a new deck.

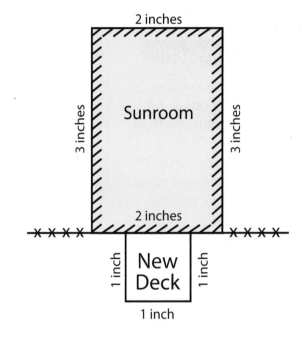

19. If the longer side of the actual sunroom is 30 feet
long, what is the scale of the map?

(1) 1 in. : 7 ft
(2) 1 in. : 8 ft
(3) 1 in. : 10 ft
(4) 1 in. : 12 ft
(5) 1 in. : 14 ft

20. If the map has a scale of $\frac{1}{2}$ in. : 6.5 ft, what are
the actual dimensions of the new deck?

(1) 6.5 feet by 6.5 feet
(2) 7 feet by 7 feet
(3) 10 feet by 10 feet
(4) 11.5 feet by 11.5 feet
(5) 13 feet by 13 feet

Circles

For use with student book pp. 94-95

① Review the Skill

A **circle** forms a closed loop in which all of the points on the circle are equidistant from the center. Most problems involving circles on the GED Mathematics Test relate to area and circumference. To solve them, use the formulas for area and circumference of a circle.

② Refine the Skill

If you know the area of a circle and need to find the radius, divide the area by 3.14, and then use your calculator to find the square root of that number. Examine the information and diagram. Then answer the questions that follow.

☑ TEST-TAKING TIPS

When finding area, either multiply 3.14 × radius × radius, or first square the radius and then multiply by 3.14.

Elizabeth created a path through her garden with identical round paving stones like those shown below. The circumference of each stone is 25.9 inches. **Ⓐ**

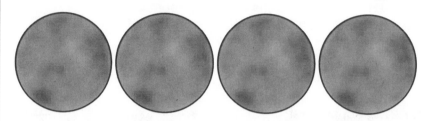

Ⓐ You know the circumference and want to find the diameter. Use the formula for circumference and then work backward.

Ⓑ Note that the information you are given is in inches. For this question, multiply the number of stones by the diameter of a stone. Then divide by 12 to find the number of feet.

1. What is the **diameter** of each stone in inches?

   (1) 2.90
   (2) 4.13
   (3) 6.48
   (4) 8.25
   (5) 17.05

2. If Elizabeth uses 35 stones, about how many **feet long** will her garden path be?

   (1) 4
   (2) 19
   (3) 24
   (4) 92
   (5) 289

UNIT 4

Directions: Choose the one best answer to each question.

3. A birdbath has a diameter of 30 inches. What is the circumference of the birdbath in inches?

    (1) 47.1
    (2) 94.2
    (3) 188.4
    (4) 706.5
    (5) 2,826.0

Question 4 refers to the information and figure below.

Lydia is using an old tractor tire to build a sandbox. She is cutting a piece of plywood to use as a cover for the sandbox.

132 cm

4. How many square centimeters of plywood does Lydia need to cover the sandbox if the cover goes to the edge of the tire?

    (1) 207
    (2) 414
    (3) 828
    (4) 13,678
    (5) 54,711

5. Mr. Dunn is painting a large circle in the middle of a gymnasium. The diameter of the circle is 12 feet. What is the area of the circle?

    (1) 18.84 ft^2
    (2) 37.68 ft^2
    (3) 75.36 ft^2
    (4) 113.04 ft^2
    (5) 452.16 ft^2

Questions 6 through 9 refer to following information and diagram.

The circular mirror below has a frame that is 2 inches wide. The diameter of the mirror and frame together is 11 inches.

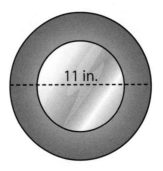

11 in.

6. What is the radius of the mirror without the frame?

    (1) 3.5 in
    (2) 4.5 in.
    (3) 7 in.
    (4) 9 in.
    (5) 11 in.

7. What is the area of the mirror only in square inches?

    (1) 34.5
    (2) 38.4
    (3) 40.8
    (4) 95.0
    (5) 379.9

8. What is the area of the frame only in square inches?

    (1) 284.9
    (2) 60.5
    (3) 56.5
    (4) 54.2
    (5) 6.3

9. What is the circumference of the mirror with the frame in inches?

    (1) 34.54
    (2) 35.64
    (3) 47.10
    (4) 94.99
    (5) 176.62

Questions 10 and 11 refer to the following information and diagram.

A circular tablecloth is shown in the diagram below.

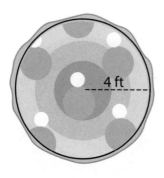

10. How many square feet is the tablecloth?

    (1) 12.56
    (2) 25.12
    (3) 50.24
    (4) 100.48
    (5) 200.96

11. Tomás places the tablecloth on a circular table that has a diameter of 6 feet. How many square feet of the tablecloth will hang over the edge of the table?

    (1) 21.98
    (2) 28.26
    (3) 50.24
    (4) 113.04
    (5) Not enough information is given.

12. Jonna is sewing a front cover for a circular pillow. The pillow has a diameter of 15 inches. To sew the front cover, she must cut the fabric two inches wider all the way around. What is the minimum area, in square inches, of the piece of fabric she will use?

    (1) 1,133.5
    (2) 706.5
    (3) 314.0
    (4) 283.4
    (5) 226.9

13. What is the difference in square inches between the two circles?

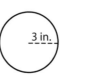

    (1) 1.0
    (2) 3.14
    (3) 6.28
    (4) 15.0
    (5) 21.98

Questions 14 and 15 refer to the following information and diagram.

Ava hung a circular sunshield in a window in her living room to block the afternoon sun.

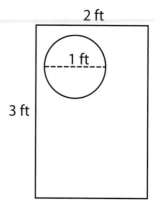

14. What is the area of the sunshield in square feet?

    (1) 6.0
    (2) 3.14
    (3) 1.57
    (4) 1.0
    (5) 0.79

15. About what percent of the area of her window is covered by the sunshield?

    (1) 13%
    (2) 17%
    (3) 25%
    (4) 50%
    (5) 78%

16. A large circle has a radius of 6 meters. A smaller circle has a radius of 2 meters. How many small circles are needed to cover the large circle?

   (1) 4.0
   (2) 9.0
   (3) 12.6
   (4) 100.5
   (5) 125.6

Question 17 refers to the following information and diagram.

   The area of the circular garden shown in the diagram is 144π square feet.

17. Russell is building a fence around the garden to keep out animals. What will be the circumference of the fence in feet?

   (1) 37.68
   (2) 47.12
   (3) 56.52
   (4) 75.36
   (5) 16,277.76

18. The area of a circle is 19.625 square centimeters. What is the diameter, in centimeters, of the circle?

   (1) 2.5
   (2) 3.1
   (3) 5.0
   (4) 6.3
   (5) Not enough information is given.

19. Dillon is building a model airplane. The front tires have a diameter of 3.5 inches. What is the total circumference of both tires?

   (1) 5.50 in.
   (2) 9.62 in.
   (3) 10.99 in.
   (4) 19.23 in.
   (5) 21.98 in.

Questions 20 and 21 refer to the following information and diagram.

   A hotel swimming pool is in the shape of the number eight.

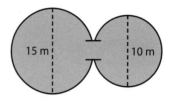

20. What is the approximate area of the swimming pool in square meters?

   (1) 40
   (2) 78
   (3) 255
   (4) 705
   (5) 1019

21. If the diameter of the smaller section is increased by 45 cm, what will be the area of the entire enlarged pool?

   (1) 93.27 square meters
   (2) 198.46 square meters
   (3) 219.85 square meters
   (4) 262.35 square meters
   (5) 342.90 square meters

22. Linda is cutting circle shapes for a bulletin board. If she wants to cut a circle that has a circumference of 25.12 inches, what should the radius be in inches?

   (1) 4
   (2) 8
   (3) 12
   (4) 16
   (5) 20

23. Jenna's sports bottle has a radius of 3 inches. What is the circumference of the sports bottle?

   (1) 4.71 in.
   (2) 9.42 in.
   (3) 18.84 in.
   (4) 28.26 in.
   (5) 37.68 in.

Solid Figures

For use with student book pp. 96-97

① Review the Skill

A **solid figure** is a three-dimensional figure such as a cube, rectangular solid, pyramid, cone, or cylinder. Most problems relating to solid figures on the GED Mathematics Test involve calculating volume.

② Refine the Skill

Understanding how to apply formulas to solid figures is an important skill for the GED Mathematics Test. For more information about formulas, see p.viii. Read the information. Then answer the questions that follow.

Genevieve wants to buy an above-ground swimming pool. She is trying to decide between two models, shown below. Each model holds the same amount of water. The height of Pool B is represented by x.

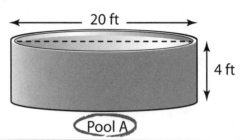

Pool A

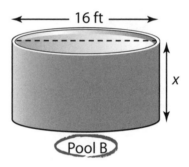

Pool B

A The volume of the two pools is the same. Since the diameter and height are both given for Pool A, find the volume of this pool.

B Remember that the formula for volume of a cylinder uses the radius, not the diameter. Divide the diameter by 2 to find the radius.

☑ **TEST-TAKING TIPS**

Questions relating to solid figures and volume may ask you to solve for diameter, radius, or area of a base, or the length, width, or height of a figure. Read the problem carefully to decide what you need to solve for.

1. What is the volume, to the nearest cubic foot, of each pool?

    (1) 125
    (2) 251
    (3) 1,004
    (4) 1,256
    (5) 5,024

2. What is the height, in feet, of Pool B?

    (1) 4.25 ft
    (2) 6.25 ft
    (3) 8.0 ft
    (4) 10.0 ft
    (5) Not enough information is given.

Directions: Choose the <u>one best answer</u> to each question.

3. A grocery store sells Italian sausage in the cylindrical tube-shaped package shown below.

10 in.

If the radius of the package is about 1.5 inches, how many cubic inches is the package?

(1) 104.67
(2) 94.20
(3) 75.25
(4) 70.65
(5) 23.55

4. A cube-shaped box has a length, width, and height of 18 inches. What is the volume of the box to the nearest cubic foot?

(1) 3
(2) 18
(3) 36
(4) 324
(5) 5,832

5. A square pyramid has a height of 9 cm and a base with an area of 36 cm. What is the volume of the square pyramid to the nearest cubic centimeter?

(1) 108
(2) 170
(3) 324
(4) 339
(5) 1,017

6. Anaya's perfume bottle is a rectangular prism. The bottle is 2.5 centimeters wide and 13 centimeters tall. If the volume of the bottle is 97.5 cubic centimeters, what is the length of the perfume bottle?

(1) 2.5 cm
(2) 3 cm
(3) 4.3 cm
(4) 7.5 cm
(5) 13 cm

Questions 7 through 9 refer to the information and figures below.

The Sno-Cone Hut sells sno-cones in three sizes. Diagrams of the three sizes are shown below.

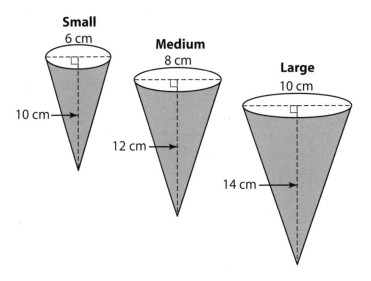

7. What is the volume of the smallest cone to the nearest cubic centimeter?

(1) 62
(2) 94
(3) 157
(4) 283
(5) 471

8. About how many more cubic centimeters does the large size hold compared to the medium?

(1) 46
(2) 128
(3) 165
(4) 211
(5) 662

9. The owner has decided to replace the smallest cone. The new cone will have a 5-centimeter diameter and a 9-centimeter height. About how many cubic centimeters larger was the old sno-cone size?

(1) 35 cm³
(2) 45 cm³
(3) 59 cm³
(4) 94 cm³
(5) 153 cm³

UNIT 4

Questions 10 and 11 refer to the figure below.

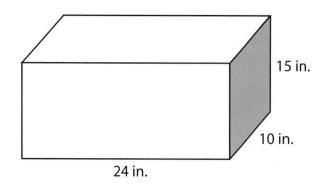

15 in.

10 in.

24 in.

10. Alyssa has the fish tank shown above. If she pours water into the tank until it is half full, how many cubic inches of water will be in the tank?

(1) 3,600
(2) 1,800
(3) 1,200
(4) 600
(5) Not enough information is given.

11. Alyssa pours water into the tank until the water reaches one inch below the top of the tank. How many cubic inches of water are in the tank?

(1) 3,599
(2) 3,360
(3) 3,240
(4) 240
(5) Not enough information is given.

12. A company makes paper cups by rolling rectangular pieces of paper stock, like the one below, into cylinders. Each cup has a height of 10 cm.

10 cm

If a cup has a radius of 3.5 cm, what is the volume of the cup in cubic centimeters?

(1) 109.9
(2) 128.2
(3) 219.8
(4) 274.8
(5) 384.7

Questions 13 through 15 refer to the text and figures below.

An ice sculpture company is experimenting with freezing blocks of ice in the shapes of square pyramids as shown in the diagram below.

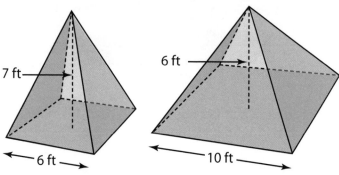

7 ft

6 ft

6 ft

10 ft

Pyramid A   **Pyramid B**

13. What is the volume of Pyramid A?

(1) 28 cubic feet
(2) 42 cubic feet
(3) 84 cubic feet
(4) 98 cubic feet
(5) 104 cubic feet

14. What is the volume of Pyramid B?

(1) 20 cubic feet
(2) 60 cubic feet
(3) 120 cubic feet
(4) 200 cubic feet
(5) 600 cubic feet

15. What is the difference, in cubic feet, between the volume of Pyramid A and Pyramid B?

(1) 84
(2) 116
(3) 200
(4) 284
(5) Not enough information is given.

16. What is the height of a can of soda that is 3 inches in diameter and holds 28.26 cubic inches?

(1) 2 in.
(2) 3 in.
(3) 4 in.
(4) 5 in.
(5) 6 in.

UNIT 4

17. A food service company ships boxes that contain 40 cans of shortening. Each can has a radius of 2 inches and a height of 5 inches. The cans are placed in a box like the one shown below. After the cans are placed in the box, how much empty space is in the box?

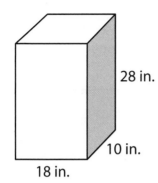

28 in.

10 in.

18 in.

(1) 2,512 cubic inches
(2) 2,528 cubic inches
(3) 3,784 cubic inches
(4) 4,202 cubic inches
(5) Not enough information is given.

18. Kaya is planting flowers in the cylindrical-shaped flowerpot shown below.

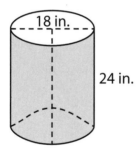

18 in.

24 in.

She begins by filling the bottom 3 inches of the flowerpot with rocks. Then she fills the rest of the pot with potting soil. About how many cubic inches of potting soil does she use?

(1) 590
(2) 1,190
(3) 5,340
(4) 6,100
(5) 21,360

19. A team of sand sculptors is building a dinosaur with spikes on its back. The shape they have chosen for the spikes is a cone. If they build spikes that contain about 565 cubic inches of sand, how many inches high are the cones they use?

(1) 12
(2) 13
(3) 14
(4) 15
(5) Not enough information is given.

20. What is the volume, to the nearest cubic foot, of a square pyramid with a side length of 2 feet 6 inches and a height of 3 feet 3 inches?

(1) 6
(2) 7
(3) 12
(4) 13
(5) 21

21. A Native American teepee is shown in the diagram below.

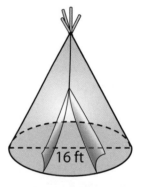

16 ft

If the space inside the teepee is 803.84 cubic feet, what is the height of the teepee to the nearest foot?

(1) 4
(2) 6
(3) 9
(4) 12
(5) 36

UNIT 4

Irregular Figures

For use with student book pp. 98-99

① Review the Skill

An **irregular figure** is made up of several shapes or parts of shapes. Irregular figures can be two- or three-dimensional. You can find the volume or area of an irregular shape by dividing it into simple figures and adding the volume or area of each simple figure. You also can find the perimeter of a plane irregular shape by adding the lengths of the sides.

② Refine the Skill

Understanding how to divide shapes, use logic to identify missing measurements, and apply formulas will help you solve problems on the GED Mathematics Test. Examine the diagram. Then answer the questions that follow.

☑ TEST-TAKING TIPS

Remember that your calculator follows the order of operations. Enter parentheses when necessary, or use several steps to perform multiple operations.

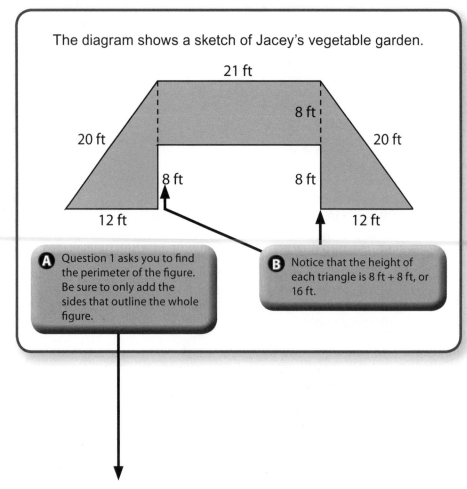

The diagram shows a sketch of Jacey's vegetable garden.

21 ft

8 ft

20 ft   20 ft

8 ft   8 ft

12 ft   12 ft

A Question 1 asks you to find the perimeter of the figure. Be sure to only add the sides that outline the whole figure.

B Notice that the height of each triangle is 8 ft + 8 ft, or 16 ft.

1. If Jacey were to put a fence around the entire outside of her vegetable garden, how many feet of fencing would she need?

   (1) 85
   (2) 101
   (3) 122
   (4) 138
   (5) 244

2. Jacey is spraying liquid compost onto her vegetable garden. She must calculate the amount of liquid compost she needs based on the number of square feet that she will cover. What is the area of her entire garden in square feet?

   (1) 216
   (2) 264
   (3) 312
   (4) 360
   (5) 552

Directions: Choose the one best answer to each question.

Questions 3 and 4 refer to the figure below.

The diagram shows Laura's living room space.

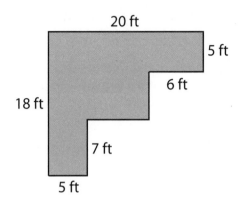

3. Laura is carpeting her living room. How many square feet of carpet will she need?

    (1) 76
    (2) 189
    (3) 219
    (4) 317
    (5) 360

4. Laura needs tacking strips to go on the floor around the outer edge beneath the carpet. How many feet of tacking strips will she need?

    (1) 72
    (2) 76
    (3) 78
    (4) 85
    (5) 90

5. Corinne ordered a pizza with a diameter of 16 in. The pizza was cut into 8 equal slices. She ate 3 slices. What is the area of the remaining pizza?

    (1) 75.36 sq in.
    (2) 100.48 sq in.
    (3) 125.6 sq in.
    (4) 200.96 sq in.
    (5) 502.8 sq in.

6. For the back-to-school season, a store is selling a container of paper clips in the shape of a pencil as shown below.

    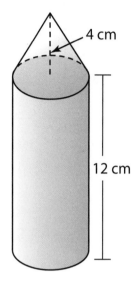

    The radius of the pencil container is 3 cm. What is the volume of the container to the nearest cubic centimeter?

    (1) 126
    (2) 144
    (3) 226
    (4) 377
    (5) 452

7. Adam is tiling the bathroom floor shown below.

    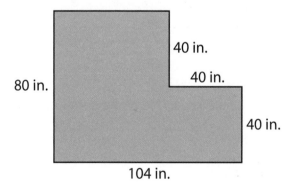

    If each tile is 8 inches by 8 inches, how many tiles does he need to cover the floor?

    (1) 64
    (2) 105
    (3) 116
    (4) 124
    (5) 840

8. A theater company built the stage shown below. What is the volume of the figure?

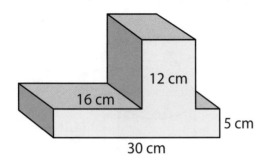

(1) 960 cm³
(2) 1,800 cm³
(3) 5,640 cm³
(4) 5,760 cm³
(5) Not enough information is given.

Questions 9 and 10 refer to the following information and diagram.

The diagram shows the setup of the main garden bed in a rose garden. The two larger circles are congruent.

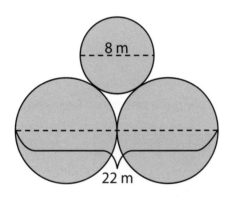

9. What is the area of one of the larger circles?

(1) 34.5 m²
(2) 95.0 m²
(3) 379.9 m²
(4) 759.8 m²
(5) 1,519.8 m²

10. About how many square meters is the garden bed?

(1) 145
(2) 190
(3) 240
(4) 290
(5) 380

Questions 11 through 14 refer to the following figure.

Stew drew the figure below. The diameter of the semicircle is also the height of the rectangle.

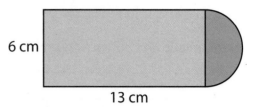

11. The semicircle at the end of the rectangle is exactly one half of a complete circle. What is the area of the semicircle?

(1) 9.42 cm²
(2) 14.13 cm²
(3) 18.84 cm²
(4) 28.26 cm²
(5) 56.52 cm²

12. What is the area of the figure?

(1) 87.42 cm²
(2) 92.13 cm²
(3) 96.84 cm²
(4) 106.26 cm²
(5) 134.52 cm²

13. What is the perimeter of the figure?

(1) 50.84 cm
(2) 47.42 cm
(3) 41.42 cm
(4) 38.00 cm
(5) 36.50 cm

14. If the figure were twice as tall, what would be the area?

(1) 156.00 cm²
(2) 174.84 cm²
(3) 184.26 cm²
(4) 193.68 cm²
(5) 212.52 cm²

Questions 15 through 18 refer to the following information and diagram.

The figure shows a triangle set on top of a rectangle.

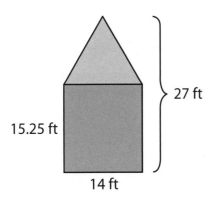

15. What is the height of the triangle?

(1) 11.75 ft
(2) 13.5 ft
(3) 14 ft
(4) 15.25 ft
(5) 27 ft

16. What is the area of the figure?

(1) 56.3 square feet
(2) 75.0 square feet
(3) 295.75 square feet
(4) 378.0 square feet
(5) 402.5 square feet

17. What is the perimeter of the figure?

(1) 56.3 feet
(2) 68.0 feet
(3) 70.3 feet
(4) 75.0 feet
(5) Not enough information is given.

18. Suppose the two shapes were pulled apart, and that the triangle were equilateral. Fencing is needed to enclose each shape. How much fencing is needed?

(1) 100.5 ft
(2) 93.75 ft
(3) 86.5 ft
(4) 71.25 ft
(5) 56.25 ft

Questions 19 through 21 refer to the following information and diagram.

The revolving restaurant on top of a downtown skyscraper is in the shape of a cylinder with a vaulted ceiling shaped like a cone, as shown in the diagram below.

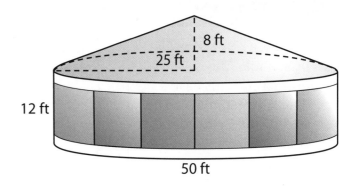

19. What is the volume of the cone-shaped section of the restaurant in cubic feet?

(1) 209.3
(2) 5,233.3
(3) 7,850.0
(4) 13,083.3
(5) 15,700.0

20. What is the approximate volume, in cubic feet, of the inside of the restaurant?

(1) 5,233
(2) 18,317
(3) 23,550
(4) 28,783
(5) 39,249

21. A design company is testing out different seating configurations. The company needs to know the square footage of the floor of the restaurant. What is the area of the floor in square feet?

(1) 50.24
(2) 654.17
(3) 1,962.5
(4) 5,000
(5) 7,500

Pythagorean Theorem

For use with student book pp. 100-101

① **Review the Skill**

As you know, a **right triangle** has a right angle. The **hypotenuse** and legs have a special relationship that can be described by the Pythagorean theorem, which states that $a^2 + b^2 = c^2$. You can use this theorem to find a missing length of a right triangle.

② **Refine the Skill**

Remember that $\frac{1}{2} \times$ base $\times$ height will give you the area of a triangle, while the Pythagorean theorem involves side lengths. Examine the diagram. Then answer the questions that follow.

☑ **TEST-TAKING TIPS**

Be sure to look for evidence that a triangle is a right triangle before you use the Pythagorean theorem. It only applies to right triangles.

A ramp was built to add wheelchair access to a public building. The ramp rises 2 feet, as shown in the diagram below.

Ramp 2 ft

10 ft

A The measurements of the legs of the right triangle are given. Solve for the hypotenuse to find the length of the ramp.

B To solve question 2, substitute 12 for 10 and solve for the hypotenuse. Remember that the hypotenuse is always the longest side of a right triangle.

A 1. If the lower edge of the ramp is 10 feet from the base of the building along level ground, what is the approximate length, in feet, of the ramp?

(1) 9.2
(2) 9.5
(3) 9.6
(4) 9.8
(5) 10.2

B 2. The owners of the building are remodeling the front entrance. They would like to modify the ramp so that it begins 12 feet from the building. What will be the length of this new ramp?

(1) 11.7 ft
(2) 11.8 ft
(3) 12.2 ft
(4) 12.4 ft
(5) 12.5 ft

UNIT 4

Directions: Choose the <u>one best answer</u> to each question.

<u>Questions 3 through 5</u> refer to the coordinate plane below.

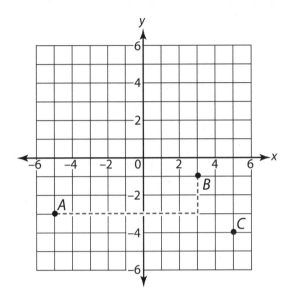

3. What is the distance between points A and B?

   (1) 6.32
   (2) 7.07
   (3) 7.28
   (4) 7.75
   (5) 8.25

4. What is the distance between points B and C?

   (1) 3.46
   (2) 3.61
   (3) 3.74
   (4) 3.87
   (5) Not enough information is given.

5. What is the distance between points A and C?

   (1) 11.18
   (2) 10.20
   (3) 10.05
   (4) 10.00
   (5) 9.95

<u>Questions 6 and 7</u> refer to the following figure.

Dana designed the quilt square shown below.

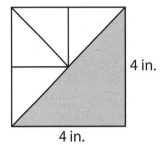

6. What is the length of the diagonal of the outside square in inches?

   (1) 5.66
   (2) 4.00
   (3) 2.83
   (4) 2.01
   (5) 1.41

7. Notice the small square in the upper left corner of the large square. One side of this small square is half the length of one side of the large square. What is the length of the diagonal of the small square?

   (1) 2.00 in.
   (2) 2.83 in.
   (3) 3.25 in.
   (4) 3.82 in.
   (5) 5.66 in.

8. What is the length of the hypotenuse of a right triangle with sides 11 cm and 15 cm?

   (1) 10.2 cm
   (2) 15.5 cm
   (3) 18.6 cm
   (4) 24.5 cm
   (5) 26.2 cm

9. A computer monitor is listed as measuring 21 inches. This is the distance across the diagonal of the screen. If the screen is 16 inches wide, what is the height of the screen to the nearest tenth of an inch?

(1) 4.5
(2) 9.1
(3) 13.6
(4) 27.2
(5) 37.1

Question 10 refers to the following diagram.

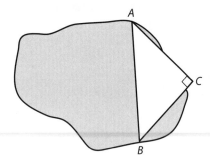

10. A surveyor wants to find the width of the pond. She placed stakes at points A, B, and C. She knows that △ABC is a right triangle. If the distance between A and C is 75 feet and the distance between B and C is 63 feet, what is the width of the pond between points A and B?

(1) 12.2 feet
(2) 40.7 feet
(3) 54.5 feet
(4) 97.9 feet
(5) 144.2 feet

11. Caleb's empty binder forms a right triangle from the side view. If the binder is 3 inches tall and 11 inches wide, what is the length of the hypotenuse?

(1) 8 in.
(2) 9.2 in.
(3) 11.4 in.
(4) 14 in.
(5) 15.3 in.

Questions 12 and 13 refer to the following diagram.

12. A 7.9-foot ramp runs from the back of a moving truck to the ground. If the ramp meets the ground 6.5 feet away from the truck, about how many feet up from the ground is the ramp?

(1) 2.0
(2) 4.5
(3) 7.1
(4) 10.2
(5) 14.4

13. If the ramp on the back of the truck were 5 feet off the ground and touched the ground at a point 8 feet away from the back of the truck, about how many feet long would the ramp be?

(1) 3.6
(2) 5.3
(3) 9.0
(4) 9.1
(5) 9.4

14. A right triangle has sides of 55 inches and 40 inches. What is the length of the hypotenuse to the nearest foot?

(1) 5
(2) 6
(3) 7
(4) 8
(5) 9

15. Which group of segments could form a right triangle?

(1) 6.5 m, 2.8 m, 7.08 m
(2) 4.25 m, 3.8 m, 5.07 m
(3) 11.5 m, 13.6 m, 16.81 m
(4) 12.75 m, 8.6 m, 14.45 m
(5) 7.25 m, 3.5 m, 10.75 m

UNIT 4

Questions 16 and 17 refer to the information and diagram below.

Henry is building a walkway through a rectangular garden as shown in the diagram below.

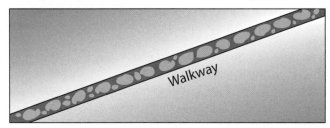

16. If the length of the garden is 30 yards and the width of the garden is 17 yards, what is the approximate length of the walkway in yards?

(1) 34.5
(2) 24.7
(3) 21.4
(4) 15.9
(5) 13.3

17. If the length of the walkway is 40 yards and the width of the garden is 12 yards, what is the approximate length of the garden in yards?

(1) 12.5
(2) 28.4
(3) 38.2
(4) 41.8
(5) 52.3

18. A 15-foot ladder is placed against the side of a building so that it reaches 12 feet up the side of the building. How far away from the building is its base?

(1) 8 feet
(2) 9 feet
(3) 10 feet
(4) 11 feet
(5) 12 feet

Questions 19 through 21 refer to the following information and figure.

The front view of a dollhouse is shown below.

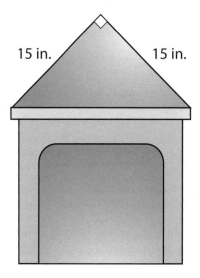

15 in.   15 in.

19. What is the width of the dollhouse in inches?

(1) 15.0
(2) 17.5
(3) 18.6
(4) 19.2
(5) 21.2

20. What is the area of the triangle roof in square inches?

(1) 51.2
(2) 112.5
(3) 159.0
(4) 225.0
(5) 318.0

21. If the height of the rectangular section is 18 inches, what is the perimeter of the front view?

(1) 69.2 inches
(2) 87.2 inches
(3) 90.4 inches
(4) 108.4 inches
(5) Not enough information is given.

Answer Key

UNIT 1 NUMBER SENSE AND OPERATIONS

LESSON 1, pp. 2–5

1. (5), 5,683 is the only number with 5 thousands; the rest have either 3 or 4 thousands.

2. (3), The two greatest values are 4,586 and 5,683, which both fall on the weekend.

3. (4), 1,107 is greater than 1,001, but less than 1,250.

4. (1), All rows have more than 200 seats except for Row A.

5. (3), Rows D, E, and F all have at least one seat in the thousands.

6. (2), 1,100 is greater than 1,097, but less than 1,105.

7. (4), The information shows that S can be found on pages 1178 to 1360. The numbers 1234 through 1287 can be found within this range.

8. (1), Twelve thousand is 12,000. Eight hundred two is 802.

9. (5), 75 has 7 tens, so it is the least, and 84 has 8 tens, so it comes next. Then focus on ones to order 92, 95, and 98.

10. (5), The first three digits are read as "one hundred fifty thousand," and the next three digits are read as "two hundred eighteen."

11. (2), The 4 in the tens place is not large enough to round up to the hundreds place.

12. (5), All the numbers are greater than 30,000 except for 14,227.

13. (4), To find the number of people between the ages of 25 and 54, 3 six-digit numbers must be added. All the other numbers have two digits.

14. (3), The 8 is in the hundreds place, and the 7 is in the ones place, so 807 is read as "eight hundred seven."

15. (4), Charlie is the tallest child, so he will be the tallest adult.

16. (2), Jake and Kiera are both 34 inches tall, so they are expected to be the same height.

17. (1), All numbers have 2 ten thousands. Order numbers by thousands: 2**0**,564; 2**2**,755; 2**3**,804.

18. (5), All numbers have 1 hundred thousand except for 305,000, which has 3 hundred thousands.

19. (3), All numbers have 6 digits except for 79,000, which has 5 digits, so it is the least. Then order numbers by ten thousands: 1**1**9,000; 1**3**1,000; 1**5**1,000.

LESSON 2, pp. 6–9

1. (4), Add 4,596 and 4,025 to find a sum of 8,621.

2. (3), Multiply 3,115 by 3 to find a product of 9,345.

3. (5), Multiply $325 by 6 to find a product of $1,950.

4. (3), Subtract $2,750 – $1,560. Regroup 7 hundreds and 5 tens as 6 hundreds and 15 tens.

5. (4), Multiply $72 by 12 to find a product of $864.

6. (1), A total of $1,080 divided by 4 people is $270 per person.

7. (5), Add $567,800 + $258,900 to find a sum of $826,700.

8. (4), Add 22 + 14 + 12 to find a sum of 48.

9. (3), To find the difference of 1,500 – 892, regroup 1 thousand and 5 hundreds as 0 thousands, 14 hundreds, 9 tens, and 10 ones.

10. (3), Add $50 + $335 + $80 + $75 to find a total cost of $540. Then divide $540 by 5 people to find a quotient of $108.

11. (5), Add $825 + $220 + $285 to find a sum of $1,330.

12. (3), To subtract $285 – $179, regroup $285 as 2 hundreds, 7 tens, and 15 ones.

13. (5), Multiply $179 by 12 to find a product of $2,148.

14. (1), Annette works 5 × 6, or 30, hours per week. 30 hours times $13 per hour = $390 per week, and $390 per week times 4 weeks = $1,560.

15. (4), Add 54 + 39 to find a total of 93 hours worked. Multiply 93 by $11 to find a product of $1,023.

16. (5), Add $458 + $397 + $492 to find a sum of $1,347.

17. (4), Divide $23,870 in sales by a price of $385 to find a quotient of 62.

18. (3), A seamstress needs 2 × 5 = 10 yards for the shirts and 5 × 5 = 25 yards for the dresses. Subtract 25 – 10 to find a difference of 15.

19. (4), Since 37 is the round-trip mileage, this figure includes driving to and from work. Multiply 5 days per week by 4 weeks to get 20 days. Then multiply 20 days by 37 miles to get a product of 740 miles.

20. (2), The charity has already collected $4,020 + $3,902, or $7,922. Subtract 7,922 from 12,500. Regroup 12,500 as 0 ten thousands, 11 thousands, 14 hundreds, 9 tens, and 10 ones.

21. (1), Divide the cost of $1,445 by 289 square feet to find a quotient of $5 per square foot.

22. (2), Since there are 12 months in a year, there are 3 × 12 = 36 months in 3 years. Divide $13,392 by 36 months to find a quotient of $372.

23. (4), Divide $270 by the cost of each share, which is $15.

24. (1), Multiply $7 profit per share by 25 shares to find a product of $175.

LESSON 3, pp. 10–13

1. (2), Round $810 to $800, and $720 to $700; $800 + $700 = $1,500.

2. (1), The Ryersons expect to pay $810 + $720, or $1,530, for food and lodging. Subtract $1,650 – $1,530 to find a difference of $120.

3. (3), José has eaten 1,250 + 780, or 2,030, calories so far. Subtract this from 3,500. Regroup 3,500 as 3 thousands, 4 hundreds, 10 tens, and 0 ones.

4. (2), 2,012 production employees + 157 shipping employees = 2,169 employees. Subtract this from 2,391 to find a difference of 222.

5. (4), Multiply $126 by 12 months to find a product of $1,512. The $57 for monthly auto insurance is not needed to solve the problem.

6. (3), $95 divided by 5 people is $19 per person.

7. (5), Add 6 + 5 + 7 + 8 + 8 to find a total of 34 hours for the week. Multiply 34 hours by $8 to find a product of $272.

8. (4), 34 hours last week + 6 more hours = 40 hours in all, and 40 hours × $9 = $360.

9. (5), The amount of the tip is unknown, so the total cost cannot be determined.

10. (1), After the deposit, Naomi has $913 + $130, or $1,043, in her account. The amount of checks and withdrawals is $75 + $75 + $50, or $200. Subtract 200 from 1,043 by regrouping 1,043 as 0 thousands, 10 hundreds, 4 tens, and 3 ones.

UNIT 1 (continued)

11. (1), Subtract 97,634 – 41,868 to find a difference of 55,766, which is the number of miles Marla drove using the new tires. Subtract 40,000 from this number to find the number of miles driven above 40,000.

12. (2), 16 gallons × $3 per gallon = $48 to fill the tank. To drive 800 miles, she needs to fill her tank 800 ÷ 400, or 2, times. Multiply $48 by 2 to find a product of $96.

13. (5), Multiply $950 by 3 to find a product of $2,850.

14. (1), Subtract 4,598 – 1,354 to find a difference of 3,244. Then divide this number by 4 (Trisha + 3 siblings), to find a quotient of 811.

15. (3), Round 4,208 to 4,000 and 983 to 1,000. Subtract 4,000 – 1,000 to find a difference of 3,000.

16. (2), Add 3,156 + 2,634 + 4,208 to find a total of 9,998 red, blue, or white skeins. Add 1,920 + 983 + 732 + 531 + 1,828 + 935 to find a total of 6,929 skeins of other colors. The difference of 9,998 – 6,929 is 3,069, which rounds to 3,100.

17. (3), The payment plan will cost $150 × 12, or $1,800. Subtract $1,620 from this amount to get a difference of $180.

18. (2), Cody earned $50 × 4, or $200, on televisions and $30 × 3, or $90, on speakers. He earned $200 + $90 = $290 in all.

19. (5), The cost of mulch is unknown, so the cost of mulch and blocks cannot be determined.

20. (2), $1,476 divided by 12 months = $123 per month.

21. (3), Gretchen ordered 3 + 8 + 14 = 25 boxes of men's shirts and 5 + 6 + 5 = 16 boxes of women's shirts. Multiply 25 boxes by 25 men's shirts per box to find a product of 625 men's shirts. Multiply 16 boxes by 35 women's shirts per box to find a product of 560 women's shirts. The difference of 625 – 560 is 65.

22. (4), Women's shirts: 6 + 5 = 11 boxes; 11 boxes × 35 shirts per box = 385 shirts. Men's shirts: 3 + 8 = 11 boxes; 11 boxes × 25 shirts per box = 275 shirts. 385 women's shirts + 275 men's shirts = 660 shirts in all.

23. (2), The difference of 245 girls who play soccer – 218 girls who play basketball = 27 girls.

LESSON 4, pp. 14–17

1. (1), $\frac{2}{6}$ and $\frac{1}{3}$ are equivalent because $\frac{1}{3} = \frac{1 \times 2}{3 \times 2} = \frac{2}{6}$, and $\frac{1}{3}$ corresponds to Plant A.

2. (3), Rename the fractions as $\frac{4}{12}, \frac{2}{12}, \frac{9}{12}, \frac{8}{12}$, and $\frac{3}{12}$. The greatest fraction is $\frac{9}{12}$, which corresponds to Plant C.

3. (3), 2 male students out of 5 students = $\frac{2}{5}$.

4. (1), To simplify $\frac{16}{64}$, divide both the numerator and denominator by 16.

5. (5), $50 – $28 = $22 left, and $\frac{22 \div 2}{50 \div 2} = \frac{11}{25}$.

6. (3), To simplify $\frac{18}{72}$, divide both the numerator and denominator by 18.

7. (4), To simplify $\frac{2,000}{3,000}$, divide both the numerator and denominator by 1,000.

8. (3), 4 members who ordered ice cream out of 15 members in all is $\frac{4}{15}$, which cannot be simplified.

9. (4), $\frac{8}{18}$ is not simplified, because the numerator and denominator can both be divided by 2.

10. (3), 248 students – 172 female students = 76 male students. To simplify $\frac{76}{248}$, divide both the numerator and denominator by 4.

11. (3), 750 + 850 = 1,600 students who wore either red or white, and 2,500 – 1,600 = 900 students who wore blue. To simplify $\frac{900}{2,500}$, divide both the numerator and denominator by 100.

12. (4), Rename the fractions as $\frac{4}{10}, \frac{7}{10}, \frac{5}{10}, \frac{9}{10}$, and $\frac{8}{10}$. The greatest fraction is $\frac{9}{10}$, which corresponds to Ethan.

13. (3), Ethan completed $\frac{9}{10}$, and $\frac{4}{10} + \frac{5}{10} = \frac{9}{10}$. Dara and Miguel correspond to $\frac{4}{10}$ and $\frac{5}{10}$.

14. (4), Multiply 25 by $\frac{1}{5}$ to get 5. Then subtract 5 from 25 to get 20. Erik correctly answered 20 questions.

15. (5), Turn $7\frac{1}{2}$ into the improper fraction $\frac{15}{2}$, so there are fifteen half-cups of flour.

16. (4), There are 8 + 2 = 10 total questions. Alexandra answered $\frac{8}{10}$, which simplifies to $\frac{4}{5}$, of the questions correctly.

17. (3), Turn $1\frac{3}{4}$ into the improper fraction $\frac{7}{4}$. Quentin will fill the $\frac{1}{4}$-cup 7 times.

18. (3), Multiply the whole number 2 by the denominator 8, and then add the product to the numerator 3 to find the numerator of the improper fraction: 19. The improper fraction is $\frac{19}{8}$.

19. (5), Divide 23 by 4 to get 5 with a remainder of 3. Use the remainder as the numerator of the mixed number to get $5\frac{3}{4}$.

20. (4), Divide the numerator and denominator of $\frac{34}{85}$ by 17 to find the simplified fraction $\frac{2}{5}$.

21. (4), Simplify the fraction $\frac{825}{2,750}$ to get $\frac{3}{10}$.

LESSON 5, pp. 18–21

1. (5), Rename $3\frac{1}{4}$ as $\frac{13}{4}$ and $4\frac{1}{8}$ as $\frac{33}{8}$. Then multiply $\frac{13}{4}$ by $\frac{2}{2}$ to get $\frac{26}{8}$. Subtract to determine that Sharon will use $\frac{33}{8} - \frac{26}{8} = \frac{7}{8}$ yards more to make the extra-large dress.

2. (3), Rename $2\frac{3}{4}$ as a mixed number and then multiply by $\frac{1}{2}$. Sharon has $\frac{11}{4} \times \frac{1}{2} = \frac{11}{8}$, or $1\frac{3}{8}$, yards of fabric.

3. (3), Rename both numbers as improper fractions: $\frac{8}{1}$ and $\frac{7}{2}$. Then find the common denominator and subtract: $\frac{16}{2} - \frac{7}{2} = \frac{9}{2}$. So, Chandra has $4\frac{1}{2}$ sick days left.

4. (5), Find the common denominator of the fractions and then add the mixed numbers: $3\frac{3}{4} + 5\frac{2}{4} + 4\frac{1}{4} = 12\frac{6}{4}$. Then simplify to see that Todd used $12\frac{6}{4} = 13\frac{1}{2}$ gallons of water.

5. (4), The farmer used $6 - 1\frac{1}{3} = \frac{18}{3} - \frac{4}{3} = \frac{14}{3}$, or $4\frac{2}{3}$, more gallons last year.

6. (3), Divide $29,400 by 24 to get $1,225. Elias makes $1,225 on his semi-monthly paycheck.

7. (4), Divide 24 by $\frac{1}{4}$ to find that the chef can make $24 \div \frac{1}{4} = 24 \times \frac{4}{1} = 96$ specials.

UNIT 1 (continued)

8. (4), It takes Mike 15 minutes, or $\frac{15}{60} = \frac{1}{4}$ of an hour, to mow one lawn, so he should be able to mow $30 \div \frac{1}{4} = 30 \times \frac{4}{1} = 120$ lawns in 30 hours.

9. (2), It takes Amy 35 minutes, or $\frac{35}{60} = \frac{7}{12}$ of an hour, to edit one page of a textbook. So, it would take her $300 \times \frac{7}{12} = 175$ hours to edit a 300-page book.

10. (2), To find $\frac{2}{3}$ of $\frac{1}{2}$, multiply $\frac{2}{3}$ by $\frac{1}{2}$ to find a product of $\frac{1}{3}$.

11. (2), Find a common denominator and rename each fraction, $25\frac{7}{8} = 25\frac{21}{24}$ and $17\frac{5}{6} = 17\frac{20}{24}$, and then subtract. Ed has $25\frac{21}{24} - 17\frac{20}{24} = 8\frac{1}{24}$ yards of fencing left.

12. (2), Find the common denominator and then add each fraction: $\frac{1}{5} + \frac{1}{2} = \frac{2}{10} + \frac{5}{10} = \frac{7}{10}$. Subtract $\frac{7}{10}$ from 1, or $\frac{10}{10}$, to find that $\frac{3}{10}$ of the group sat in red seats.

13. (3), Find the common denominator and add the fractions. Luke rode his bicycle $24\frac{5}{6} + 18\frac{2}{3} = 24\frac{5}{6} + 18\frac{4}{6} = 42\frac{9}{6} = 43\frac{1}{2}$ miles over the weekend.

14. (3), Luke rode $25\frac{9}{10} - 12\frac{7}{8} = 25\frac{36}{40} - 12\frac{35}{40} = 13\frac{1}{40}$ fewer miles on Wednesday than on Monday.

15. (5), It will take Ginny $\frac{26}{1} \times \frac{1}{9} = \frac{26}{9}$, or $2\frac{8}{9}$, hours.

16. (3), The board should be $3\frac{1}{4} + \frac{3}{8} = 3\frac{2}{8} + \frac{3}{8} = 3\frac{5}{8}$ feet long.

17. (4), Multiply the whole number by the denominator, and then add the product to the numerator: $50 \times 2 + 1 = 101$. Use this as the numerator with the same denominator to make the improper fraction $\frac{101}{2}$.

18. (1), Rename each mixed number as an improper fraction, and then divide to find $4\frac{3}{4} \div 2\frac{1}{4} = \frac{19}{4} \div \frac{9}{4} = \frac{19}{4} \times \frac{4}{9} = \frac{76}{36}$. So, it took them $\frac{76}{36} = 2\frac{1}{9}$ hours to hike the trail.

19. (3), Since it takes $\frac{3}{4}$ hour to write a 200-word blog, it takes $\frac{3}{4} \times \frac{1}{2} = \frac{3}{8}$ hour to write a 100-word blog. Multiply $\frac{3}{8}$ by 5 to see that it takes $\frac{15}{8}$, or $1\frac{7}{8}$, hours to write a 500-word blog.

20. (3), Rename each mixed number as an improper fraction, and then find a common denominator. Subtract to find that Mario needs to work $32\frac{5}{6} - 19\frac{7}{8} = \frac{197}{6} - \frac{159}{8} = \frac{788}{24} - \frac{477}{24} = \frac{311}{24} = 12\frac{23}{24}$ more hours this week.

21. (4), The drive-through staff can process $18 \div \frac{2}{3} = 18 \times \frac{3}{2} = 27$ orders in 18 minutes.

LESSON 6, *pp. 22–25*

1. (2), Solve $\frac{3}{4} = \frac{x}{8}$ for x and find that $x = 6$.

2. (5), There are 4 males and $12 - 4 = 8$ females. The ratio of male to female clarinet players is $\frac{4}{8} \div \frac{4}{4} = \frac{1}{2}$.

3. (1), Olive performed $12 + 4 = 16$ total skills, and her ratio of incorrect to total skills is $\frac{4}{16} = \frac{1}{4}$.

4. (5), The ratio of games lost to games won is 4:38, which can be simplified to 2:19.

5. (3), Divide 16 by 8 to get $2 per can of soup.

6. (5), Solve $\frac{1 \text{ in.}}{3 \text{ ft}} = \frac{4 \text{ in.}}{x \text{ ft}}$ for x to find $x = 12$ feet.

7. (4), The ratio of miles driven on Monday to miles driven on Tuesday is $\frac{96}{60} = \frac{8}{5}$.

8. (1), Solve $\frac{12}{30} = \frac{x}{10}$ to find that $x = 4$ eggs, so the ratio is 4 to 10, or 2 to 5.

9. (3), Solve $\frac{8}{3} = \frac{24}{x}$ for x to find that $x = 9$.

10. (2), The ratio of full-time to part-time employees is 30:12, or 5:2.

11. (3), Solve $\frac{2}{150} = \frac{6}{x}$ for x to find that $x = 450$ miles.

12. (2), Solve $\frac{5}{15} = \frac{275}{x}$ for x to find that $x = 825.

13. (4), Solve $\frac{1}{5} = \frac{x}{35}$ for x to find that $x = 7$ dogs were adopted.

14. (1), Trevor drove $\frac{48 \text{ miles}}{3 \text{ hours}} = 16$ miles per hour.

15. (3), The recipe calls for $2 + 3 = 5$ teaspoons of sauce. Solve $\frac{3}{5} = \frac{x}{20}$ for x to find that $x = 12$ teaspoons of caramel sauce.

16. (3), Subtract $\frac{4}{5}$ from 1 to find that $\frac{1}{5}$ of the students do not ride the bus. Solve $\frac{1}{5} = \frac{x}{450}$ for x to find that $x = 92$.

17. (3), Solve $\frac{2}{5} = \frac{x}{30}$ to find that $x = 12$ people.

18. (2), Solve $\frac{14}{1} = \frac{406}{x}$ for x to find that $x = 29$ teachers.

19. (5), Solve $\frac{110}{1} = \frac{x}{4.5}$ for x to find that $x = 495$ calories.

20. (1), Subtract 16 from 30 to find that 14 people do not drive to work. The ratio of drivers to non-drivers is $16:14 = 8:7$.

21. (3), Solve $\frac{2}{3} = \frac{26}{x}$ for x to find that $x = 39$ parking spots.

22. (3), Solve $\frac{414}{18} = \frac{x}{1}$ for x to find that $x = 23$ miles per gallon.

23. (5), Add Leila's mileage to find that she drove a total of 2,040 miles over 5 weeks. The ratio of Week 1 to total weeks is $420:2,040 = 7:34$.

24. (4), Solve $\frac{1}{22} = \frac{x}{176}$ for x to find that $x = 8$ lifeguards.

25. (1), Solve $\frac{3}{8} = \frac{387}{x}$ for x to find that $x = 1,032$ people.

26. (5), Solve $\frac{8}{24} = \frac{12}{x}$ to find that $x = 36.

27. (4), The ratio of applicants to openings for a staff writer is $48:4 = 12:1$.

28. (3), Solve $\frac{27}{3} = \frac{x}{5}$ for x to find that $x = 45$ applicants for the art researcher position. Subtract 27 from 45 to find that 18 additional people will apply for the position.

LESSON 7, *pp. 26–29*

1. (2), Compare the whole numbers and then the decimal places to find that Tay's bowling ball is the lightest.

2. (4), Compare the whole numbers and then the decimal places to determine that two of the bowling balls have a mass greater than 6.25 kg.

3. (5), Add $5.8 + 5.2 + 6.2 + 7.2 + 6.6$ to find the total weight of the bowling balls is 31 kg.

4. (3), Mr. Peterman's ball weighs $7.2 - 5.2 = 2$ kg more than Tay's ball.

5. (1), Compare the whole numbers and then the decimal places to find that Kate drove the least number of miles on Monday.

6. (2), Compare the whole numbers and then the decimal places to find the order from least to greatest is 37.5, 37.7, 37.8, 38.1, and 38.3.

UNIT 1 (continued)

7. (3), Morgan's time could be 218.45 because it is greater than 218.15, but less than 218.65.

8. (3), The scores 15.965 and 15.97 are less than Natalia's score of 15.975, so she came in third place.

9. (3), Milk costs $3.89; round up to $4. Divide $12 by $4 to find that Anne can buy 3 gallons of milk.

10. (5), Strawberries cost $2.99 ≈ $3 and 5.17 ≈ 5 pounds, so it would cost about $15 for 5.17 pounds.

11. (4), A soft drink costs $1.79 ≈ $2. Divide $8 by $2 to find that Dylan can buy 4 soft drinks.

12. (4), Book number 35.783 is greater than 31.858 and less than 35.784, so it would be in Floor 3, Section B.

13. (2), Book number 17.778 is greater than 17.655 and less than 21.584, so the shelf is in Floor 1, Section B.

14. (4), The digit in the hundredths place of 42.468 is greater than 4, so 42.468 rounds to 42.5 pounds.

15. (3), Sample C weighs 1.121 kg, which is greater than the maximum weight of 1.103 kg, so Isaiah would reject it.

16. (2), Compare the whole numbers and then the decimal places to find that Player B has the highest batting average.

17. (5), Compare the whole numbers and then the decimal places to find that Players D, C, and B have the highest batting averages in order from least to greatest.

18. (5), Compare the whole numbers and then the decimal places to find that Stop and Gas has the lowest price for gas.

19. (4), The digit in the hundredths place of $2.45 is greater than 4, so $2.45 rounds to $2.50.

20. (2), Compare the whole numbers and then the decimal places to find that Shauna's scores from lowest to highest are 8.75, 9.25, and 9.50.

21. (3), The weight 8.37 pounds is greater than 7.86, but less than 10.95, so it will cost $8.99.

22. (5), The weight 16.54 pounds is greater than 15.41, but less than 25.00, so it will cost $15.75, which is more than $15.

23. (5), Since $49.88 ≈ $50 per month, Rachel pays about $50 × 12 = $600 a year.

LESSON 8, pp. 30–33

1. (2), Multiply $1.59 by 10 to find that $15.90 was spent on 10 iced teas.

2. (5), Lydia spent $4.99 + $1.29 = $6.28 in all, so she received $10.00 – $6.28 = $3.72 in change.

3. (5), Multiply $112.43 by 2 to get a product of $224.86.

4. (2), Divide $5.89 by 8 to find that a can of beans costs $0.74.

5. (4), Evan spent $589.45 + 82.32 + 14.99 = $686.76 in all.

6. (2), Subtract $75.45 from $89.79 to find that chairs at In the Woods cost $14.34 less. William saved $14.34 × 4 = $57.36.

7. (2), The cost of a single package is $7.62 ÷ 6 = $1.27.

8. (4), Ariana spent $17.95 + $3.27 = $21.22 total. She has $15.78 remaining.

9. (3), Carmen has $163.60 ÷ 8 = $20.45 deducted from her paycheck each week.

10. (1), Russell spent $5.69 + $3.98 + $1.99 = $11.66 on lunch.

11. (1), Timothy pays $143 ÷ 52 = $2.75 per week.

12. (4), Add $597.16 and $217.98 to get a sum of $815.14. Subtract $45.00 from the sum to get a new balance of $770.14.

13. (1), Without sales tax, 2.3 pounds of salami cost $3.95 × 2.3 = 9.085 ≈ $9.09.

14. (1), Divide $675 by 12 to find the monthly payment of $56.25.

15. (1), Terese spent a total of $14.89 + $2.38 + $0.79 = $18.06. She should receive $20.00 – $18.06 = $1.94 in change.

16. (4), Lisa's total cost is $22.95 + $ 66.25 = $89.20.

17. (3), Subtract $14.85 from $22.95 to find that Mark would save $8.10.

18. (3), Tim has a combined total of 95.75 + 92.5 + 98.25 = 286.50 on his three exams.

19. (2), Subtract $85.04 from $124.53 to find the difference of $39.49.

20. (5), Jonah spent $124.53 + $118.92 + $95.41 + $88.73 + $85.04 + $86.29 = $598.92 from July to December.

21. (1), Lorenzo saved $2.29 – $2.05 = $0.24 per box, so he saved $0.24 × 5 = $1.20 in all.

22. (3), The total score of all three judges is 8 + 8.5 + 7.5 = 24, so his total score is 24 × 3.2 = 76.8.

23. (2), Divide 115.02 by 5.4 to find a quotient of 21.3 miles per hour.

24. (4), Alexis spent $2.65 × 6 = $15.90 in all and should receive $20.00 – $15.90 = $4.10 in change.

25. (2), Walt pays $1,556.28 ÷ 12 = $129.69 per month.

26. (5), Multiply 60.2 by 3.5 to get a product of 210.7 miles.

LESSON 9, pp. 34–37

1. (2), Divide 8 by the total number of votes, 50, to find 0.16, which equals 16%.

2. (5), The fraction $\frac{14}{50}$ is equivalent to $\frac{28}{100}$, or 0.28.

3. (1), Hamilton and Carlotti will receive 12 + 8 = 20 votes altogether. Divide 20 by 50 to get 0.4 = 40%.

4. (2), Sanchez and Hamilton would receive 12 + 14 = 26 votes altogether. Divide 26 by 50 to find that they would receive 0.52 = 52% of the votes, which is the majority.

5. (4), There is a percentage of $\frac{1}{8}$ = 1 ÷ 8 = 0.125 = 12.5% first-graders dropped off at school.

6. (3), Since $\frac{2}{50} = \frac{4}{100}$, 4% of the students work full time while attending college.

7. (5), Since 85% = $\frac{85}{100}$, this can be simplified to $\frac{17}{20}$.

8. (3), Divide 3 by 25 to get 0.12 = 12%.

9. (5), Customers will pay 90% = $\frac{90}{100} = \frac{9}{10}$ of the original price.

10. (2), Employees pay 70% = 0.70 of the original price, so Sam will pay $580 × 0.7 = $406.

11. (1), It will cost 500 × $2 = $1,000 for the flyers. Marie's down payment will be $1,000 × 0.3 = $300.

12. (2), The fraction of science-related questions is 45% = $\frac{45}{100} = \frac{9}{20}$.

13. (3), The unit price is $22\frac{1}{2}$ cents = 22.5 cents = $0.225.

14. (2), Subtract 22.8 from $54\frac{1}{2}$ = 54.5 to find that Nina biked 31.7 miles on the second day.

15. (2), Self-employment taxes are $\frac{5.5}{100} = \frac{55}{1,000} = \frac{11}{200}$ of her income.

16. (2), Divide 82 by 100 to find that 82% = 0.82.

UNIT 1 (continued)

17. (2), The Panthers won $\frac{22}{34} = 0.647 = 64.7\%$ of their games.

18. (3), Ted answered $\frac{41}{50} = 0.82 = 82\%$ of the questions correctly.

19. (4), $1,230 \times 0.2 = $246 down payment. Subtract $246 from $1,230 = $984 owed on the computer after the down payment.

20. (1), Jim makes a profit of $10.50 − $7 = $3.50 per knapsack. His percentage of profit margin is $3.50 ÷ $7 = 0.5 or 50%.

21. (4), Maya paid 70% $= \frac{70}{100} = \frac{7}{10}$ of the original price.

22. (4), Carlos will save 40% $= \frac{40}{100} = \frac{4}{10} = \frac{2}{5}$ of the original price.

23. (3), Add $\frac{1}{6} = \frac{10}{60}$ for food and $0.35 = \frac{35}{100} = \frac{21}{60}$ for housing to get a total of $\frac{31}{60}$. Subtract this from 1, or $\frac{60}{60}$, to find the fraction of her remaining earnings is $\frac{29}{60}$.

24. (3), Elliott's friends pay 90% $= \frac{9}{10}$ of the original price.

25. (4), The Kickers won $24 \times 0.75 = 18$ matches.

26. (1), The interest rate $5\frac{1}{2}\%$ can be written as $5.5 ÷ 100 = 0.055$.

LESSON 10, pp. 38–41

1. (2), Solve $\frac{6.10}{40.66} = \frac{x}{100}$ for x to find that $x = 15.002$, which is about 15% of the subtotal.

2. (5), The customer's tip is $40.66 \times 0.2 = $8.13, so the total bill is $40.66 + $8.13 = $48.79.

3. (2), Theo now pays $615 − $585 = $30 more for his rent. Solve $\frac{30}{585} = \frac{x}{100}$ for x to find the percent increase is $x \approx 5.128 \approx 5\%$.

4. (5), Solve $\frac{2.86}{x} = \frac{8}{100}$ for x to find that $x = $35.75.

5. (2), Use the formula: $I = prt$. Ezra will pay $3,000 \times 0.03 \times 1.5 = $135 in interest.

6. (3), Dan's down payment was $16,584 \times .2 = $3,316.80. He has to pay $16,584 − $3,316.80 = $13,267.20 over the next 24 months. Dan's monthly payment is $13,267.20 ÷ 24 = $552.80.

7. (4), The discount for the jacket is $152.60 \times 0.4 = $61.04. Noelle paid $152.60 − $61.04 = $91.56 for the jacket.

8. (3), Solve $\frac{2,025}{x} = \frac{4.5}{100}$ for x to find that $x = $45,000.

9. (3), The interest on Remy's loan is $10,000 \times 0.056 \times 3 = $1,680. She paid a total of $10,000 + $1,680 = $11,680.

10. (2), $22,000 \times 0.2 = $4,400. Subtract $4,400 from $22,000 to find an owed balance of $17,600. Divide $17,600 by 36 months to find a monthly car payment for Jae of $488.89.

11. (4), Solve $\frac{72}{x} = \frac{6}{100}$ to find that $x = $1,200.

12. (5), $\frac{308,205 \text{ parts}}{1,158,675 \text{ in all}} \approx 0.2659$, and $0.2659 \approx 27\%$.

13. (4), $\frac{545,380}{1,158,675} \approx 0.47069$, which is about 47%.

14. (2) Using the formula $I = prt$, $I = $210,000 \times 0.05 \times 4 = $42,000 in interest. $42,000 interest + a loan of $210,000 = $252,000 in all

15. (4), The increase is $11 \times 0.04 = $0.44 per hour. $11.00 + an increase of $0.44 = $11.44.

16. (3), The decrease in passengers was $5,478 − 4,380 = 1,098$. Solve $\frac{1,098}{5,478} = \frac{x}{100}$ to find that there was about a 20% decrease.

17. (2), Michelle's new salary = 115% × her old salary, so $86,250 = 1.15x$; $x = $75,000.

18. (3), Solve $\frac{x}{35} = \frac{20}{100}$ to find that the class size increased by 7 students. There are now $35 + 7 = 42$ students.

19. (3), Using the formula $I = prt$, $787.50 = 10,500(3)r$; $r = 0.025$, which is 2.5%.

20. (1), Solve $324 = 0.72x$ to find that there were 450 teachers in the union. Then subtract $450 − 324$ to find that 126 teachers were against it.

21. (5), He pays 95% of the first shirt, 85% of the second, and 75% of the third. $0.95(12) + 0.85(12) + 0.75(12) = $30.60.

22. (2), They hired $850 \times 0.08 = 68$ more employees.

23. (2), The population decreased by $756 − 711 = 45$ students. Solve $\frac{45}{756} = \frac{x}{100}$ to find a decrease of about 6%.

24. (5), The interest rate is unknown.

25. (2), In Maryland, the computer game would cost $31.80, which is less than Delaware's price of $32.

UNIT 2 MEASUREMENT/DATA ANALYSIS

LESSON 1, pp. 42–45

1. (3), Convert 45 mg to 4.5 cg and 2 g to 200 cg. The printmaker used $4.5 + 200 + 85 = 289.5$ cg.

2. (2), Convert 50 mg to 0.05 g and 55 cg to 0.55 g and add them together for a sum of 0.6 g. The mass of the red pigment is $3 − 0.6 = 2.4$ g greater than the combined mass of the blue and green pigments.

3. (3), Since 2 cups = 1 pint, Cedric will need 3×1 pint = 3 pints of orange juice.

4. (4), Since 4 pints = 2 quarts, Cedric will need 3×2 quarts = 6 quarts of carbonated water.

5. (5), Since 5 pints = 10 cups, Cedric will need 3×10 cups = 30 cups of ginger ale.

6. (4), Divide 700 by 1,000 to find that Sabrina marked 0.7 km on Day 1.

7. (2), Sabrina marked $700 + 600 + 800 + 1,000 = 3,100$ m by Day 4. Divide 3,100 by 1,000 to find that she marked 3.1 km.

8. (3), The runners must race $700 + 600 + 800 + 1,000 + 900 = 4,000 = 4$ km.

9. (1), Jason threw the javelin $63 − 54 = 9$ feet more than Hector. Divide 9 by 3 to find 3 yards.

10. (3), Hannah walked $(875)(3) + (2,625)(2) = 7,875$ yards. Divide 7,875 by 1,760 to find $4.47 \approx 4.5$ miles.

11. (2), Mara will need $\frac{18 \times 24}{12} = \frac{432}{12} = 36$ ft of ribbon.

12. (2), George ran $\frac{2,640}{1,760} = 1.5$ miles.

13. (3), Kyle will need $\frac{(3)(448) + (2)(236)}{1,000} = \frac{1,816}{1,000} = 1.816$ kL of water.

14. (4), They gathered $\frac{(5)(10) + (5)(1) + (5)(0.1)}{10} = \frac{55.5}{10} = 5.55$ cL of pond water.

15. (1), The soccer team consumed $17 ÷ 1,000 = 0.017$ kL of water.

16. (2), The tallest sapling is $121 ÷ 100 = 1.21$ m tall.

17. (1), The difference in height is $\frac{57 − 33}{100} = \frac{24}{100} = 0.24$ m.

UNIT 2 *(continued)*

18. (5), The data from the following summer are missing, so there is not enough information.

19. (2), One box of cereal contains $\frac{45 \times 8}{1,000} = \frac{360}{1,000} = 0.36$ kg of carbohydrates.

20. (1), Jim consumed $250 \div 2 = 125$ mg of sodium. So, he consumed $125 \div 10 = 12.5$ cg.

21. (3), Darlene's drawing will be $\frac{50 \times 4}{10} = \frac{200}{10} = 20$ cm tall.

LESSON 2, *pp. 46–49*

1. (4), The perimeter is $40 + 40 + 40 + 40 = 160$ yd.

2. (5), The perimeter of the plot of land is $120 + 80 + 120 + 80 = 400$ yd.

3. (1), Subtract $2 \times 16 = 32$ from 72 to get a difference of 40. Divide 40 by 2 to find a width of 20 ft.

4. (3), The perimeter of Erica's garden is $(4)(4) = 16$ ft.

5. (5), Erica will need $16 + 72 = 88$ ft of fencing.

6. (3), Solve $C = 3.14d$ for C when $d = 24$ in. to find a circumference of 75.36 in.

7. (4), The perimeter of the square piece of wood is $(4)(24) = 96$ in.

8. (2), The difference between the perimeter of the wood and the circumference of the mirror is $96 - 75.36 = 20.64$ in.

9. (2), Subtract $2 \times 12 = 24$ from 56 to get a difference of 32. Divide 32 by 2 to find a length of 16 ft.

10. (3), The perimeter of one triangle is $16 + 12 + 20 = 48$ ft.

11. (1), The total measurement of the two missing sides is $54 - (2)(16) = 22$ cm. So, the width is $22 \div 2 = 11$ cm.

12. (3), The length of one side of one triangle is $15 \div 3 = 5$ in.

13. (3), The perimeter of one triangle is $(5)(3) = 15$ in.

14. (4), The perimeter of the parallelogram is $15 + 5 + 15 + 5 = 40$ in.

15. (3), The new length will be $15 + 5 = 20$ in., and the new perimeter will be $20 + 5 + 20 + 5 = 50$ in.

16. (2), The circumference of the small triangle is $(3.14)(2)(3) = 18.84$ in.

17. (3), The diameter of the larger circle is $(2)(3 + 4) = 14$ in.

18. (5), The circumference of the larger circle is $(3.14)(14) = 43.96$ in.

19. (2), The perimeter of the triangle is $8 + 8 + 8 = 24$ ft.

20. (2), Subtract $2 \times 8 = 16$ from 36 to get a difference of 20. Divide 20 by 2 to find a width of 10 ft.

21. (4), The perimeter of the shaded area is $10 + 8 + 10 + 8 + 8 = 44$ ft.

LESSON 3, *pp. 50–53*

1. (2), There will be $(80)(60) = 4,800$ yd² of grass needed for the rectangular area.

2. (2), There will be $\frac{1}{2}(80)(60 + 105) = 6,600$ yd² of grass seed needed.

3. (4), The area of Ian's living room is $(25)(25) = 625$ ft².

4. (5), One dimension of the vent is missing, so there is not enough information.

5. (4), The area of the wall is $(10)(14) = 140$ ft².

6. (4), The combined area of the two windows is $(2)(3)(3) = 18$ ft².

7. (2), The area of the wall that will be painted is $140 - 18 = 122$ ft².

8. (4), The area of the rectangular piece of wood is $(18)(32) = 576$ in².

9. (4), The base of one triangle is $40 - 32 = 8$ in. The area of one triangle is $\frac{1}{2}(8)(18) = 72$ in². The area of both triangles is $72 + 72 = 144$ in².

10. (3), The area of the parallelogram is $(40)(18) = 720$ in².

11. (4), The total area of the backyard is $\frac{1}{2}(10)(40 + 16) = 280$ ft².

12. (1), The area of the lot that will be paved is $280 \div 2 = 140$ ft².

13. (2), The cost of pavers will be $(140)(\$3) = \$420$.

14. (5), They would spend $(\$420)(2) = \$840$ to pave their entire backyard.

15. (2), Solve $A = bh$ for b when $A = 48$ and $h = 4$ to find that $b = 12$ ft.

16. (1), The area of one triangle is $\frac{1}{2}(3)(4) = 6$ ft².

17. (3), The total area of the triangles is $\frac{1}{2}(3)(4)(2) = 12$ ft².

18. (2), The area of the shaded region is $48 - 12 = 36$ ft².

19. (4), The area of the shaded section is $\frac{1}{2}(30)(22) = 330$ ft².

20. (4), The area of the unshaded section is $(30)(22) - 330 = 330$ ft².

21. (5), The area of the entire billboard is $(30)(22) = 660$ ft².

22. (2), Solve $A = \frac{1}{2}bh$ for h when $A = 33.84$ and $b = 14.1$ to find that $h = 4.8$ cm.

LESSON 4, *pp. 54–57*

1. (2), Calculate volume to find the space inside a three-dimensional figure.

2. (3), The volume of the storage bin is $(6)(8)(12.5) = 600$ ft³.

3. (4), The volume of swimming pool A is $(15)(20)(4) = 1,200$ ft³.

4. (2), Solve $1,200 = (16)(15)x$ for x to find that $x = 5$ ft.

5. (2), The volume of her pool will be $1,200 \div 2 = 600$ ft³.

6. (4), The volume of the smallest container is $(12)(12)(12) = 1,728$ cm³.

7. (3), The difference in volume between containers A and B is $(15)(15)(24) - (12)(12)(20) = 5,400 - 2,880 = 2,520$ cm³.

8. (4), The volume of Angela's living room is $(10)(16)(14) = 2,240$ ft³.

9. (3), The volume of the room minus the sealed-off area is $2,240 - (4)(10)(14) = 1,680$ ft³.

10. (4), The volume of the box is $(3)(5)(10) = 150$ ft³.

11. (4), The volume of Box 1 is $(12.5)(12.5)(12.5) \approx 1,953.13$ cm³.

12. (1), The length of one side of Box 2 is $(2)(12.5) = 25$ cm. The area of Box 2 is $(25)(25)(25) = 15,625$ cm³.

13. (4), The difference in volume between Boxes 1 and 2 is $15,625 - 1,953.13 = 13,671.87$ cm³.

14. (5), The volume of the old toolbox is $(48)(18)(16) = 13,824$ in³.

15. (4), The volume of the new toolbox is $(54)(24)(12) = 15,552$ in³.

16. (2), The difference in volume between the old and new toolboxes is $15,552 - 13,824 = 1,728$ in³.

17. (4), The volume of Owen's garage without the addition is $(10)(12)(14) = 1,680$ ft³.

18. (2), The volume of the addition is $x^3 = 512$ ft³, and $8^3 = 512$, so $x = 8$ ft.

19. (1), The new height would be $10 - 2 = 8$ ft. So, the new volume would be $(8)(12)(14) = 1,344$ ft³.

LESSON 5, *pp. 58–61*

1. (5), The range of the data set is $9 - 1 = 8$.

2. (3), The mean of the data is $(3 + 9 + 3 + 4 + 7 + 5 + 6 + 3 + 1 + 5) \div 10 = 4.6$.

3. (1), The range of the grades is $97 - 68 = 29$.

4. (3), The score 85 is the most frequent, so it is the mode.

5. (3), Subtract Elena's grade, 75, from the median grade, 85, to find a difference of 10.

6. (1), The median for January through June is ($11,820 + $18,560) ÷ 2 = $15,190.

7. (3), The total sales for July through December is $24,450 + $22,110 + $23,450 + $19,300 + $15,340 + $16,980 = $121,630. The mean is $121,630 ÷ 6 ≈ $20,272.

8. (4), The range of sales throughout the year is $26,890 − $7,200 = $19,690.

9. (5), The range for the data set is 7.5 − 0.25 = 7.25.

10. (4), The result 5.5 occurs the most frequently, so it is the mode of the data set.

11. (3), The median number of hours is (5.5 + 6) ÷ 2 = 5.75.

12. (3), The range for the number of hours is 7 − 2.25 = 4.75.

13. (2), The median term is 1.5.

14. (4), The mean of Wednesday's data is (5 + 5.5 + 0.5 + 5 + 1) ÷ 5 = 3.4. The mean of Sunday's data is (6 + 5.5 + 3 + 7 + 7.5) ÷ 5 = 5.8. The difference is 5.8 − 3.4 = 2.4.

15. (3), The average number of points is (24 + 7 + 13 + 12 + 0 + 36) ÷ 6 ≈ 15.33.

16. (2), The median = (12 + 14) ÷ 2 = 13.

17. (3), The fastest runner is Ana because she had the lowest time.

18. (3), The median time is 23:27.

19. (1), The set where the greatest value minus the least value is equal to $6\frac{1}{2}$ is choice 1.

20. (3), The number 3 is the mode because it has the most tally marks.

21. (3), The median for the data set is 3.

22. (1), The mean for the data set is [(1)(2) + (2)(5) + (3)(7) + (4)(2) + (5)(1)] ÷ 17 ≈ 2.7.

23. (2), The mean would be [(1)(2) + (2)(5) + (3)(7) + (4)(2) + (5)(2)] ÷ 18 ≈ 2.83.

LESSON 6, *pp. 62–65*

1. (3), The sections for 1, 4, and 5 make up more than half of the spinner, so spinning one of them is likely.

2. (4), The probability of spinning a 3 is $\frac{1}{5}$.

3. (3), The probability of spinning a white or striped wedge is 6:8 = 3:4.

4. (4), The probability of spinning a red or striped wedge is $\frac{5}{8}$.

5. (2), The probability of picking one of the 5 black marbles out of 12 total marbles is $\frac{5}{12}$.

6. (3), There are now 6 striped + 4 black = 10 total marbles. The experimental probability of picking a striped marble is $\frac{6}{10}$ = 60%.

7. (2), Out of three picks, she selected a striped marble twice. The experimental probability at this point of picking a striped marble is $\frac{2}{3}$.

8. (4), The probability of selecting a red wedge or an odd number is 100%.

9. (3), Marta has 1 chance of spinning a 4 out of 6 possibilities, for a probability of 1:6.

10. (4), There are 5 chances of spinning a 6, 2, or white wedge. The probability is 5:6.

11. (1), The probability of landing on a 2 out of the 6 sides is 1:6.

12. (5), Chuck landed on 2 odd numbers in 2 rolls so the probability is 2:2 = 1:1.

13. (3), The probability of rolling an even number is $\frac{3}{6}$ = 50%.

14. (2), The probability that the next car will be blue or red is (15 + 25) ÷ (32 + 15 + 25 + 18 + 10) = 40 ÷ 100 = 0.40.

15. (2), The probability of seeing a car of a different color is $\frac{10}{100}$ = 10%.

16. (3), Black cars have been seen the most, so the probability of seeing a black car is greatest.

17. (4), Julian has picked 2 red marbles out of 3 picks, so the probability is $\frac{2}{3}$.

18. (5), There is not enough information because we do not know how many black or red marbles there are.

LESSON 7, *pp. 66–69*

1. (5), Good Morning and Puffs have the least calories.

2. (3), Puffs has the most dietary fiber with 6 g.

3. (4), Ernesto has driven 636 + 91 = 727 miles altogether.

4. (4), Ernesto will have to drive 165 + 154(3) = 627 miles.

5. (3), Between the years 1999 to 2001, the "2 to 3" category increased by 13.

6. (5), In 2003, (77 + 29 + 15) ÷ (19 + 60 + 77 + 29 + 15) = 121 ÷ 200 = 60.5% of commuters who spend 2 or more hours commuting.

7. (1), All of the categories show an increase except "1 or less."

8. (2), On Day 2, there are 90 cars, which is twice as many as bikes and motorcycles combined (20 + 25 = 45; 45 × 2 = 90).

9. (4), The data first increased from 175 to 221, and then decreased from 221 to 61.

10. (4), Solve 175 = 3x for x to find that x = 58.3. Day 5 has a total of 61.

11. (4), The percentage of employees polled that were male was $\frac{25 + 30}{15 + 30 + 25 + 30} = \frac{55}{100}$ = 55%.

12. (5), There was a percentage of $\frac{15 + 25}{100} = \frac{40}{100}$ = 40% who favored extending hours.

13. (5), There was a percentage of $\frac{30}{45}$ = 0.667 ≈ 67% of women who opposed extending hours.

14. (2), Since $\frac{40}{100}$ favor and $\frac{51}{100}$ are needed to change the hours, 11 more votes are needed.

15. (3), There were 3 + 5 = 8 bowlers who scored between 100 and 139.

16. (4), The scores between 160 and 179 are the most frequent.

17. (5), Because of how the intervals are organized, we cannot be sure of how many bowlers scored between 157 and 189.

18. (3), The percentage of bowlers who scored between 160 and 179 is $\frac{9}{3 + 5 + 8 + 9 + 5} = \frac{9}{30}$ = 30%.

19. (5), Between September and October, the sales are almost twice the July to August sales.

20. (1), The difference between the November through December sales and January through April sales is $1,141.85 − ($483.70 + $586.81) = $1,141.85 − $1,070.51 = $71.34.

21. (4), Sales at the end of the year are highest because the sales in September through December have the greatest values.

UNIT 2 *(continued)*

LESSON 8, *pp. 70–73*

1. (2), Sales changed from about $650 to $450, which is a $200 decrease.

2. (3), Hot dog sales decreased from $800 to $300, which is the greatest decrease.

3. (4), The sharpest decrease occurred from 1980 to 1990.

4. (2), The bars for 1950 and 1990 are closest in height.

5. (3), The heights of the bars increase and then decrease.

6. (4), According to the scatter plot, workers at age 55 earn the highest annual salaries.

7. (2), Up to a certain age, greater levels of experience generally lead to higher annual earnings by employees.

8. (1), Gray squirrels show the only increase.

9. (5), There is no bar for the opossum, so it was not seen in 2000.

10. (4), The striped bar for deer is the same height as the solid bar for raccoons.

11. (4), The lines almost meet in September, so the rainfall is about the same.

12. (3), The widest gap between lines is in May, so the difference between rainfalls is greatest.

13. (2), The line for Anchorage is always below the line for the United States because its rainfall is consistently lower.

14. (2), About 7,500 – 2,500 = 5,000 more women work in education.

15. (4), The bar for computer specialist is twice as tall as the bar for retail.

16. (5) There is not enough information, because this bar graph does not indicate future trends.

17. (3), The points for June through August are above 17.

18. (4), The approximate difference between the number of daylight hours in August and December is 17 – 6 = 11.

19. (2), March has about 10 hours more daylight than the 5 hours in January.

LESSON 9, *pp. 74–77*

1. (3), The section for ice cream is about half of 25%, or about 12%.

2. (4), The cheeseburger section of the graph shows about 30%, which is closest to $\frac{1}{3}$.

3. (4), Together, fuel oil and gas occupy 60% of the circle, which is greater than 50%.

4. (5), The wood stove and electricity are both used 15%.

5. (4), The percentage of the population that does not use gas is 100% – 25% = 75%.

6. (3), The Democrat section occupies half of the graph.

7. (4), The percentage of the population that voted Independent or Republican is slightly less than 50%, which is closest to 45%.

8. (3), Together, walking and running occupy half of the circle.

9. (3), Running occupies $\frac{1}{4}$ of the circle, and $\frac{4}{4} - \frac{1}{4} = \frac{3}{4}$.

10. (5), There is not enough information, since skiing is not on the graph.

11. (5), Red maples occupy more than 30% and less than 50% of the circle, so about 40%.

12. (3), Expect about (300)(0.40) = 120 red maple trees.

13. (5), The percentage of students who speak more than two languages is 25% + 40% = 65%.

14. (4), The percentage of students who do not speak Chinese is 20% + 15% = 35%.

15. (3), English is included on each section of the graph.

16. (3), Diego should spend (100)(0.25) = $25 on food.

17. (4), Diego should put (2,200)(0.05) = $110 toward savings.

18. (5), Food and rent are the two largest sections of the graph, so they make up the largest percentage.

LESSON 10, *pp. 78–81*

1. (4), There were 3.2 hours that passed between 10:28 A.M. and 1:40 P.M.

2. (1), Solve 1,190 = 3.2r for r to find that the rate is 371.9 ≈ 372.

3. (3), Solve 10 = 7t for t to find that the time it will take is 1.43 ≈ 1 hour 26 minutes. He will need to leave at 3:30 – 1:26 = 2:04 P.M.

4. (3), The distance from Cheryl's house to Bob's house is 40 + 20 = 60 miles. Solve 60 = 45t for t to find that t = 1.33 hours ≈ 1 hour 20 minutes. She will arrive at 2:30 P.M. + 1:20 = 3:50 P.M.

5. (4), Solve 40 = 50t for t to find that it took Cheryl 0.8 hour to get to Max's house. Solve 20 = 35t for t to find that it took Cheryl 0.57 hour to drive to Bob's house. Her total journey took about 0.8 + 0.5 + 0.57 = 1.87 ≈ 1 hour and 52 minutes.

6. (2), There are 4 hours and 40 minutes between 7:30 A.M. and 12:10 P.M.

7. (4), Solve $d = 65 \left(\frac{45}{60} \right)$ for d to find that he will travel 48.75 miles.

8. (4), Solve 100 = r × 1.5 for r to find that his average speed is 66.67 mph.

9. (3), Solve 20 = 18t for t to find that t = 1.111 hour ≈ 1 hour 6 minutes, which is Stacey's time.

10. (1), Solve 20 = r × 1.5 for r to find that Jared's rate was 13.33 mph. To find who rode 13.33 + 2 = 15.33 mph, solve 20 = 15.33t for t to find that t = 1.3 hours ≈ 1 hour 18 minutes, which is Hector's time.

11. (3), Stacey crossed the finish line at 2:38 – 0:24 = 2:14 P.M.

12. (2) The total travel time between Midtown and Northside is 1 hour and 25 minutes.

13. (5), Add the wait time of 1 hour 30 minutes to the travel time of 17 minutes for a total time of 1 hour 47 minutes.

14. (5), There is not enough information, because the mileage is unknown.

15. (3), Solve $5 = \frac{45}{60}r$ to find that Nick ran 6.67 mph.

16. (4) Solve 5 = 7t for t to find that t = 0.714 hour ≈ 42.8 minutes. Nick ran the course in about 43 minutes.

17. (2), Nick will finish at 11:35 A.M. + 0:43 = 11:78 = 12:18 P.M.

18. (3), Convert 1 hour 12 minutes to 1.2 hours. Solve 25 = r × 1.2 for r to find that Anna's average rate of speed is 20.8 mph.

19. (2), Convert 1 hour 4 minutes to 1.0667 hours and 1 hour 23 minutes to 1.383 hours. Solve 25 = r × 1.0667 for r to find that Hannah's average rate of speed is 23.44 mph. Solve 25 = r × 1.383 for r to find that Brian's average rate of speed is 18.08 mph. The difference is 23.44 – 18.08 = 5.36 ≈ 5.4 mph.

20. (5), Kyle crossed the finish line at 12:30 P.M. + 1:34 = 1:64 = 2:04 P.M.

UNIT 3 ALGEBRA, FUNCTIONS, AND PATTERNS

LESSON 1, *pp. 82–85*

1. (1), The change in temperature is $65 - 68 = -3°F$.
2. (5), The temperature at 8:00 P.M. would be $76 - 4 = 72°F$.
3. (3), The football team has gone $8 - 10 + 43 = 41$ yards.
4. (5) The change is $11,416 - 11,498 = -82$.
5. (4), She is at $8,453 - 2,508 + 584 = 6,529$ feet.
6. (4), The diver's position is $3 + 2 - 8 = -3$ meters.
7. (4), Deshon has a score of $-145 + 80 + 22 = -43$ points.
8. (2), Anna has a balance of $784 - (\$23 + \$69 + \$90) + \$129 = \$731$.
9. (2), Donna's score was $5 + (-10) + (-10) = -15$ points.
10. (5), Dorothy scored $15 + 5 + 0 = 20$ points. Nikki scored $0 + 10 + (-15) = -5$ points. Dorothy scored $20 - (-5) = 25$ more points than Nikki.
11. (4), The submarine's new position is $-3,290 + 589 - 4,508 = -7,209$.
12. (4), The mountain is $10,549 + 872 = 11,421$ feet above sea level.
13. (1), The balance of Jordan's account is $\$890 - (\$45 \cdot 3) = \$890 - \$135 = \$755$.
14. (4), Solve $-2x + 2 = 0$ for x to find that the original number is $x = 1$.
15. (1), The team members have $-120 \cdot 4 = -480$ points.
16. (2), The rock climbers descended 363 feet, which means they descended $363 \div 3 = 121$ feet. Since the rock climbers were descending, their change in height in each phase was -121 feet.
17. (1), Erik was $12 - 8 = 4$ miles from home.
18. (1), Don scored $-10 - 3 = -13$ points.
19. (5), The final product is $(-7)(-1)(-1)(-1) = (7)(1) = 7$.
20. (5), Since $156 is taken out of her account each month, the final product is $-\$156 \cdot 12 = -\$1,872$.
21. (3), Karen will pay her sister $\$1,554 \div 6 = \$259$.
22. (1), When Jumana deposited $25, her balance was $105. The total of the two checks was $\$75 \times 2 = \$150$. Her new balance is $\$105 - \$150 - \$25 = -\$70$.
23. (3), Janet is on floor $54 - 22 + 5 = 37$.
24. (4), Cheryl receives $\$527 \times 6 = \$3,162$.
25. (1), Connor's monthly payment is $\$3,228 \div 12 = \$269$, which is taken out of his account, so the integer is $-\$269$.
26. (2), Solve $x - (-10) = 6$ for x to find that $x = -4$.

LESSON 2, *pp. 86–89*

1. (3), Elizabeth's grandparents' house is represented by $3(29) + 23 = 110$ miles away.
2. (1), The distance to her grandparents' house is $\frac{4(7) - 3}{5} = \frac{28 - 3}{5} = \frac{25}{5} = 5$.
3. (4), Let $b =$ the number of boys; then there are $2b - 15$ girls.
4. (2), Let $a =$ the number of adult tickets; then $\frac{1}{3}a + 56 = \frac{a}{3} + 56$ represents the number of children's tickets sold.
5. (2), There are $3(12)(50)p - 1$ pencils left.
6. (5), Let Wednesday $= x$ and Thursday $= y$; then Tuesday can be described by $4(x + y)$.
7. (2), Let $y =$ the sophomore class; then the freshman class can be described by $\frac{3y}{4}$.

8. (3), The perimeter can be represented by $(2b + 1) + b + (-4 + 3b) = (2b + b + 3b) + (1 - 4) = 6b - 3$.
9. (1), Let $x + y =$ the two grandchildren together; then Nick's grandfather can use the expression $5 + 2(x + y)$ to describe his age.
10. (4), The cyclist rode $3(30) - 20 = 70$ miles on Monday.
11. (2), Simplify $3(x + 2x)$ to $3(3x)$. So $3(3 \cdot 4) = 3(12) = 36$.
12. (3), Leo is $2(23) - 21 = 46 - 21 = 25$ years old.
13. (3), The theater takes in $15(\$207) + 25(\$134) = \$3,105 + \$3,350 = \$6,455$.
14. (2), There are $\frac{1}{2}(374) + 56 = 243$ female students.
15. (5), Let $m =$ the number of men's shoes sold; then $12 + 4m$ represents the number of women's shoes sold. The value of m is unknown.
16. (3), If $b =$ the base, then $3b - 3 = h$, so $A = \frac{1}{2}b(3b - 3)$.
17. (1), Let $t = \frac{1}{2}B - 45$ and solve for B to find $B = 2t + 90$.
18. (3), The first number is represented by $\frac{1}{2}(x + y) = \frac{x + y}{2}$.
19. (4), Sean swam $2(15) - 8 = 22$ laps.
20. (5), The expression $4y - 8(3 - 2(-3))$ is equal to $4y - 8(3 - (-6)) = 4y - 8(9) = 4y - 72$.
21. (2), There were $2(45) - 34 = 56$ students who scored above average.
22. (4), Jada paid $\frac{1}{2}(\$84) - \$5 = \$37$ for gas.
23. (5), Let $\frac{x}{y}$ represent the quotient of the second and third numbers; then $3\left(\frac{x}{y}\right)$.
24. (1), The perimeter of the rectangle can be represented by $2w + 2\left(6 + \frac{2}{3}w\right) = 2w + 12 + \frac{4}{3}w = 12 + \frac{10}{3}w$.

LESSON 3, *pp. 90–93*

1. (2), The lobster price can be represented by $t = \frac{1}{3}(10) + 4$.
2. (5), Let $t =$ the price of lobster tails; then their bill is represented by $2(\$8) + 3t = \$70$. Solve for t to find that the lobster tails cost $54.
3. (5), The first number can be found by using the equation $x + 5x = 72$, which simplifies to $6x = 72$.
4. (3), The equation $r = 55 + 2g$ can be used. Let $g = \$228$ to find $r = 55 + 2(228)$.
5. (5), Let $p =$ the price before sales tax. The price of the printer can be found using $p + 0.06p = 105.97$.
6. (2), The price of the adult's admission can be found by solving $\frac{1}{2}a - 3 = 26$.
7. (1), Let $h =$ Rachel's husband's income; then together they earn $2h + h = \$1,050$, which simplifies to $3h = \$1,050$.
8. (2), Steven worked $2 + \frac{1}{3}(33) = 13$ hours.
9. (3), If the number of yards is multiplied by 36, you will find the number of inches, so $36y = i$.
10. (5), Use the formula $d = rt$ to find $60 = 15t$.
11. (3), Let $x =$ the number of miles Brian biked; then Ben biked $11 + x$ miles. So, solve $11 + x + x = 107$ for x to find that $x = 48$.
12. (2), Let $d =$ desks and $c =$ chairs. Use $12d + 20c = 1,260$. Solve for d with $c = 30$ to find that each desk cost $55.
13. (4), Solve $\$2.69x = \$53.80$ for x to find that there are 20 boxes per carton.
14. (5), Solve $x + \frac{2}{3}x = 55$ to find $x = 33$.

UNIT 3 (continued)

15. (1), Let m = the amount Karleen's mother spent; then solve $m + 65.25 + \frac{1}{4}m = 659$ for m to find that her mother spent $475. So, Karleen spent $65.25 + \frac{1}{4}(475) = \$184$.

16. (2), Solve $3(2.29) + 3.35b = 23.62$ for b to find that Emma bought 5 boxes of crackers.

17. (4), Solve $4 - 2(3x - \frac{1}{2}) = 5x - 2\frac{1}{3}$ for x to find $x = \frac{2}{3}$.

18. (3), Solve $5s + 0.87 = 15.37$ for s to find that each ice cream cone cost $2.90.

19. (1), Solve $2(49.99) - 10$ to find that the cell phone costs $89.98 at Store A.

20. (4), A children's ticket costs $2 + \frac{1}{2}(9) = \$6.50$. Solve $4(9) + 6.50c = 75$ for c to find that 6 children's tickets were purchased.

21. (2), Solve $200 + 0.15x = 300 + 0.10x$ for x to find that Juan's sales need to be $2,000.

22. (3), Let m = Michael's contribution. Solve $m + 2m - 25 = 200$ for m to find that Michael contributed $75. So, Andrew contributed $2(\$75) - \$25 = \$125$.

23. (2), Let m = Madeleine's age and solve for m to find that she is 16 years old. So, Xavier is $4 + \frac{1}{2}(16) = 12$ years old, and he will be $12 + 2 = 14$ years old in 2 years.

24. (1), Solve $s + 4s - 74 = 486$ for s to find that Beth's student loan payment is $112.

25. (3), Ann's weekly salary is $2(874) - 543 = \$1,205$.

LESSON 4, pp. 94–97

1. (2), The length of one side of Meredith's garden is $\sqrt{121} = 11$ ft.

2. (4), Meredith planted $3 \times (2.3 \times 10^3) = (3 \times 2.3) \times 10^3 = 6.9 \times 10^3$ broccoli seeds.

3. (1), Move the decimal point four places to the right to find 5.0×10^{-4}.

4. (4), There are $3 \times 3 \times 3 \times 3 = 81$ items, which is approximately 80.

5. (3), There are $\sqrt{144} = 12$ questions.

6. (3), The total number of students is $3^4 + 2^6$.

7. (4), Move the decimal point nine places to the right to find Saturn is 1,433,500,000 km from the sun.

8. (2), Jupiter is $(7.786 \times 10^8) - (1.082 \times 10^8) = (7.786 - 1.082) \times 10^8 = 6.704 \times 10^8$ km farther from the sun.

9. (2), The number rounded to the nearest hundredth is $\sqrt{7,788} = 88.24965 \approx 88.25$.

10. (3), The volume of the cube is $(29)(29)(29) = 24,389$ cm³.

11. (1), Since any number raised to the zero power is equal to 1, $4^0 = 5^0$.

12. (3), The number with the greatest power of ten is Jupiter.

13. (1), The numbers with the least power of ten are Mercury, 3.3×10^{23}, and Mars, 6.42×10^{23}. Since $3.3 < 6.42$, Mercury has the least mass.

14. (1), Divide the masses: $\frac{1.899 \times 10^{27}}{6.42 \times 10^{23}} = 0.29 \times 10^4$. Round 0.29 to 0.3 and then write the answer in scientific notation, 3.0×10^3.

15. (4), Multiply each term in the parentheses by $4x$ to find that $4x(x^2 + 2y) = 4x^3 + 8xy$.

16. (3), Since 10 is to the fifth power, place 5 zeros after 1 to find that $10^5 = 100,000$.

17. (2), The expression b^{-4} is equal to $\frac{1}{b^4}$.

18. (2), The length of the square is $\sqrt{6.7} \approx 2.6$.

19. (5), Move the decimal point the left 10 spaces to find that the marbled lungfish weighs 0.00000000013283 grams.

20. (2), The square root of 25 is 5, and the square root of 36 is 6. Since 33 falls between 25 and 36, the square root of 33 falls between 5 and 6.

21. (3), Move the decimal point nine places to the left to find 4.435×10^9.

22. (3), When the decimal point is moved one place to the left, the exponent becomes one digit greater, so $4.404 \times 10^9 = 0.4404 \times 10^{10}$.

23. (4), Since $81 = 9 \times 9 = 3 \times 3 \times 3 \times 3$, $x = 4$.

24. (3), The area of the square is $7.8^2 = 60.84$ sq in.

25. (3), The number of students at Sunnyside High School is $3 \times 2^9 = 3 \times 512 = 1,536$.

26. (2), The volume of the cube is $15^3 = 3,375$ cm³.

27. (2), A negative × a negative = a positive. A negative × a negative × a negative = a negative. So, if x equals an even number, the answer will be positive.

LESSON 5, pp. 98–101

1. (4), As t increases by 1, d increases by 60, so $260 + 60 = 320$ km.

2. (1), To find d when $t = 0$, find $80 - 60$. So, $d = 20$ km.

3. (1), To find y, multiply x by 3 and then subtract 2 from the product, so $y = 3x - 2$.

4. (3), Solve $y = 3x - 2$ with $x = 6$ to find that $y = 16$.

5. (3), Multiply the previous term by 2 to get the next term.

6. (2), Multiply 27 by 3 to get 81, and then multiply 81 by 3 to find that the sixth term is 243.

7. (2), The pattern is $1^2, 2^2, 3^2, 4^2,\ldots$ So, the next term is $5^2 = 25$.

8. (1), Multiply the previous term by 2 to get the next term, so $-80 \times 2 = -160$.

9. (4), Let $x = 1$; then $50 - 1^2 = 49$.

10. (5), Solve $1 = \frac{1}{2}x$ for x to find that $x = 2$.

11. (2), The pattern is subtract 2. Since $5 - 2 = 3$ and $3 - 2 = 1$, the fifth term will be 1.

12. (2), The pattern is subtract 3, so the sixth term is $-15 - 3 = -18$, and the seventh term is $-18 - 3 = -21$.

13. (5), For $f(x) < 1$, x must be greater than 8. So, $x = 9$.

14. (3), The next term of the sequence has 16 triangles.

15. (4), Solve $250 = 1,000(r)(5)$ for r to find that the rate is $0.05 = 5\%$.

16. (5), Solve $220 = 55t$ for t to find that $t = 4$.

17. (4), Solve $I = 0.01(5,000)$ to find that there is an increase of 50 people.

18. (5), Solve $80 = \frac{9}{5}C + 32$ for C to find that $80°F \approx 26.7°C$.

19. (4), The equation $h = d - 0.2d^2$ works for each point.

20. (5), Solve $h = 5 - 0.2(5)^2$ for h to find that the height is 0 meters.

21. (4), Kara's answer was $3(1^2) + 1 = 4$. Solve $4 = 3x^2 + 1$ for x to find that another value of x is -1.

22. (1), For the function $y = x^3$, $1 = 1^3$.

23. (2), The rule is multiply by -2, so the eighth term is -256.

24. (5), Since $y = x^2$, we know that $x^2 = 4$, so $x = 2$.

25. (2), As d increases by 10, p increases by 14.7. To get p, multiply by 1.47, and then add 14.7 to the product. So, $p = 1.47d + 14.7$ or $p = \frac{14.7d}{10} + 14.7$.

UNIT 3 (continued)

LESSON 6, pp. 102–105

1. (2), Since $A = lw$, $48 = w(w - 2)$, which is equal to $48 = w^2 - 2w$.

2. (4), Factor $48 = w^2 - 2w$ to find that $w = -6$ or 8, and since distance cannot be negative, the distance is 8 ft.

3. (3), Use FOIL to find $(x + 5)(x - 4) = x^2 + x - 20$.

4. (4), Use FOIL to find that the area is $(x - 4)(x - 4) = x^2 - 8x + 16$.

5. (2), Let $x =$ the number of pencils per student; then there are $(x - 5)x$ pencils in all.

6. (1), Factor $x^2 - 4x - 21$ to find $(x - 7)(x + 3)$.

7. (5), Factor $x^2 + 8x - 20$ to find $(x - 2)(x + 10)$.

8. (1), Factor $x^2 - 5x - 6$ to find $(x - 6)(x + 1)$.

9. (2), Factor $x^2 - 7x - 30$ to find $(x - 10)(x + 3)$.

10. (1), $A = lw$, so $(x + 2)(x - 5) = x^2 - 3x - 10$.

11. (4), Factor $x^2 - 16$ to find that $x = 4$ and $x = -4$.

12. (2), Factor $x^2 + 6x + 9$ to find $(x + 3)(x + 3)$. So, each side is represented by $(x + 3)$.

13. (2), If the product of two consecutive integers is 42, then $x(x + 1) = 42$. So, the equation is $x^2 + x - 42 = 0$.

14. (4), Use FOIL to find that $(x + 4)(x + 4) = x^2 + 8x + 16$. Set the expression equal to 49 to find that $x^2 + 8x - 33 = (x + 11)(x - 3)$. So, $x = -11$ and $x = 3$. Since length cannot be negative, use $x = 3$.

15. (4), Solve $x^2 + (x + 1)^2 = 113$ for x to find that $x = -8$ and $x = 7$. All answers are positive, so 7 and 8.

16. (4), Solve $x(x + 2) = 35$ for x to find that $x = -7$ and $x = 5$. Since the product is 35, the factors must be positive. So, 5 is the first integer and $x + 2 = 7$ is the second integer.

17. (3), Use FOIL to find that $(x - 3)(x - 3) = 81$ is equivalent to $x^2 - 6x - 72 = (x + 6)(x - 12)$. So, $x = -6$ and $x = 12$.

18. (1), Multiply x by $2x$ and set the expression equal to 32 to find $2x^2 - 32 = 0$.

19. (4), Factor $2x^2 - 32 = 0$ to find that $x = 4$ and $x = -4$. The lengths of the sides are 4 m and $2(4) = 8$ m.

20. (4), Solve $0 = t^2 - 2t - 8$ for t to find $t = -2$ and $t = 4$.

21. (2), Solve $x(x + 1) = 110$ for x to find $x = -11$ and $x = 10$. So, $x = -11$ and -10.

22. (1), Use FOIL and then solve $x^2 + 7x - 8x - 56 - 4x + 4$ and simplify to $x^2 - 5x - 52$.

23. (4), Solve $x(x + 2) = 10 + 5(x + x + 2)$ for x to find the positive value of x is 10, so $x + 2 = 12$.

24. (1), Solve $x(2x + 4) = 160$ for x to find $x = -10$ and $x = 8$.

25. (4), Multiply x by $x + 2$ and set the expression equal to 48 to find $x^2 + 2x - 48 = 0$.

26. (4), Solve $x(x + 1) = 12$ for x to find $x = -4$ and $x = 3$. The answer is -4 and -3.

27. (3), Divide both sides of the equation by 2 to find $x^2 - 4x - 5$. Factor to find $x = -1$ and $x = 5$.

28. (1), Solve $(x - 2)(x - 2) = 64$ for x to find $x = -6$ and $x = 10$.

29. (1), Solve $w(w + 8) = 84$ for w to find $w = -14$ and $w = 6$.

30. (3), The length is $w + 8 = 6 + 8 = 14$ ft.

LESSON 7, pp. 106–109

1. (5), To find the minimum width of plywood, use $25w \geq 100$.

2. (3), Divide both sides by 25 to find $w \geq 4$.

3. (2), –3 and all numbers greater are plotted.

4. (5), Subtract 5 from both sides to find $x < 9$.

5. (3), The expression $x \geq 3$ uses a closed circle because it is greater than *or* equal to.

6. (4), Solve for x to find $x \geq 3$.

7. (2), Solve for x to find $-\frac{1}{3} \geq x$ or $x \leq -\frac{1}{3}$.

8. (5), The numbers –1 and lower are graphed, so $x \leq -1$.

9. (1), Solve for x to find $x \geq 11$.

10. (1), The situation is represented by the inequality $4x + 3 > 5x - 2$.

11. (3), Solve $12 + 0.10x \leq 25$ for x to find $x \leq 130$.

12. (3), Solve $3g > 9$ for g to find $g > 3$, so the lowest price is $3.01.

13. (4), Solve $\frac{45 + 38 + 47 + x}{4} \geq 44$ for x to find $x \geq 46$.

14. (5), Solve $\frac{450 + 550 + x}{3} \geq 600$ for x to find $x \geq 800$.

15. (2), Solve $15 + 0.75x \leq 25$ for x to find the possible number of games Cole can play.

16. (5), Add 156 to both sides to find that $x < 190$.

17. (4), Solve $1,500 + 0.03x \geq 3,000$ for x to find $x \geq 50,000$.

18. (2), Solve $\frac{14,000 + 9,000 + x}{3} > 10,000$ for x to find $x > 7,000$.

19. (4), Solve $1.60 + 0.95x \leq 4.50$ for x to find $x \leq 3.05$. Then add the quantities of the differently priced packages to arrive at the answer.

20. (2), Solve $b + 2.5b \leq 157.50$ for b to find $b \leq 45$.

21. (1), Solve $m + 3m - 400 < 2,000$ for m to find $m < 600$.

22. (3), Solve $\frac{0.266 + x}{2} > 0.300$ for x to find $x \geq 0.334$.

23. (3), Solve $2x - 30 \leq 100$ for x to find $x \leq 65$.

24. (1), Let $y =$ the second round. Then $y < 2(10)$, so $y < 20$.

25. (4), Solve $3x < 45$ to find $x < 15$, so the greatest amount is $14.99.

26. (4), Solve $\frac{78 + 85 + 82 + 74 + x}{5} \geq 80$ for x to find $x \geq 81$.

LESSON 8, pp. 110–113

1. (4), Point G is 3 units right and 3 units down, so $(3, -3)$.

2. (4), Point G would move 6 units up to $(3, 3)$.

3. (5), Point D is 2 units right and 5 units up, so $(2, 5)$.

4. (2), Six units down from point C is $(1, -5)$.

5. (2), To get from point F to point E, move 3 units down and 2 units left. So, move 3 units down and 2 units left from point C to find the point with coordinates $(-1, -2)$.

6. (1), Point D would be $(2 + 2, 5 - 5)$, so $(4, 0)$.

7. (5), Point C would be 1 unit below the x-axis instead of 1 unit above, so $(1, -1)$.

8. (3), Quadrant 2 has negative x-coordinates and positive y-coordinates, so $(-2, 5)$.

9. (1), Frank landed at $(4 + 2, -3 - 1) = (6, -4)$.

10. (3), The y-coordinate would decrease by 3, so $(x, -6 - 3) = (x, -9)$.

11. (2), The new location of point M is $(-3 + 3, -2 + 2) = (0, 0)$.

12. (3), Point M is moved 4 units right and 4 units up.

13. (3), Point K will be 1 unit to the left of the y-axis instead of 1 unit to the right, so $(-1, 2)$.

14. (4), Quadrant 3 has negative x- and y-coordinates, so $(-3, -2)$.

15. (1), The bottom point should be 3 units down from the top, so $(-3, -5)$.

16. (5), When the dots are connected, they form a right triangle.

UNIT 3 (continued)

17. (5), To move from point S to point P, move left 2 units and up 2 units. If rotated, move right 2 units and down 2 units.
18. (5), The location of point P' would be $(-4, 4 - 4) = (-4, 0)$.
19. (3), The point would be 5 units to the left of the y-axis, so $(-5, -2)$.
20. (1), $\overline{WZ}$ would be 6 units long instead of 3 units. Six units to the right of W is $(-2 + 6, 2) = (4, 2)$.
21. (2), $\overline{ZY}$ would be 1 unit long instead of 3 units long. So, 1 unit down from $(1, 2)$ is $(1, 1)$.

LESSON 9, pp. 114–117

1. (2), The x- and y-coordinates are always opposites, and the sum of opposites is zero, so $x + y = 0$.
2. (3), Use the distance formula to find $\sqrt{(2 - (-3))^2 + (-2 - 3)^2} = \sqrt{50} \approx 7.1$.
3. (3), The ordered pair whose x-value is double the y-value is $(4, 2)$.
4. (1), Solve $-2 = y + 1$ to find $y = -3$.
5. (2), Solve $2x + 2(-3) = -8$ to find $x = -1$.
6. (5), The graph would pass through $(2, -2)$ because $-2 = 4 - 3(2)$ is true.
7. (1), Solve $3x - 1 = 5$ to find $x = 2$.
8. (3), For the equation $x + 2y = 2$, when $x = 0$, $y = 1$. The only line that passes through $(0, 1)$ is choice 3.
9. (4), Use the distance formula to find $\sqrt{(4 - 0)^2 + (7 - 0)^2} = \sqrt{65} \approx 8.1$.
10. (5), The x- and y-values of each point have a sum of 5, so $x + y = 5$.
11. (1), Use the distance formula to find $\sqrt{(-3 + 2)^2 + (-8 + 5)^2} = \sqrt{10} \approx 3.2$.
12. (1), The graph would pass through $(1, -3)$ because $-3 = -2(1) - 1$ is true.
13. (3), Use the distance formula to find $\sqrt{(-2 - (-4))^2 + (-4 - 3)^2} = \sqrt{53} \approx 7.3$.
14. (3), Use the distance formula to find $\sqrt{(4 - (-4))^2 + (4 - 3)^2} = \sqrt{65} \approx 8.1$.
15. (4) Find QR: $\sqrt{(4 - (-2))^2 + (4 - (-4))^2} = \sqrt{100} = 10$. Add all sides to find the perimeter is $7.3 + 8.1 + 10 = 25.4$.
16. (5), Ordered pair $(4, 5)$ is a solution because $2(4) - 3 = 5$ is true.
17. (3), The line contains the points $(0, 1)$ and $(1, 3)$. Both points satisfy the equation $2x + 1 = y$.
18. (5), Point $(3, -2)$ is found on the graph because $-2 = 4 - 2(3)$ is true.
19. (3), Use the distance formula to find $\sqrt{(4 - 2)^2 + (0 - 4)^2} = \sqrt{20} \approx 4.5$.
20. (4), Count 7 units up, so the police officer drove 7 miles straight north.
21. (2), Use the distance formula to find $\sqrt{(5 - (-5))^2 + (5 - 1)^2} = \sqrt{116} \approx 10.8$.

LESSON 10, pp. 118–121

1. (4), The slope of line G is $\dfrac{\text{rise}}{\text{run}} = \dfrac{3}{6} = \dfrac{1}{2}$.
2. (3), The y-intercept is 2, so the equation of the line is $y = \dfrac{1}{2}x + 2$.

3. (1), The slope of line H is $\dfrac{3 - 4}{2 - (-4)} = \dfrac{-1}{6}$.
4. (2), The slope of the line is $\dfrac{-4 - (-2)}{-3 - (-1)} = \dfrac{-2}{-2} = 1$.
5. (2), The only graph with a slope of $\dfrac{1}{2}$ is $y = \dfrac{1}{2}x - 3$.
6. (3), Solve $-2 = -1(4) + b$ to find that $b = 2$. So, the equation is $y = -x + 2$. If $x = 2$, then $y = 0$, so $(0, 2)$.
7. (1), The y-intercept is $y = 3$, and the slope is $\dfrac{\text{rise}}{\text{run}} = \dfrac{4}{-10} = -\dfrac{2}{5}$. So, the equation is $y = -\dfrac{2}{5}x + 3$.
8. (5), Solve $1 = 2(4) + b$ to find $b = -7$, so $y = 2x - 7$.
9. (4), The initial fee $= b = \$20$, and the slope is $\dfrac{\text{rise}}{\text{run}} = \dfrac{30}{1} = 30$. So, $y = 30x + 20$.
10. (2), The slope of line T is $\dfrac{-2 - (-3)}{3 - (-3)} = \dfrac{1}{6}$.
11. (4), Solve $\dfrac{1}{3} = \dfrac{4}{x}$ for x to find that $x = 12$. The span is $12 \times 2 = 24$.
12. (1), Solve $-3 = -\dfrac{1}{2}(-4) + b$ to find $b = -5$. So, $y = -\dfrac{1}{2}x - 5$.
13. (4), Line D is the only line that rises from left to right.
14. (5), Line E is the only horizontal line.
15. (3), Line C is the only vertical line.
16. (1), Lines A and B are always an equal distance apart.
17. (1), The slope would be $\dfrac{-3 - 3}{-2 - (-4)} = \dfrac{-6}{2} = -3$.
18. (5), The only line with slope $\dfrac{1 - (-3)}{3 - (-2)} = \dfrac{4}{5}$ is $y = \dfrac{4}{5}x - 2$.
19. (4), The slope would be $\dfrac{1 - 3}{3 - (-4)} = \dfrac{-2}{7}$.

UNIT 4 GEOMETRY

LESSON 1, pp. 122–125

1. (3), $\angle JKL$ and $\angle MKL$ are complementary, so $90° - 30° = 60°$.
2. (4), $\angle MKN$ is a straight angle, which has a measure of $180°$.
3. (2), $\angle 2$ and $\angle 4$ are vertical, so they are congruent.
4. (5), $\angle 1$ and $\angle 3$ are vertical angles.
5. (4), $\angle 3$ and $\angle 4$ are supplementary, so $180° - 52° = 128°$.
6. (4), If two angles are congruent and complementary, then one angle has a measure of $90° \div 2 = 45°$. The supplement is $180° - 45° = 135°$.
7. (2), The angles are supplementary, so $180° - 115° = 65°$.
8. (3), The measures of $\angle DBA$, $\angle ABC$, and $\angle CBE$ have a sum of $180°$; $180° - 90° = 90°$, and $90° \div 2 = 45°$.
9. (4), $m\angle CBA + m\angle ABD = m\angle CBD$, so $m\angle CBD = 90° + 45° = 135°$.
10. (4), If $b = $ the measure of $\angle B$, solve $b + 20 + 3b = 180$ for b to find that $b = 40°$. Then $m\angle A = 180° - 40° = 140°$.
11. (4), $\angle 2$ and $\angle 3$ are adjacent and supplementary because they share a side and have measures that add up to $180°$.
12. (3), $\angle 7$ and $\angle 8$ are supplementary; $180° - 60° = 120°$.
13. (3), $\angle 6$ is an exterior angle and is on the other side of the transversal from $\angle 4$.
14. (5), $\angle 3$ and $\angle 7$ are corresponding because they are in the same relative position.
15. (1), $\overline{EJ}$ and $\overline{EF}$ form the angle, so it is called $\angle JEF$.
16. (5), We do not have enough information.
17. (2), $m\angle 1 + m\angle 2 = 90°$, so they are complementary.
18. (4), $\angle 1$ and $\angle 2$ are supplementary, so $m\angle 2 = 180° - 35° = 145°$; $145° + 145° = 290°$.

UNIT 4 (continued)

19. (4), ∠1 and ∠2 are supplementary, and ∠3 and ∠4 are supplementary, so 180° + 180° = 360°.
20. (4), ∠4 and ∠3 are supplementary, so 180° – 30° = 150°.
21. (3), Each angle is 90°, so 90° + 90° = 180°.
22. (1), Figure A shows perpendicular lines, which form two adjacent 90° angles.
23. (4), Figure D shows a right angle split into two angles.
24. (5), Figure E shows at least one pair of vertical angles.

LESSON 2, pp. 126–129

1. (3), To find y, subtract 70° from 180° to find 110°.
2. (2), The 85° angle and x are alternate interior angles, so they are congruent.
3. (2), $x = 70°$, because opposite angles of parallelograms are congruent.
4. (3), Two side-by-side angles of a parallelogram have measures that sum to 180°, so $y = 180° – 70° = 110°$.
5. (1), Opposite angles of parallelograms are congruent, so the missing angle is 110°.
6. (4), The measure of the obtuse angle is 180° – 45° – 35° = 100°.
7. (2), All rectangles have four 90° angles.
8. (3), The measure of the obtuse angle is 180° – 35° – 35° = 110°.
9. (2), A right triangle has one 90° angle, so 180° – 90° – 40° = 50°.
10. (2), A right angle has a measure of 90°, so half the measure would be 45°; 180° – 90° – 45° = 45°.
11. (3), m∠XYZ = 180° – 130° = 50°, and m∠Y = 90°; 180° – 50° – 90° = 40°. The larger acute angle is 50°.
12. (4), Subtract 40° from 90° to get 50°.
13. (1), The angle has a measure of 180° – 90° – 60° = 30°.
14. (5), ∠KLJ ≅ ∠LHI because they are corresponding angles, so the angle measure is 60°.
15. (4), The top and bottom sides are parallel, which are $\overline{LM}$ and $\overline{NO}$.
16. (4), The sum of the measures of the interior angles of any quadrilateral is 360°.
17. (3), Since ∠R ≅ ∠Q and ∠T ≅ ∠S, 360° – 105° – 105° = 150°, and 150° ÷ 2 = 75°.
18. (2), The sum of the measures of the interior angles of a triangle is 180°, which also is the measure of a straight angle.
19. (2), An isosceles right triangle has one right angle and two congruent acute angles; 180° – 90° = 90°, and 90° ÷ 2 = 45°.
20. (1), ∠BDC ≅ ∠BEF because they are corresponding angles.
21. (2), ∠FCD ≅ ∠BFE because they are corresponding angles.
22. (4), The measure is 120° because 360° – 90° – 90° – 60° = 120°.

LESSON 3, pp. 130–133

1. (1), $\overline{JK} \cong \overline{TU}$ because corresponding parts of congruent figures are congruent.
2. (3), $\overline{KJ} \cong \overline{VW}$, so m$\overline{VW}$ = 12 cm.
3. (1), ∠L ≅ ∠F because they are corresponding parts.
4. (4), $\overline{CF}$ corresponds to $\overline{ML}$.
5. (4), The perimeter is 4.5 + 4.5 + 4.5 + 2 = 15.5 cm.
6. (3), ∠A ≅ ∠H because corresponding angles of similar figures are congruent.

7. (2), The sides of Triangle 2 are half the length of the sides of Triangle 1. The measure of $\overline{AC}$ is 1.5 in., so the corresponding side is 1.5 ÷ 2 = 0.75 in.
8. (5), We do not know the measure of $\overline{AB}$, and the Pythagorean theorem has not yet been introduced.
9. (3), Answer choice 3 states that the two right triangles are similar.
10. (4), Corresponding sides of similar figures are proportional, and corresponding angles are congruent.
11. (3), An obtuse triangle cannot have a right angle; triangles can be either obtuse, right, or acute.
12. (2), Find 180° – 75° – 45° to find a difference of 60°.
13. (3), ∠I ≅ ∠C because corresponding angles of similar triangles are congruent.
14. (5), We do not have enough information.
15. (3), $\overline{HI}$ corresponds to $\overline{CD}$, so m$\overline{CD}$ = 20 m.
16. (2), Find 180° – 75° – 75° to find a difference of 30°.
17. (3), The perimeter is 20 + 20 + 5 = 45 m.
18. (4), Multiply 18 by $\frac{2}{3}$: $\frac{18}{1} \times \frac{2}{3} = \frac{6}{1} \times \frac{2}{1} = 12$.
19. (1), The width of the smaller carpet is $\frac{9}{1} \times \frac{2}{3} = \frac{3}{1} \times \frac{2}{1} = 6$. The difference in areas is (18 × 9) – (12 × 6), or 162 – 72 = 90 sq ft.

LESSON 4, pp. 134–137

1. (3), Solve $\frac{1 \text{ in.}}{5 \text{ ft}} = \frac{x}{8 \text{ ft}}$ to find that x = 1.6 in.
2. (4), Use proportions to find that the length is 20 ft and the width is 15 ft, so the area is 300 sq ft.
3. (4), Solve $\frac{6}{4} = \frac{x}{12}$ to find that x = 18 in.
4. (5), Solve $\frac{1 \text{ in.}}{5.5 \text{ mi}} = \frac{3.5 \text{ in.}}{x}$ to find that x = 19.25 miles.
5. (1), Solve $\frac{1 \text{ in.}}{25 \text{ mi}} = \frac{x}{350 \text{ mi}}$ to find that x = 14 miles.
6. (4), Solve $\frac{2 \text{ cm}}{6.5 \text{ km}} = \frac{3.25 \text{ cm}}{x}$ to find that $x \approx$ 10.6 km.
7. (5), Blue Harbor to Dodgeville through Westfield is a map distance of 6.25 cm, but through Crawford is a map distance of 6 cm. The difference is 0.25 cm. Solve $\frac{2 \text{ cm}}{6.5 \text{ km}} = \frac{0.25 \text{ cm}}{x}$ to find that $x \approx$ 0.81 km.
8. (4), Solve $\frac{0.5 \text{ in.}}{5 \text{ ft}} = \frac{1.5 \text{ in.}}{x}$ and $\frac{0.5 \text{ in.}}{5 \text{ ft}} = \frac{1 \text{ in.}}{x}$ to find that the dimensions are 15 ft and 10 ft.
9. (1), Note that $\frac{7}{8}$ = 7 ÷ 8 = 0.875. Solve $\frac{0.5 \text{ in.}}{5 \text{ ft}} = \frac{0.875 \text{ in.}}{x}$ to find that x = 8.75 ft, which also equals $8\frac{3}{4}$ ft.
10. (1), Solve $\frac{0.5 \text{ in.}}{5 \text{ ft}} = \frac{0.75 \text{ in.}}{x}$ to find that the width is 7.5, or $7\frac{1}{2}$, ft. From question 9, the length is $8\frac{3}{4}$ ft.
11. (3), Solve $\frac{2 \text{ in.}}{3.2 \text{ mi}} = \frac{x}{19.2 \text{ mi}}$ to find that x = 12 in.
12. (2), Solve $\frac{48 \text{ km}}{4 \text{ cm}} = \frac{x}{1 \text{ cm}}$ to find that x = 12 km; the scale is 1 cm : 12 km.
13. (5), Solve $\frac{22}{31.9} = \frac{55}{x}$ to find that x = 79.75 ft, which rounds to 79.8 ft.
14. (1), Solve $\frac{4.2}{3.8} = \frac{x}{6.8}$ to find that $x \approx$ 7.5 ft.
15. (3), Solve $\frac{1}{32} = \frac{x}{108.8}$ to find that x = 3.4 in.
16. (5), Use two proportions to find that the shorter side is 13.5 ft, and the longer side is 18.75 ft. The area is 13.5 × 18.75 = 253.125 sq ft.

UNIT 4 (continued)

17. (2), Solve $\frac{3\text{ cm}}{18.6\text{ km}} = \frac{10\text{ cm}}{x}$ to find that Stacey drove 62 km. Use $d = rt$ to find that Stacey drove for about 0.689 hours, or about $0.689 \times 60 = 41.3$ minutes.

18. (4), A square has four congruent sides. If the perimeter is 22 cm, then each side is $22 \div 4 = 5.5$ cm long. Solve $\frac{2\text{ cm}}{5\text{ yd}} = \frac{5.5\text{ cm}}{x}$ to find that $x = 13.75$ yd.

19. (3), Solve $\frac{3\text{ in.}}{30\text{ ft}} = \frac{1\text{ in.}}{x}$ to find that $x = 10$ ft, so the scale is 1 in. : 10 ft.

20. (5), Solve $\frac{0.5\text{ in.}}{6.5\text{ ft}} = \frac{1\text{ in.}}{x}$ to find that both the length and width are 13 ft.

LESSON 5, pp. 138–141

1. (4), Using the formula for circumference, solve $25.9 = 3.14d$ to find that $d \approx 8.248$ in.

2. (3), Multiply 35 stones by a diameter of 8.25 in. to get a total length of 288.75 in. Divide 288.75 in. by 12 in. per foot to get a quotient of 24 ft.

3. (2), Solve $C = 3.14(30)$ to find that the circumference is 94.2 in.

4. (4), The radius is $132 \div 2$, or 66 cm. Solve $A = 3.14 \times 66^2$ to find an area of 13,677.84 sq cm, which rounds to 13,678 sq cm.

5. (4), The radius is $12 \div 2$, or 6, ft. Solve $A = 3.14 \times 6^2$ to find an area of 113.04 sq ft.

6. (1), Find $11 - 2 - 2 = 7$, which is the diameter of the mirror without the frame. If $d = 7$, then $r = 3.5$.

7. (2), Solve $A = 3.14 \times 3.5^2$ to find an area of 38.465 sq in, which rounds to 38.4 sq in.

8. (3), Subtract the area of the mirror from the area of the entire frame and mirror: $(3.14 \times 5.5^2) - 38.465 = 56.52$ sq in.

9. (1), The circumference is $3.14 \times 11 = 34.54$ in.

10. (3), The tablecloth is $3.14 \times 4^2 = 50.24$ sq ft.

11. (1), Subtract the area of the table from the area of the tablecloth: $50.24 - 3.14 \times 3^2 = 50.24 - 28.26 = 21.98$ sq ft.

12. (4), The diameter will be $15 + 2 + 2 = 19$ in., so the radius will be 9.5 in. The area is $3.14 \times 9.5^2 = 283.385$ sq in. , which rounds to 283.4 sq in.

13. (5), Subtract the area of the small circle from the area of the large circle: $(3.14 \times 4^2) - (3.14 \times 3^2) = 50.24 - 28.26 = 21.98$ sq in, which rounds to 283.4 sq in.

14. (5), The area is $3.14 \times 0.5^2 = 0.785$ sq ft, which rounds to 0.79 sq ft.

15. (1), Divide the area of the circle by the area of the rectangle, and multiply by 100: $0.785 \div (2 \times 3) \approx 0.13$, and $0.13 \times 100 = 13\%$.

16. (2), Divide the area of the large circle by the area of the small circle: $(3.14 \times 6^2) \div (3.14 \times 2^2) = 113.04 \div 12.56 = 9$.

17. (4), Since $A = 3.14 \times r^2$, and $A = 144(3.14)$, solve $144(3.14) = 3.14r^2$ for r to find that $r = 12$ ft. If $r = 12$, then $d = 24$, and $C = 3.14 \times 24 = 75.36$ ft.

18. (3), Solve $19.625 = 3.14\,r^2$ for r to find that $r = 2.5$. If $r = 2.5$, then $d = 5$ cm.

19. (5), The circumference is $3.14 \times 3.5 = 10.99$, so the circumference of both tires is $10.99 \times 2 = 21.98$ in.

20. (3), Add the areas of the two circles: $(3.14 \times 7.5^2) + (3.14 \times 5^2) = 176.625 + 78.5 = 255.125$ sq m, which rounds to 255 sq m.

21. (4), The diameter of the small section would increase to 10.45 m, which gives a radius of 5.225 m. Add the two areas: $(3.14 \times 7.5^2) + (3.14 \times 5.225^2) \approx 176.625 + 85.724 = 262.349$ sq m, which rounds to 262.35 sq m.

22. (1), Solve $25.12 = 3.14d$ to find that $d = 8$, so $r = 4$ in.

23. (3), The circumference is $3.14 \times 6 = 18.84$ in.

LESSON 6, pp. 142–145

1. (4), Determine the volume of Pool A by using the formula for the volume of a cylinder: $V = 3.14 \times 10^2 \times 4 = 1{,}256$ ft³.

2. (2), The volume of Pool B is 1,256 because the pools have the same volume. Solve $1{,}256 = 3.14(8^2)h$ to find that $h = 6.25$ ft.

3. (4), Use the formula for the volume of a cylinder: $V = 3.14 \times 1.5^2 \times 10 = 70.65$ cubic inches.

4. (1), Since the question asks for the volume in cubic feet, rename 18 in. as 1.5 ft. The volume is $1.5 \times 1.5 \times 1.5 = 3.375$ ft³, which rounds to 3 ft³.

5. (1), The (base edge)² would be 36, so $V = \frac{1}{3} \times 36 \times 9 = 108$ cm³.

6. (2), Solve $97.5 = 2.5(13)l$ to find that $l = 3$ cm.

7. (2), The volume is $V = \frac{1}{3} \times 3.14 \times 3^2 \times 10 = 94.2$ cm³, which rounds to 94 cm³.

8. (3), Subtract the volume of the medium from the volume of the large. The large is $V = \frac{1}{3} \times 3.14 \times 5^2 \times 14 \approx 366.33$, and the medium is $V = \frac{1}{3} \times 3.14 \times 4^2 \times 12 = 200.96$, so $366.33 - 200.96 = 165.37$ cm³, which rounds to 165 cm³.

9. (1), From question 7, the volume of the original small is 94.2 cm³. The volume of the replacement is $V = \frac{1}{3} \times 3.14 \times 2.5^2 \times 9 = 58.875$, so $94.2 - 58.875 = 35.325$, which rounds to 35 cm³.

10. (2), Divide the volume of the full tank by 2: $V = 24 \times 10 \times 15 = 3{,}600$, and $3{,}600 \div 2 = 1{,}800$ in³.

11. (2), The height of the water would be $15 - 1 = 14$ in., and the volume would be $V = 24 \times 10 \times 14 = 3{,}360$ in³.

12. (5), The volume of a cup would be $V = 3.14 \times 3.5^2 \times 10 = 384.65$ cm³, which rounds to 384.7 cm³.

13. (3), The volume is $V = \frac{1}{3} \times 6^2 \times 7 = 84$ cubic feet.

14. (4), The volume is $V = \frac{1}{3} \times 10^2 \times 6 = 200$ cubic feet.

15. (2), The difference is $200 - 84 = 116$ cubic feet.

16. (3), Solve $28.26 = 3.14 \times 1.5^2 \times h$ to find that $h = 4$ in.

17. (2), The volume of the box is $V = 18 \times 10 \times 28 = 5{,}040$ in³. The volume of one can is $V = 3.14 \times 2^2 \times 5 = 62.8$ in³, so $5{,}040 - (40 \times 62.8) = 2{,}528$ in³.

18. (3), The height of the soil is $24 - 3$, or 21, in. The volume of the soil is $V = 3.14 \times 9^2 \times 21 = 5{,}341.14$ in³, which rounds to 5,340 in³.

19. (5), The radius is unknown, so we cannot determine the height.

20. (2), Rename the side length as 2.5 ft, and the height as 3.25 ft. The volume is $V = \frac{1}{3} \times 2.5^2 \times 3.25 = 6.7708$ cubic feet, which rounds to 7 cubic feet.

21. (4), Solve $803.84 = \frac{1}{3}(3.14)(8^2)h$ to find that $h = 12$ ft.

UNIT 4 *(continued)*

LESSON 7, *pp. 146–149*

1. (3), The perimeter is $12 + 20 + 21 + 20 + 12 + 8 + 21 + 8 = 122$ ft.

2. (4), Add the areas of the two triangles and the rectangle. One triangle has an area of $A = \frac{1}{2} \times 12 \times 16 = 96$, so two triangles = 192 sq ft. The rectangle is $21 \times 8 = 168$ sq ft, so the total area is $192 + 168 = 360$ sq ft.

3. (3), Divide the figure into three horizontal rectangles. The top is $20 \times 5 = 100$ sq ft, the middle is $14 \times 6 = 84$ sq ft, and the bottom is $5 \times 7 = 35$ sq ft. The total area is $100 + 84 + 35 = 219$ sq ft.

4. (2), The perimeter is $18 + 20 + 5 + 6 + 6 + 9 + 7 + 5 = 76$ ft.

5. (3), The area of the whole pizza is $A = 3.14 \times 8^2 = 200.96$ sq in. If she ate three pieces, then $\frac{5}{8}$ are left, and $\frac{5}{8} = 5 \div 8 = 0.625$, and $0.625 \times 200.96 = 125.6$ sq in.

6. (4), Add the volume of the cone and the volume of the cylinder. Cone: $V = \frac{1}{3} \times 3.14 \times 3^2 \times 4 = 37.68$ cm³. Cylinder: $V = 3.14 \times 3^2 \times 12 = 339.12$ cm³. The combined volume is $37.68 + 339.12 = 376.8$ cm³, which rounds to 377 cm³.

7. (2), Each tile has an area of 64 in², so divide the area of the figure by 64. Divide the figure into a top rectangle and a bottom rectangle. The top is $40 \times 64 = 2,560$ in², and the bottom is $40 \times 104 = 4,160$ in², so the total is $2,560 + 4,160 = 6,720$ in². Adam needs $6,720 \div 64 = 105$ tiles.

8. (5), The width of the stage is unknown, so the volume cannot be determined.

9. (2), The diameter is 11 m, and the radius is 5.5 m; $A \approx 3.14 \times 5.5^2 \cong 94.99$ sq m, which rounds to 95.0 sq m.

10. (3), The area of the small circle is $A = 3.14 \times 4^2 = 50.24$ sq m, so the total area is about $95 + 95 + 50.24 = 240.24$ sq m, which rounds to 240 sq m.

11. (2), Divide the area of a circle with diameter 6 in half: $A = 3.14 \times 3^2 = 28.26$, and $28.26 \div 2 = 14.13$ cm².

12. (2), The rectangle is $13 \times 6 = 78$ cm², so $14.13 + 78 = 92.13$ cm².

13. (3), The perimeter is $13 + 6 + 13$, plus the circumference of the semicircle, which is $\frac{1}{2} \times 3.14 \times 6 = 9.42$ cm. The perimeter is $13 + 6 + 13 + 9.42 = 41.42$ cm.

14. (5), The new diameter would be 12 cm, so the new radius would be 6 cm. Semicircle = $\frac{1}{2} \times 3.14 \times 6^2 = 56.52$ cm²; Rectangle = $12 \times 13 = 156$ cm², and $56.52 + 156 = 212.52$ cm².

15. (1), The height of the triangle is $27 - 15.25 = 11.75$ ft.

16. (3), The triangle is $\frac{1}{2} \times 14 \times 11.75 = 82.25$ ft², and the rectangle is $14 \times 15.25 = 213.5$ ft², so the total area is $82.25 + 213.5 = 295.75$ ft².

17. (5), We do not know the lengths of two sides of the triangle.

18. (1), Add the perimeter of the triangle and the perimeter of the rectangle: $14 + 14 + 14 + 14 + 15.25 + 14 + 15.25 = 100.5$ ft.

19. (2), The volume is $\frac{1}{3} \times 3.14 \times 25^2 \times 8$, which is about 5,233.33 cubic feet.

20. (4), The volume of the cylinder-shaped section is $3.14 \times 25^2 \times 12 = 23,550$ cubic feet, so the total volume is $5,233.33 + 23,550 = 28,783.33$ cubic feet, which rounds to 28,783 cubic feet.

21. (3), The floor is a circle, and the area is $3.14 \times 25^2 = 1,962.5$ square feet.

LESSON 8, *pp. 150–153*

1. (5), Solve $10^2 + 2^2 = c^2$ to find that $c^2 = 104$ and $c \approx 10.2$ ft.

2. (3), Solve $12^2 + 2^2 = c^2$ to find that $c^2 = 148$ and $c \approx 12.17$ ft, which rounds to 12.2 ft.

3. (5), Imagine that $\overline{AB}$ is the hypotenuse of a right triangle with vertices A, B, and $(3, -3)$. Solve $8^2 + 4^2 = c^2$ to find that $c \approx 8.25$.

4. (2), Imagine that $\overline{BC}$ is the hypotenuse of a right triangle with vertices B, C, and $(3, -4)$. Solve $2^2 + 3^2 = c^2$ to find that $c \approx 3.61$.

5. (3), Imagine that $\overline{AC}$ is the hypotenuse of a right triangle with vertices A, C, and $(5, -4)$. Solve $1^2 + 10^2 = c^2$ to find that $c \approx 10.05$.

6. (1), Solve $4^2 + 4^2 = c^2$ to find that $c^2 = 32$ and $c \approx 5.66$ in.

7. (2), Solve $2^2 + 2^2 = c^2$ to find that $c^2 = 8$ and $c \approx 2.83$ in.

8. (3), Solve $11^2 + 15^2 = c^2$ to find that $c^2 = 346$ and $c \approx 18.6$ cm.

9. (3), Solve $16^2 + b^2 = 21^2$ to find that $b^2 = 185$ and $b \approx 13.6$ in.

10. (4), Solve $75^2 + 63^2 = c^2$ to find that $c^2 = 9,594$ and $c \approx 97.9$ ft.

11. (3), Solve $3^2 + 11^2 = c^2$ to find that $c^2 = 130$ and $c \approx 11.4$ in.

12. (2), Solve $6.5^2 + b^2 = 7.9^2$ to find that $b^2 = 20.16$ and $b \approx 4.49$ ft, which rounds to 4.5 ft.

13. (5), Solve $5^2 + 8^2 = c^2$ to find that $c^2 = 89$ and $c \approx 9.43$ ft, which rounds to 9.4 ft.

14. (2), Solve $55^2 + 40^2 = c^2$ to find that $c^2 = 4,625$ and $c \approx 68$ in. Rename 68 in. as $68 \div 12 \approx 5.67$ ft, which rounds to 6 ft.

15. (1), Since $6.5^2 + 2.8^2 \approx 7.08^2$, the segments could form a right triangle.

16. (1), Solve $30^2 + 17^2 = c^2$ to find that $c^2 = 1,189$ and $c \approx 34.48$ yd, which rounds to 34.5 yd.

17. (3), Solve $12^2 + b^2 = 40^2$ to find that $b^2 = 1,456$ and $b \approx 38.16$ yd, which rounds to 38.2 yd.

18. (2), Solve $12^2 + b^2 = 15^2$ to find that $b^2 = 81$ and $b = 9$ yd.

19. (5), Solve $15^2 + 15^2 = c^2$ to find that $c^2 = 450$ and $c \approx 21.2$ in.

20. (2), The area is $\frac{1}{2} \times 15 \times 15 = 112.5$ square inches.

21. (2), The perimeter would be $15 + 15 + 18 + 18 + 21.2 = 87.2$ in.

Index

Note: Page numbers in **boldface** indicate definitions or main topic discussion. Page ranges indicate example problems and practice.

linear, **114**, 114–117, **118**, 118–121
quadratic, 102
slope-intercept form of a line, **118**, 118–121
solving, 90–93, 102
writing, 90
Estimating decimals, 26, 30
Evaluating algebraic expressions, **86**, 86–89
Exponents, **94**, 94–97
Expressions, **86**, 86–89
factors of, **102**, 102–105
Extending patterns, **98**, 98–101
Exterior angles, 126

F

Faces
of cube, 54
of rectangular prism, 54
Factoring, **102**, 102–105
FOIL method, 102
Foot, 42
Formulas
for area, viii, 50, 106, 138, 150
for circumference, viii, 46
for distance between two points, viii, 114
for distance traveled, viii
as equations, 90
for mean, viii
for median, viii
for mode, viii
for perimeter, viii, 46
Pythagorean theorem, viii, **150**
for simple interest, viii
for slope of a line, viii, 118
for total cost, viii
use of on GED test, vii
for volume, viii
Fractions, **14**, 14–17, 34
converting to/from decimals/percents, 34
equivalent fractions, 14
improper, 14, 18
minutes converted to, 78
mixed numbers and, 14, 18
operations with, **18**, 18–21
ratios written as, 22
reducing, 18
values on circle graphs as, 74
Frontmatter
About the GED Tests, iv–v
subject-area breakdown, iv
About *GED Xcelerator,* vi
About *Xcelerator Mathematics,* vii
Calculator Directions, x–xi
Copyright/Acknowledgements, ii
Formulas for GED Mathematics Test, viii
Response Options, ix
Study Skills, 1
Table of Contents, iii
Test-Taking Tips, xii
Title Page, i
Functions, **98**, 98–101

G

Gallon, 42
GED Tests
construction of, iv
number of people taking/year, vi
number of people who passed in 2007, vi
preparation for, 1
response options, ix
scoring of, ix
subjects tested/number of questions per subject, iv
time limits for, iv
Geometry
angles, **122**, 122–125
circles, **46**, 46–49, 74, **138**, 138–141
congruent/similar figures, **130**, 130–133
indirect measurement, 122, 126, 130, **134**, 134–137, 146, **150**, 150–153
irregular figures, **146**, 146–149
lines, 110, 114–125
proportions, 130, **134**, 134–137
Pythagorean theorem, **150**, 150–153
quadrilaterals, 46, 50, 94, 126, **126**, 126–129
solid figures, 54, **142**, 142–145
triangles, **126**, 126–129, **150**, 150–153
See also Area; Perimeter; Volume
Gram, 42
Graphing
equations, **114**, 114–117
inequalities, 106–109
points, 110–113
Graphs
bar, **70**, 70–73
circle, **74**, 74–77
line, **70**, 70–73
Greater than or equal to symbol (≥), 106
Greater than symbol (>), 2, 106

H

Height of a figure, 50, 146
Horizontal axis, 70
Horizontal line, 114
Hour, 78
Hypotenuse, **150**, 150–153

I

Identifying patterns, 98
Impossible outcomes, 62
Improper fractions, 14, 17
Indirect measurement, **134**, 134–137
of angles, 122, 126, 130
of area of irregular figures, 146
with proportions, 134–137
of sides of congruent/similar figures, 130
using Pythagorean theorem, 150–153
of volume of irregular figures, 146
Inequalities, **106**, 106–109
graphing, 106–109
solving, 106–109

Integers, **82**, 82–85
Interest problems, 38–40
Interior angles, 126
Inverse operations, 6, 90
Irregular figures, **146**, 146–149

K

Kilogram, 42
Kiloliter, 42
Kilometer, 42

L

Legs of right triangles, 150–153
Length
perimeter/circumference and, 46–49
units of measure, 42
Less than or equal to symbol (≤), 106
Less than symbol (<), 106
Like fractions, 14, 18
Linear equations, **114**, 114–117
slope-intercept form, **118**, 118–121
Line graphs, **70**, 70–73
Lines, **114**, 114–117, 122–125
on coordinate grid, 114
graphing, 110, 114
linear equations generating, 114
slope-intercept form of, **118**, 118–121
slope of, **118**, 118–121
Line segment, 130–133
Liter, 42

M

Mean, **58**, 58–61
Measurement
area, **50**, 50–53
circumference, 46
perimeter, 46
units/systems of measure, **42**, 42–45
volume, **54**
Measurement systems, **42**, 42–45
Median, **58**, 58–61
Meter, 42
Metric system, **42**, 42–45
Milligrams, 42
Milliliter, 42
Millimeter, 42
Minutes, 78
Mixed numbers
changing to/from improper fractions, **14**, 14–17
operations with, **18**, 18–21
Mode, **58**, 58–61
Multiple-step solutions, 10, 22, 134, 146
Multiplication, 6
checking answers, 6
in conversion of metric units, 42
with decimals, 30
of fractions, 18

with integers, 82, 82–85
inverse operation of, 6, 90
as repeated addition, 6, 10
by ten, 26, 30
word clues indicating, 6, 18, 86

N

Negative exponents, 94
Negative numbers, 110, 118
Negative slope, 118
Number line, 82, 106–107
Number sense
decimals, **26**, 26–29
fractions, **14**, 14–17
fractions/decimals/percents
relationships, 34–37
operations with decimals, 30–33
operations with fractions, **18**, 18–21
operations with whole numbers, **6**, 6–9
percent problems, 38–41
ratios/proportions, **22**, 22–25
whole numbers, 2–5
word problems, **10**, 10–13
Numerator, 14, 34

O

Obtuse angles, 126
One, as denominator of unit rate, 22
Operations
with decimals, 30–33
with fractions, 18
with integers, **82**, 82–85
inverse of, 6, 90
order of, 82, 86, 146
with whole numbers, **6**, 6–9
Ordered pairs, 110
graphing a line with, 114
Ordering
decimals, 26
whole numbers, 2
Order of operations
on calculator, 146
evaluating algebraic expressions and, 86
with integers, 82
Outcomes
certain, 62
likely, 62
possible, 62
unlikely, 62

P

Parallelograms, 50, 126
Parentheses, 146
Part (percentage of), **38**
Patterns, **98**, 98–101
Percents, **34**, 34–37, 62
converting to/from fractions/decimals, 34
probability expressed as, 62

problems with, 34, 38–41
values on circle graphs as, 74–75, 77
Percent sign (%), 34
Perimeter, **46**, 46–49
of irregular figures, 146
Pi (π), 138
Place value
of decimals, 26
of whole numbers, 2
Points, 110
determining slope with two, 118
drawing a line with two, 114
Polygons
area, **50**, 50–53
congruent/similar, **130**, 130–133
perimeter of, 46
See also Parallelograms; Quadrilaterals;
Rectangles; Squares; Trapezoids;
Triangles
Positive exponents, 94
Positive numbers, 110, 118
Positive slope, 118
Pound, 42
Powers of numbers, 94–97
Probability, **62**, 62–65
Proportions, **22**, 22–25
finding length of missing side of similar
figures, 130
indirect measurement using, **134**, 134–137
solving percent problems with, 38
Pyramids, 142, 144
Pythagorean theorem, **150**, 150–153

Q

Quadratic equations, 102
Quadrilaterals, **126**, 126–129. *See also*
Parallelograms; Rectangles; Squares;
Trapezoids
Quotient, 30

R

Radius, 138
calculating from area of circle, 138
finding from diameter, 142
Range, **58**, 58–61
Rate, **38**, 78
Ratios, **22**, 22–25
percents, 34
probability expressed as, 62
reducing, 22
unit rates, **22**
ways of writing, 22
Reciprocal, 18
Rectangles, 126
area of, 50
perimeter of, **46**
sides of, 46
Rectangular prism, 54
Reducing fractions, 18
Reflections, 110
Regrouping, 6

Right angles, **122**, 126
Right triangles
Pythagorean theorem and, **150**, 150–153
sides/angles of, 150
Rotations, 110
Rounding
decimals, 26
Rows in tables, 66
Rule, 98

S

Scale, 74
Scale drawings, 134, 136–137
Scientific notation, **94**, 94–97
Sequence of numbers, 98–101
Shadows, 134, 136
Sides
of congruent/similar figures, 130
indirect measurement of, 130, 134
of parallelograms, 50
of quadrilaterals, 126
of right triangles, 150–153
of trapezoids, 50
of triangles, 126
Similar figures, **130**, 130–133
Simple interest, 38–40
Single-bar graph, **70**, 70–71, 73
Slope-intercept form of a line, **118**, 118–121
Slope of a line, **118**, 118–121
finding from two points, 118
formula for, 118
Solid figures, **142**, 142–145
cones, 142–143, 145
cubes, 54, 142, 144–145
cylinders, 142–143, 145
pyramids, 142, 144
volume of, **54**, 54–57
Solving, 102, 106–109
equations, 90–93, 102–105
inequalities, 106–109
multiple-step problems, 10, 22, 134, 146
proportions, 22
word problems, 10–13
Square roots, **94**, 94–97
Squares, 50
area of, 51, 53, 94
Square/square root key, 138
Square units, 50
Straight angle, 122
Subtraction, 6
checking answers, 6
with decimals, 30–33
of fractions, 18–21
of integers, 82
inverse operation of, 6, 90
word clues indicating, 10, 18, 82
Sum, 6
Supplementary angles, **122**
Symbols, 106
greater than or equal to symbol (≥), 106
greater than symbol (>), 106
for "is congruent to" (≅), 130
for "is similar to" (~) 130